FREEDOM!

THE CASE FOR OPEN BORDERS

BY JOSS SHELDON

Cover design by Maida Yaqoob and Khatoon Bibi.

Beta Readers: Amelija Kasum, Roxy W, Alits.
Science Consultant: Elisa Cabrales.
Philosophy Consultant: Stephanie Seppi.

Proofread by Sadia Khan.

Even until quite recently, many of the world's inhabitants were not quite sure of what country they were citizens, or why it should matter.

My mother, who was born a Jew in Poland, once told me a joke from her childhood: There was a small town located along the frontier between Russia and Poland. No-one was ever quite sure to which it belonged. One day, an official treaty was signed. Not long after, surveyors arrived to draw a border.

Some villagers approached them where they had set up their equipment on a nearby hill:

"So where are we, Russia or Poland?"

"According to our calculations, your village now begins exactly thirty-seven meters into Poland."

The villagers immediately began dancing for joy.

"Why?" the surveyors asked. "What difference does it make?"

"Don't you know what this means?" they replied. "It means we'll never have to endure another one of those terrible Russian winters!"

DAVID GRAEBER

The metaphors for immigration are usually aquatic: We talk of floods and tides, of being swamped and drowned. We might do better to think of Britain as a lake refreshed by one stream that bubbles in, and another that trickles out. The fish might squabble, and at times attack one another. Conditions sometimes favour the pike, sometimes the minnow. Every so often, the incoming stream stirs the still pond. But over time, the lake adapts and develops a new, unexpected ecology. Without the oxygen generated by (the) fresh water (from the stream), it would stagnate."

ROBERT GUEST

CONTENTS

INTRODUCTION

"The bosom of America is open to receive not only the opulent and respected stranger, but the oppressed and persecuted of all nations and religions; whom we shall welcome to a participation of all our rights and privileges."
George Washington

It's the 16th of June, back in 2015.

Donald Trump is riding an escalator in the Manhattan tower he's named after himself. The skin beneath his chin is sagging over a generic red tie. His face is reddish-purple.

He holds his left hand aloft, and offers a thumbs-up to the press.

In the background, a couple of dozen people are standing on the level from which Trump is descending, pressed up against a golden handrail. Some wave at the reality TV star, whilst others snap photos on their phones. A few of these spectators have wandered in off the street; curious to see what's afoot. Others are being paid $50 to attend.

Trump follows his wife, Melania, who is sporting a white dress and a stoic face. He clambers up onto a makeshift stage, positions himself, and begins in the style to which the world will soon become accustomed:

"Our country is in serious trouble. We don't have victories anymore. We used to have victories, but we don't have them. When was the last time anybody saw us beating, let's say, China in a trade deal? They kill us. I beat China all the time. All the time.

"When did we beat Japan at anything? They send their cars over by the millions, and what do we do? When was the last time you saw a Chevrolet in Tokyo? It doesn't exist, folks. They beat us all the time.

"When do we beat Mexico at the border? They're laughing at us, at our stupidity. And now they are beating us economically. They are not our friend, believe me. But they're killing us economically.

"The US has become a dumping ground for everybody else's problems.

"Thank you. It's true, and these are the best and the finest. When Mexico sends its people, they're not sending their best. They're not sending you. They're not sending you. They're sending people that have lots of problems, and they're bringing those problems with us. They're bringing drugs. They're bringing crime. They're rapists. And some, I assume, are good people.

"But I speak to border guards and they tell us what we're getting. And it only makes common sense. It only makes common sense. They're sending us not the right people.

"It's coming from more than Mexico. It's coming from all over South and Latin America, and it's coming probably... probably... from the Middle East. But we don't know. Because we have no protection and we have no competence, we don't know what's happening. And it's got to stop."

***

These were the opening remarks from the speech that launched Trump's campaign for office.

He'd started as he meant to go on.

Less than two weeks later, when NBC dumped Trump for "Derogatory statements... regarding immigrants", the future president doubled down, claiming:

"We must have strong borders and not let illegal immigrants enter the United States... Public reports routinely state great amounts of crime are being committed by illegal immigrants."

Trump insisted that the solution was a border wall:

"I will build a great wall. And nobody builds walls better than me, believe me. And I'll build them very inexpensively. I will build a great, great wall on our southern border, and I will make Mexico pay for that wall."

And Trump took things to the next level, in December of that year – saying he'd implement a "Total and complete shutdown of Muslims entering the United States":

"Our country cannot be the victims of horrendous attacks by people that believe only in Jihad, and have no sense of reason or respect for human life."

***

Things *were* pretty dire, for a significant number of Americans...

Jobs had been shipped off abroad, wages had stagnated, and

living costs were spiralling out of control. The aftermath of the Global Economic Crash had been devastating for everyday folk: Around ten-million Americans had lost their homes, nine-million had lost their jobs, and over 45 million had been plunged into poverty. (Shallby, 2018).

Trump was tapping into this seam of discontent, and offering a deliciously simple answer: It's the immigrants! *They're* the bogeymen. They're the ones who are pillaging your prosperity.

But that malaise hadn't been caused by immigrants. It was caused by the policies of Ronald Reagan, George Bush Senior, Bill Clinton and George W. Bush. They were the ones who'd put corporate profits before the welfare of the American people – cutting regulation, abolishing trade barriers, and reducing union power. (Gerstle, 2022).

And the Global Economic Crash wasn't caused by immigrants either. It was the work of unscrupulous investment bankers, the credit agencies that gave triple-A ratings to subprime loans, and successive governments, who'd rolled back the very legislation which was designed to prevent that type of meltdown.

Most of the bankers at Lehman Brothers and Bear Stearns weren't immigrants. Most of the politicians who put profit before people, were born and raised in the States. It wasn't immigrants who closed around seventy-thousand American factories, and outsourced five-million manufacturing jobs. Those decisions were made by fat cat chief executives. And it wasn't immigrants who profited from the slash-and-burn approach to managing the economy. It was a tiny cabal of shareholders. (Scott et al, 2022).

But none of that mattered. In politics, the truth is secondary. *Narrative* wins the day.

If you can pick at people's discontent, work your audience into a frenzy, say you've identified the issue, say you have the solutions, and promise to make life better – then you'll rack up the votes.

Donald Trump did that.

Hillary Clinton did not.

THE FACTS WHICH DISAPPEARED

But what if Hillary *had* tried such an approach? What if she had acknowledged the suffering of the American people? What if she'd gone as far as to say that immigration policy *was* to blame?

Imagine the scene, if you will...

Clinton and Trump have won their parties' nominations. Trump's rhetoric is well-known. But Hillary has been fighting fire with fire – taking an unashamedly *pro-immigration* stance. Her campaign has been just as controversial as Trump's. And it's attracted the same sort of passionate following – from regular Americans who feel they've been left behind, and who've been energised by the changes Clinton is proposing.

There are tens-of-thousands of them, packed inside this arena – a metallic old thing, which has been spruced up with blue drapes and glittery ribbons. Some of Hillary's supporters are holding placards. Others are waving an array of flags, which represent hundreds of nations and regions. Several are wearing baseball caps, decorated with four white letters: "IMAG". It stands for, "Immigrants Make America Great" – a reference to the immigration-fuelled prosperity that Clinton is promising to deliver.

A hush descends, as the audience anticipates their candidate's arrival.

There's a brief moment of confusion. Had they been mistaken? Would they have to wait for another five minutes? Another ten? Some people have been standing in here for hours.

A banner unfurls above the stage, a little haphazardly – unravelling on one side, while the other remains hidden. But the delay doesn't last for long. And now the banner can be seen – red, white and blue – star-spangled, with a three-word demand: "Open the borders!"

The crowd cheers:

Open the borders!

Make America the Land of the Free!

Clinton enters from stage left. But she doesn't just walk the boards. She doesn't just jog. She begins with a skip and ends in a sprint – sucked in towards the adoring masses, who are already chanting her name:

Hillary! Hillary! Hillary!

And then:

We want jobs!

Immigrants create jobs!

Clinton savours the moment. She turns to her left, waves towards the supporters at the front, and then waves towards those at the back. She arcs around, ever so slowly – saluting the middle section, before gesturing towards her right.

She only speaks when she's ready – screaming out loud and punching the air:

"The United States is a nation of immigrants!"

Cheers.

"Thank-you, thank-you. Yes. Haven't you heard? America was built by immigrants, for immigrants. Immigrants built America. Immigrants made America great. And immigrants will make it even greater!"

Applause.

A pause.

An impatient hush.

"The founding fathers were immigrants! George Washington was an immigrant. George Washington's maternal grandfather, Joseph Ball, came here from England. George Washington was an immigrant. A third-generation immigrant.

"Thank-you... Thank-you... And he wasn't alone. Thomas Jefferson was also an immigrant. A *second*-generation immigrant. His very own mother, Jane, moved to this great nation from Shadwell, near London.

"Thank-you! You're wonderful. You're the best audience in the world. The best!

"Just like Benjamin Franklin. The best! Yes. Benjamin Franklin, the son of Josiah Franklin, a fabric dyer from Ecton, Northamptonshire, Great Britain.

"John Jay was an immigrant. Yes! John Jay was an immigrant. His father, Peter, was a French Huguenot. His mother, Mary, was Dutch. An immigrant! A second-generation immigrant.

"Alexander Hamilton was born on the island of Nevis. A *first-generation* immigrant! A first-generation immigrant! He came here as a boy. The first ever treasury secretary was an immigrant!"

Cheers.

Hillary takes a long, slow breath.

She lifts her chin, and gazes towards the bleachers, doing little to suppress a grin.

Immigrants! Immigrants! Immigrants!

"George Washington?" Clinton wails.

"Immigrant!" The crowd responds.

"Thomas Jefferson?"

Immigrant!

"Benjamin Franklin?"

Immigrant!

"John Adams?"

Immigrant!

"Alexander Hamilton?"

Immigrant!

"John Jay?"

Immigrant!

"James Maddison?"

Immigrant!

"Immigrant! Immigrant! Immigrant! Thank-you. Immigrants built America. Immigrants made America great. And immigrants will make it even greater!"

Hillary nods.

She closes and reopens her eyes:

"Immigrants built this nation.

"Chinese immigrants built the railroads! The Chinese brought their food. Such great food. American Chinese food! The best Chinese food in the world. The Chinese opened restaurants, shops and laundries. The best laundries in the world. American laundries! The best!

"Do we have any Chinese Americans in the house?"

Cheers.

"The best! The best of the best. The best Chinese people in the world come to America. The ones back in China? Not so great. Pretty mediocre. But the ones who come to America? Great! Out of this world!

"And what about the Germans? Who here had German ancestry?"

Cheers.

"Is that all? I bet there's more. One-in-seven Americans descend from German immigrants. You might be German yourself, and have absolutely no idea!

"Ah yes, the German Americans. You headed west, opening farms, feeding the nation. You gave us the kindergarten. You gave us hamburgers, frankfurters, and some of the finest American cars."

Cheers.

"Thank-you. Thank-you. And what about the Scandinavian Americans? Who has Swedish or Norwegian heritage?"

Cheers.

"Wow! Love you gals. Love you guys... A million Scandinavians have moved to this great land. Charles Lindbergh's family was from Sweden. Conrad Hilton's father came from Norway. And he set up Hilton Hotels, who employ sixty-thousand Americans. Yes! One immigrant. Sixty-thousand American jobs. Immigrants create our jobs!"

Immigrants create jobs!

The noise is deafening. But Clinton doesn't flinch. She puffs her chest, and screams over the hubbub, like the singer in a rock band:

"Don't listen to those charlatans who tell you otherwise. Those frauds. Those liars. Those cheats.

"Immigrants create way more jobs than they fill!

"Immigrants are 80% more likely to start businesses than local folk. Half the people who've set up tech firms in Silicon Valley, came here from overseas. Immigrants create new products, with loads of patents. Loads. The most patents ever. More patents than anyone else. Yes. Immigrants are the lifeblood of invention. Immigrants create jobs.

Immigrants create businesses. Immigrants pay higher wages than anyone else!

"That's what we need, America. That's what we need: More immigrants. More businesses. More jobs. Higher wages. Employment for all. A pay rise for everyone here.

"Open the borders! Open the borders! Let the entrepreneurs in. Allow them to create our jobs. Allow them to boost our wages."

Open the borders!

Make America the Land of the Free!

Hillary nods, stops somewhat abruptly, and taps her lower lip – as though she's struck upon an idea. The question that follows is probably scripted. But she speaks as though it's only just popped into her mind:

"Do we have any foreign-born entrepreneurs in the house tonight?"

Most of the responses are inaudible, but a few can be heard:

My mummy is an enter-the-preen-air.

This man from Guatemala gave me a job.

Without this Ugandan, my family would be homeless.

Hillary smiles, rests a hand on the rostrum, and arches her back:

"Did you hear that? This couple has only been here for thirteen years, and they already employ over a hundred people. Thirteen years! A hundred people! Wow! Immigrants? Wow! Immigrants create our jobs.

"We shouldn't be surprised, mind you. If you have the gumption to up sticks, wave goodbye to your loved ones, leave everything behind, and travel thousands of miles... Well, you're going to have something about you. Some good old American 'Get up and go'. You're going to be the sort of go-getter who starts businesses, creates jobs, and pays the best wages. High, high wages. Great, American wages!"

The crowd is still cheering, "*Immigrants create jobs*", but Clinton is moving on:

"Immigrants save lives... Over 1.5 million immigrants work in healthcare. Yes, that's right: Three-in-ten of our doctors were born overseas. They get out of bed each morning, with one thing on their mind: *Saving your life.* Saving your mama's life. Saving your papa's life. Saving your nana's life. Saving your children's lives.

"Yes. Immigrants save lives. Immigrants save lives.

"Let's hear it for the foreign-born doctors!"

Wahoo.

"Let's hear it for the paramedics who travelled across the globe, to save your daughter's life."

Whoop. Whoop.

"Let's hear it for the immigrant dentists, nurses, opticians, therapists and pharmacists!"

Hooray.

"Immigrants build the homes we live in. They build our homes! Real American homes, made from the best American timber. And, by Jove, don't we need more homes? Am I right? Am I right? Have you seen the state of our housing market? Have you seen house prices? Have you seen rents? We need more immigrants, to build more houses, so that everyone can have a home.

"9.5% of immigrants work in construction. More immigrants work in construction than in any other industry. And we need them. Yes, we need more immigrants. We need more immigrants to build more homes. We need more immigrants to build more schools. We need more immigrants to build more hospitals, railroads, libraries, community centres, basketball courts and swimming pools.

"Open the borders! Allow the nation-builders to come!"

Open the borders.

Make America the Land of the Free!

The lighting dims. Then it dims a little more.

A shadow engulfs the stage.

Hillary scowls:

"Not everyone agrees... No. Not everyone is so intelligent... My opponent..."

Boo.

"My opponent... He says that immigrants are *bad*. Can you believe that? He wants to waste billions of dollars of your money. Yes, *your* money. He wants to waste your hard-earned cash, extending the border wall. He wants a big, bad, bloated nanny state. He wants to waste your money on a wall!

"This so-called 'Donald Trump' wants to stop Iraqi doctors from coming here, to save your nana's life. He wants to stop Mexican entrepreneurs from coming here, to create jobs for your siblings. He wants to stop Latino builders from crossing the border, to build homes for your children.

"This man hates America. Donald Trump hates America! He hates you. And he hates everything this country stands for."

Boooooo.

"But we *love* America. We know what America needs: We need *more* immigrants. We need more freedom. We need the right to work wherever we want. The right to travel wherever we choose. The right to retire wherever we damn well like!

"So, let's demolish the wall! Let's demolish every last darned wall on the planet! Let's welcome absolutely everyone, no matter where they were born. Let's make America the 'Land of the Free'!"

THE BETRAYAL

You can bet your bottom dollar that Fox News would've gone into meltdown, had Clinton run with such a campaign. Barack Obama would've been scratching his head, thinking "Who is this Hillary?" And such an approach would've alienated anyone who subscribed to an anti-freedom agenda.

But those people had already been won over by Trump. Clinton was *never* going to win their votes.

Other votes were on the table.

Such a campaign would've won support from millions of foreign-born residents. It would've won their children's and grandchildren's votes. It would've attracted voters who were friends with foreign nationals, voters whose lives had been saved by foreign doctors, and voters who were employed by immigrant entrepreneurs.

Come election day, 39.9% of the electorate remained at home. A campaign with some energy, *with a narrative*, could have persuaded them to get up, march to the ballot box, and cast the decisive votes.

But no such campaign existed.

***

Clinton did offer a few concessions.

At the launch of her campaign, she promised to "Offer hard-working, law-abiding immigrant families a path to citizenship". Her website still declares that she'd "Introduce comprehensive immigration reform", "Expand access to affordable healthcare to all families... regardless of immigration status", "Close private immigration detention centres", "Promote naturalisation", and "Support immigrant integration".

There were some clear differences. Clinton was being kinder to those immigrants *who were already in America*. But she didn't want to encourage *more* immigration. Like Trump, she still wanted to police the Mexican border. The only difference was *how*: Trump wanted to extend the border wall, whilst Hillary wanted to rely upon technology and border patrols. She didn't have any plans to remove the sections of wall which existed at the time – which had existed whilst she was secretary of state. Clinton wanted to "Enforce immigration laws *humanely*". But she still wanted to enforce those laws. She still bought into the idea that there were such things as "Legal" and "Illegal" immigrants. Rather than shout out that "No human is illegal", she essentially agreed with Trump – thereby validating his claims, and the policies he was proposing.

***

A politician might take one of five positions, when it comes to our right to move:

1) FULL-FAT LIBERTARIANISM: They might champion free movement.

2) DIET LIBERTARIANISM: They might open our borders a little.

3) STATUS-QUO-ISM: They might tinker with the current system.

4) DIET AUTHORITARIANISM: They might restrict our ability to move.

5) FULL-FAT AUTHORITARIANISM: They might close the borders and trap us all inside.

Trump placed himself somewhere between the fourth and fifth options. He did allow *some* kinds of movement, for the "Right" sort of person. But he also built a border wall – the kind of structure which is synonymous with authoritarian regimes, in places like the USSR, North Korea and Israel. And he would go on to pass Executive Order 13769 – closing the borders to people from six nations with Muslim majorities.

Hillary placed herself somewhere around the third option. She wanted to improve the system – to make it nicer, more humane, and more efficient. But she refused to challenge the status quo.

Neither candidate championed either of the first two options. Neither provided an alternative for voters who valued freedom.

Between them, Trump and Clinton narrowed the conversation. And that cannot be good for democracy.

***

I only singled out Hillary, because she just happened to be standing against Trump. Her policies weren't terrible in isolation. And we should remember that she did win the popular vote.

It's perhaps more telling to see how Clinton responded *in the years which followed*, when the presidency wasn't up for grabs, and she was free to speak her mind.

Clinton didn't fight back. She didn't become more libertarian – campaigning for our right to move. She became more authoritarian – echoing the Trumpian sentiment.

Talking to The Guardian newspaper, two years after her defeat, she remarked:

"I think Europe needs to *get a handle on migration*... I admire the very generous and compassionate approaches that were taken, particularly by leaders like Angela Merkel, but I think it's fair to say Europe has done its part, and must send a very clear message: 'We are not going to be able to continue to provide refuge and support'."

She even called for deportations:

"You deport the bad actors, you deport the criminals, you deport people who (pose) some other kind of threat to our national security...

For people who then keep coming, you turn them back."

And she demanded that immigrants assimilate:

"People who have been here for a long time, you have a cutoff point, and after that point they have to learn English, they have to pay taxes, they have to follow the law, they have to wait in line."

Clinton even went on to talk about "Solutions to migration" – normalising this idea that movement is bad – a problem that needs to be "Solved".

***

In that same article, Tony Blair – the former British prime minister – also demanded a more authoritarian stance:

"You cannot possibly stand for election unless you've got a strong position on immigration... You've got to answer those *problems*. If you don't... you leave a large space into which the populists can march." (Wintour, 2018).

Tony Blair was not a member of the Conservative Party – the British equivalent of the Republicans. He was a member of *Labour*. And here he was, buying into this Trumpian sentiment – this belief that immigration was a "Problem".

Blair and Clinton had stepped into the fourth square. They weren't even pretending to be moderates – suggesting we tinker with the status quo. They were taking a firmly authoritarian line. And they'd left a gaping chasm behind them.

None of these mainstream politicians were saying that immigrants create more jobs than they fill, that they pay more into the exchequer than they receive in return, that they build the homes we so desperately need, that they farm the food we eat, or that they save our families' lives. No-one was demanding that we open our borders, and make it *easier* for people to move. Such opinions had been gagged.

<u>OTHER WORLDS ARE POSSIBLE</u>

This book fills the void which was created by this shift towards authoritarianism – to share the ideas which are missing from the mainstream narrative – making the case *for* free movement.

I want to arm you with the information you'll need to challenge the anti-freedom agenda. So that when someone repeats a Trumpian falsehood – these ideas that "Immigrants take our jobs", or that "They're not like us" – you can respond with the facts that debunk their lies.

I want to help you to challenge the politics of fear and hatred, so that we may usher in a new politics based on the humanity we all hold in common, no matter where we were born.

***

Does that sound crazy? Perhaps it does!

But let's not forget that this narrowing of the political spectrum has been a relatively recent occurrence. Politicians *were* willing to extend a warm welcome to their international guests, in the not-too-distant past.

Do you recall the George Washington quote at the beginning of this chapter? When he said the USA was open to strangers from "All nations and religions"? Well, that kind of statement used to be *the norm*.

Harry Truman won the 1948 presidential election, after promising to *overturn* controls on migration. He later stated: "We do not need to be 'Protected' against immigrants... On the contrary, we want to stretch out a helping hand, to save those who have managed to flee (from the USSR)... To welcome and restore them." (Volner, 2019).

John F Kennedy once said: "Immigrants have enriched and strengthened the fabric of American life."

He also declared: "We are a nation of immigrants."

And Barack Obama echoed his predecessor, when he stated: "We are and always will be a nation of immigrants."

***

But it wasn't only Democrats who used to speak in such a manner. Take these quotes from the three *Republican* presidents who preceded Donald Trump, beginning with Ronald Reagan, who said this in 1980:

"(Rather than) talking about putting up a fence, why don't we work out some recognition of our mutual problems, make it possible for them to come here legally with a work permit, and then, while they're working and earning here, they pay taxes."

Reagan's successor, George Bush Senior, reminded the nation that the USA was built by immigrants, when he said this in 1990:

"Our nation is the enduring dream of every immigrant who ever set foot on these shores, and the millions still struggling to be free. This nation, this idea called America, was and always will be a new world — *our* new world."

And Bush's son, George Junior, extolled the immigrant work ethic, while speaking in 2004:

"As a Texan, I have known many immigrant families, mainly from Mexico, and I've seen what they add to our country. They bring to America the values of faith in God, love of family, hard work, and self-reliance – the values that made us a great nation."

George W. Bush also admitted that, "Nearly all Americans have ancestors who braved the oceans – liberty-loving risk takers in search of an ideal... Immigration is not just a link to America's past – it's also a bridge to America's future." (Ortiz, 2016).

***

If these *Republican* politicians – who certainly weren't a bunch of "Bleeding heart liberals" – could've spoken so glowingly about immigration in the recent past, then they should be able to do so again in the future. You never know: This book might swing them back in the right direction!

EVERYONE HAS A STORY

I suppose I have skin in the game...

I was born in Barnet – a fairly anonymous suburb on London's outermost fringe. My father grew up in the area. But my mother moved around a little – she grew up in Oxford, went to study in Liverpool, and headed down to London when she began her career. My grandparents were also born in England. So, it'd be easy for me to consider myself British through-and-through. My family speak English with an English accent. We eat fish and chips, go to football matches, and whinge about the weather. I've never heard any of my relatives refer to themselves as "Immigrants".

In reality, all eight of my great-grandparents moved to England from Eastern Europe, between the two World Wars – fleeing from antisemitism. If they hadn't made that journey, they might've been murdered by the Nazis. I wouldn't be here today, writing this book.

How many other lives were saved, thanks to similar journeys? And how many of the six-million Jews who *were* slaughtered, would've been saved had there been open borders, providing them with a passageway to safety? It's sobering to think.

But free movement, for me, isn't something that's limited to the dark annals of history. It'd be fair to say that without international travel, you wouldn't be reading this book for a *second*, entirely different reason...

In December 2012, I left my job at Northampton Town Football Club. I was determined to write and release my debut novel. But I only had a few thousand pounds in the bank.

Would that money have sufficed, had I remained in England? No way! I'd have spent it in a few months, whilst I was only a fraction of the way through the first draft, and I'd have been forced to get another job to pay the bills. Perhaps I could've written part-time. But that book – "Involution & Evolution" – took almost two years to complete. Distracted by a job, and by fatigue, it would've taken even longer. Given that it was a bit of a flop, I'd have probably lacked the motivation to keep writing. The chances are that I wouldn't have made it to book number eight, and you wouldn't be reading it today.

So, what happened?

Well, I "Moved", of course.

I put the word in quotation marks, because I didn't take up permanent residence abroad. I was more of a *nomad*. I went to India – one of the cheapest countries on the planet. I rented a rather basic room, for around £70 a month. I washed my clothes by hand, on the floor beneath the shower. I cooked porridge in a kettle for breakfast, and ate my other meals at the cheapest restaurants. All in all, I survived on about £5 a day. Even when you add in the cost of flights and visas, it's not hard to see how I made my money last for around eighteen months – enough time to complete the first two drafts of my novel.

Moving to another country, helped me to launch my new career. It also helped me to put down roots...

Even as a relatively successful author, there was no way I could've bought a house back in Barnet. According to Right Move, the average property in my hometown sold for £891,938 (in 2022). The average apartment cost £509,664. At the same time, according to Words Rated, the average indie author was only making a thousand dollars a year. You do the maths!

So, what did I do?

I wrote my first two books in India and Nepal, before writing my third – "The Little Voice" – while house-sitting for friends in Spain. When that began to sell, I treated myself. I wrote my fourth novel – "Money Power Love" – in the food-lovers paradise of Thailand. It was there that I met my (now) wife. We moved to the Philippines and then to Bulgaria, where we bought a three-bedroom house on the edge of the Pirin National Park. With beautiful mountain views, that little slice of paradise was a short drive away from a ski resort and an assortment of hot springs. It cost me around £30,000 – the sort of price that a moderately successful indie author *could* afford to pay.

After a few years, my wife began to miss the land of her birth – the Philippines. I could tell that she'd be happier if we returned to that island nation.

So here we are today. We've bought a little under two hectares of land, for about £25,000, and a team of builders are erecting our home as I type – replete with a well, water-filtration system, solar panels and wind turbine. We plan to grow our food, live off-grid, and be fairly self-sufficient.

It's not the sort of life everyone would wish for themselves, and it certainly has its downsides. But it's the life we've chosen. And there's no way we could've afforded it back in Britain.

We *had* to move, to enjoy this lifestyle. We've been incredibly fortunate, to be able to do such a thing. The British passport is a powerful tool – it makes it easy for Brits to relocate. But still, there's a part of me that feels conflicted. I feel like a spoilt brat, hopping from one place to the next, whilst other people are forced to remain where they are, and accept circumstances which were imposed upon them at birth.

There's one rule for one group of people, and another rule for everyone else. That's not right, it's not just, and it's not fair.

***

Everyone has a story. They tend to be fairly unique. And the nuance is often lost.

We rarely hear about those people who move abroad to enjoy a cheaper cost of living. We seldom speak about those people who move for the sake of a homesick spouse. Have you ever come across anyone else who moved from Britain to India, to launch a career as an author?

Discussions about migration tend to focus on the negatives. But not everyone who moves is a victim – a "Refugee", "Asylum Seeker", or an impoverished "Economic Migrant". People relocate for thousands of reasons – most of which we never stop to consider – most of which are *positive* and *beautiful*. People move to study, retire, or make a fresh start – to experience different cultures, climates and lifestyles. It's true that some of us only make single journeys – emigrating from one place, and immigrating into another. But plenty of "Returnees" do head back in the other direction. Other people are more "Nomadic". Some move around their regions, whilst others traverse the globe. They might settle down for a few weeks, a few years, or a few decades.

Whatever the case, one fact remains: No-one chooses the place where they were born. It's a lottery. You might be fortunate. You might be born in the perfect nation for you – one with all the opportunities you'll need to become the best version of yourself. Then again, you might not.

It seems inherently unjust to trap people in particular lands, simply because they were born there, when they could attain self-fulfilment elsewhere.

It's also a historic anomaly...

THE CONTENTS OF THIS BOOK

Our love of exploration is nothing new. *Homo sapiens* have been moving about, establishing homes in various locations, for at least eighty-thousand years. Earlier humans, such as *Homo habilis*, were wandering the Earth around two-million *years* ago!

Unless you live in a few specific places in Africa, you're not truly indigenous to the land you call "Home". You're the descendant of ancient travellers – people who left Africa, found new places to reside, moved on again, and established communities in different territories – spreading out further and wider, until they'd populated most of the globe.

The first chapter of this book will recount their journey – showing how we became who we are by moving about – free from the artificial restraints that borders try to impose. And it'll document the history of the border, the border wall, and the passport – recounting the ways in which we shackled ourselves to the lands of our births.

***

Having established that humans have always liked to travel, the following three chapters shall ask *why*: Why do we want to move, visit new regions, and live in different locales?

Is it a matter of *nature*?

Do some of us have a genetic inclination to explore the world, live in new places, and experience different cultures? Are we *all* built with the propensity to move – with a curious imagination, that makes us wonder, "What's over there?" – and the physical attributes, that enable us to go and find out? Or should we be kept apart? Are there any genetic differences, between the groups of people who live on either side of a border?

Is it a matter of *nurture*?

Do the members of some societies *encourage* their offspring to get restless and take to the road? Shouldn't we respect the cultures of nomadic people such as the Kazakh horsemen, and their modern equivalents – the digital nomads? Why are countries like Canada and Japan enticing people to their shores? Why are "Returnees" heading back to China and India? And why is there a culture in the Philippines, which inspires people to leave?

Or is it a matter of *necessity*?

What about all those individuals who are forced to move – to escape from poverty, disease, war, persecution, and environmental disasters? Could we eradicate global poverty, by allowing impoverished people to move to wealthier nations? Could we bring down despotic regimes, by opening our doors to their dissidents?

***

Those three chapters champion *emigration* and *circular migration*.

The next four chapters will flip things on their head. Rather than ask why *we* should have the right to move, they'll look at the benefits we'll enjoy when we welcome *others* – making the case for *immigration* and *internal migration*.

In the chapter entitled "Integrate? Or Contribute?", we'll look at how foreign nationals have enriched our *cultures*. Did you know that British labourers took football to Brazil? Or that fish and chips, the UK's national dish, was introduced by Portuguese refugees? Where do you think our languages came from? Who do you think invented Hollywood, and the idea of the "American dream"? And how many genres of music, do you think were invented by people who'd moved from one place to another?

In "They Create Our Jobs", we'll revisit the ideas we introduced in Hillary's speech: Immigrants launch businesses, which create millions of jobs. They inspire *other* entrepreneurs. They launch platforms, such as YouTube, which create a second tranche of jobs. And they create jobs as *consumers* – spending their money, and creating consumer demand – forcing firms to recruit more workers.

The next chapter – "It's Win, Win, Win" – introduces some of the other economic benefits which accrue from inward migration. Overseas workers tend to do highly skilled work, or arduous physical labour – plugging shortages in our labour supply. They *complement* the work we're already doing, making our economies more efficient. This boosts economic output, and leads to higher wages. Immigration is also a boon for the government. New arrivals tend to pay more in taxes than they receive back from the state. They plug a demographic timebomb. And abolishing borders would also save us a fortune – because we wouldn't have to pay for border walls, guards, detention centres, or deportation flights.

The final chapter in this section – "But Why? (Oh Why, Oh Why?)" – looks at the *reasons* our foreign-born cousins offer so much more than you might expect: "Travel opens the mind" – it gives us new perspectives. With a foot in two cultures, international citizens can draw lessons from both. They're also uniquely positioned to trade across borders – using the contacts they've accrued in various lands. They receive support from their diaspora networks. And if they don't get ahead themselves, there's a strong chance that they'll propel their children on to success – overachieving, relative to their peers, thanks to the "Second generation advantage".

***

Having stated the historical, biological, cultural, political and economic cases for free movement – and having dedicated several pages, extolling the virtues of both emigration *and* immigration – our journey will be drawing to an end.

We'll just have a couple of loose ends to tie.

In the penultimate chapter, we'll examine the *philosophical* case for open borders, asking: "Why freedom?" Why should we have the right to move about, and live wherever we choose? Why not cocoon ourselves within the confines of a single territory?

We'll consider both the *capitalist* and *anti-capitalist* cases for free movement. We'll look at the religious arguments for open borders. And we'll introduce some secular philosophies.

Finally, we'll wrap things up with a conclusion – suggesting some of the ways through which we might usher in another era of free movement – by shifting public opinion, applying pressure on our governments, and taking direct action – helping people to cross borders ourselves.

We'll also discuss the infrastructure we'd need to make life easier for people *after* they've reached their destination – granting them equal rights – including the right to vote in whichever country they choose, the right to buy a home wherever they like, and the right to claim welfare no matter where they live – with international passports and driving licences, which would allow us to become genuine citizens of the world.

***

Without any further ado, let's get things underway...

THE HISTORY OF MOVEMENT

"And what is a border, if not a story? It is never simply a line, a marker, a wall, an edge. First, it's an idea. An idea that is then presented as a reality. It doesn't just exist in the world. It can only ever be made. It can only ever be told."

James Crawford

Boom!

No, that doesn't do it justice.

BOOM!

No, that doesn't even come close.

The universe didn't begin with a big bang. It began with a *massive* bang. The sort of explosion that's impossible to conceive. A melee of gamma rays, heat and light.

This massive bang dispersed all the physical matter that's ever existed, at more than a billion kilometres per hour. That matter would go on to form stars, planets, trees, animals and humans – but it would never stop moving. *Every gram of matter that exists today*, has been in constant motion for 13.8 billion years – travelling away from the site of the big bang.

Our galaxy, the Milky Way, is no exception: It travels 2.1 million kilometres every single hour.

Planet Earth is also beholden by this rule of constant motion. It's orbiting the sun – travelling 107 million kilometres in an hour.

Our solar system is also moving around the Milky Way.

And there's more: That's because the Earth is rotating on its axis. If you're standing on the equator, you'll be travelling 1,600 kilometres each hour, thanks to this phenomenon alone.

All this means one thing: *You're migrating right now*. It might not seem that way. You might be very comfortable, relaxing on a sofa, sipping a cup of cocoa. Everything might *feel* pretty stable. But in reality, you're whizzing through space at a mind-boggling velocity. You've never been where you are at this moment, and you'll never be there again.

This has always been the case.

The history of the universe, is a history of *continuous travel* through space. (Fraknoi, 2007).

EVERYTHING HAS ALWAYS BEEN MOVING

The ground beneath your feet is also on the move, albeit at a rather pedestrian pace...

The science of "Plate tectonics" tells us that Earth's lithosphere – its two outermost layers – is comprised of seven or eight major "Plates", as well as several smaller "Platelets". These have been moving across the planet's surface for 3.4 billion years.

Sometimes, these continents come together, to form a single supercontinent.

We're talking about the likes of "Columbia" – a landmass shaped like a piece of pizza, which formed two-billion years ago. Columbia broke up into smaller continents, which then reunited to form "Rodinia". This process repeated itself – resulting in "Pannotia" – a supercontinent located around the South Pole. The most recent supercontinent was called "Pangea". It formed around 335 million years ago, was home to the dinosaurs, and broke up after another 135 million years – forming Asia, Africa and the Americas – continents which continue to migrate today; travelling just under ten centimetres a year. (Li et al, 2008). (Read & Watson, 1975).

***

Plants appeared on Earth a fair while after the continental plates – just under half-a-billion years ago.

And you'd never guess what: They also move around! Their seeds are so light, they can be carried by the breeze – in rivers and oceans – within birds' stomachs, claws and feathers.

They've been known to make some rather long expeditions...

Around 1.4 million years ago, a seabird carried the seeds from acacia trees in Hawaii – either in its stomach or in its wings – before depositing them on Réunion Island, *eighteen-thousand kilometres* away! (Le Roux et al, 2014).

The chances are that only a few seeds survived the journey. They took root, multiplied, and began to evolve.

But plant migration doesn't only occur when a few plants travel alone. Sometimes, a great number of plants move together...

The most recent *Great Tree Migration* occurred at the end of the last Ice Age, ten-thousand years ago. As the ice receded, the trees which had survived in more temperate locales – further from the poles, at altitude, and in protected pockets of land – began to spread across the newly unfrozen terrain.

Fossilised pollen shows that oak trees migrated across Scotland at a rate of one kilometre per year. Beach trees moved from one side of the Great Lakes to the other. Norwegian spruces circumnavigated both the North Sea and the Baltic. (Bridle, 2022).

It's not quite the acacia. These trees didn't travel eighteen-thousand kilometres in a single journey. But they experienced a *mass* migration – moving together, along with their peers.

***

The sweet potato offers an example of a *vegetable* which migrated...

When Europeans first arrived in Polynesia, they were surprised to find the starchy tuber. It bore a remarkable resemblance to a familiar foodstuff – one which they associated with Peru. But Peru was thousands of kilometres away.

Captain Cook's crew collected leaves from those sweet potatoes, took them home, and donated them to London's Natural History Museum. When they were tested, some centuries later, DNA analysis showed that they had been evolving differently from their American cousins for 111,000 years.

The sweet potato couldn't have been transported by people. They'd arrive in Polynesia several millennia *before* the first human beings. They must have made that journey by themselves. (Muñoz-Rodríguez et al, 2018).

***

The point should be obvious: *The only constant is change.*

When Dutch researchers drilled down into the Bogotá basin, in the Colombian Andes, they extracted pollen which had been preserved by the sediment. That gave them a snapshot of what the surface foliage would've looked like two-million years before.

The results were revealing: None of the vegetation that covered the Earth back then, would look familiar to us today.

Those plants didn't stick around. They evolved, perished or moved – because that's how nature works: Nature is always changing, improving and *moving*. (Thompson, 2014).

***

Animals also have a long history of migration...

When the Indian subcontinent smashed into Asia, around forty to fifty-million years ago, there were barely any mammals on that land. Scientists have discovered condylarth fossils that predate this event. But they haven't found fossils from any of the mammals that live on the subcontinent today, that are anywhere near as old.

This suggests that those animals migrated from other locations, *after* that historic event.

The seven types of langur monkeys that live in modern-day India, each descend from an older form of monkey, who travelled south up to 7.5 million years ago. Gerbils, antelope and lions wandered across from Africa, before making their homes in the deserts of Western India. Brown rats left Southeast Asia – arriving in India within the last four-thousand years. (Zeng et al, 2018). (Vaidyanathan, 2013).

***

Flat-nosed monkeys are thought to have travelled from Africa to Latin America, approximately fifty-million years ago. This was a fair while after those continents split apart, and a fair while before humans stepped foot upon Earth. Those monkeys probably made the journey atop some kind of raft.

Likewise, rodents travelled across the Panamanian isthmus, long before the two American continents came together. There was no land bridge back then. And so they must have travelled by sea. (De Queiroz, 2014).

***

In the more recent past, several animals have hitched a ride *with us...*

Scientists have proposed that humans transported the grove snail, *Cepaea nemoralis*, from the Iberian Peninsula to Ireland – to eat and possibly to farm – around eight-thousand years ago.

Pre-Neolithic humans are thought to have taken boar to Cyprus, from mainland Greece, two-thousand years before that. (Grindon & Davison, 2013). (Vigne et al, 2009).

Humans domesticated wild cats in Turkey. The Romans and Vikings adopted the furry fellows – using them to control the rodents aboard their ships. Cats were brought to Japan, to protect valuable manuscripts. And they were taken around the world – to control pests, and to offer companionship. (Ottoni et al, 2017).

In fact, pretty much every species of farmyard animal and household pet we're familiar with today, would've been transported to its current location by humans, at one time or another. Because we have a history of travel ourselves...

OUT OF AFRICA

Most cells in our body contain "Mitochondria" – structures which produce the chemical energy we need to grow, move, and remain alive. Mitochondria contain short strands of DNA, known as "Mitochondrial DNA". And this is pretty exceptional stuff: Mitochondrial DNA is passed down from mother to child, it has a high mutation rate, and mutations are carried on by each successive generation. This means that we can trace mitochondrial DNA back up the generations – from daughter to mother to grandmother – all the way to its source.

The conclusion?

At some point in the past, around 200,000 years ago, there was a woman whose mitochondrial DNA was the source of all the mitochondrial DNA that exists in humans today. That woman was the mother of humankind – a real-life "Eve".

Unlike the biblical Eve, this Eve was not the first human, or even the first *Homo sapiens*. And she certainly wasn't made from one of her husband's ribs! But she was our most recent *common* ancestor – one of about ten-thousand humans who were alive at the time. Those people all lived in Africa – their very own "Garden of Eden". But they didn't stay put. Their descendants left that mother continent – moving from place to place – establishing homes across the globe. (Gugliotta, 2008).

Scientific research supports the theory...

A 2007 study – which tested Aboriginal Australians, and Melanesians from New Guinea – found that their mitochondrial DNA shared common features with those people who were living in Africa, over fifty-thousand years before. There was no evidence to suggest they'd evolved independently. (Hudjashov et al, 2007).

A more extensive study, conducted a year later, looked at genetic material gathered from over nine-hundred unrelated individuals, in fifty-one different regions. Checking 650,000 locations within the genome, scientists found enough commonality to suggest "A serial founder" with a "Single origin in sub-Saharan Africa". (Li et al, 2008).

***

But this "Out of Africa" theory isn't the only game in town...

An alternative, the "Multiregional Hypothesis", argues that different groups of modern humans (*Homo sapiens*) evolved in different places, at different times. Australian Aboriginals may have evolved from Java Man (*Homo erectus*), whilst Europeans may have evolved from Neanderthals, and perhaps from Cro-Magnons.

Such a view is controversial. But even if it were true, it wouldn't affect the story of human migration. The Multiregional Hypothesis still traces *Homo sapiens* back to the first ever humans – *Homo habilis* – who appeared in Southern and Eastern Africa, around two-million years ago.

Homo habilis never left Africa. But they were the common ancestor of *all* the varieties of humans who've followed. And these humans *did* move about.

Homo erectus left Africa around 1.9 million years ago. They reached Java, 1.7 million years ago, and Western Europe, 1.2 million years ago. Neanderthals and Denisovans also evolved in Africa before migrating. The former headed to Europe and Northern Asia, while the latter headed east. (Carotenuto et al, 2016). (Fleagle, 2010).

Whether we all descend from a small group of *Homo habilis*, who lived in Africa two-million years ago, or from a small group of *Homo sapiens*, who evolved there more recently – the two theories both agree that we all have these common ancestors, who lived in a small part of Africa. We're all members of a single human family. And, unless you're still living in the same place as those first humans, then you are the descendant of emigrants yourself – of some ancient human beings, who left their African homeland, wandered the Earth, and settled down in a new location.

Let's take a look at their journey...

***

The "Omo One" bones, which were discovered in modern-day Ethiopia, are the oldest *Homo sapiens* remains to have ever been unearthed. They feature the rounded skulls and pointed chins which separate us from other humans. And new research – which compared the volcanic ash on these fossils, with ash from historic eruptions in the region – suggests that these humans were walking the Earth around 233,000 years ago. (Vidal et al, 2022).

The oldest *Homo sapiens* remains to be found *outside* Africa – in caves in modern-day Israel – are less than 100,000 years old. The people who lived there appear to have perished, without travelling any further.

It was only around eighty-thousand years ago, that up to fifty-thousand humans left Africa for good – probably using a land bridge which crossed the Red Sea.

***

Why would they do such a thing, after barely leaving the mother continent during the previous 150,000 years?

University of Cape Town archaeologist, John Parkington, argues that our ancestors left Africa soon after they began to eat seafood. He points to the seashells, found in the caves they inhabited around this time, and claims that the fatty acids in that food would've fuelled their oversized brains, making them "More cognitively aware, faster-wired, faster-brained, smarter."

Paleoanthropologist Richard Klein, of Stanford University, reckons that the early *Homo sapiens* experienced a genetic mutation, which improved their brainpower, and maybe gifted them with the ability to speak.

Language would've certainly inspired movement: It would've enabled our ancestors to coordinate hunts across wider tracts of terrain, and it would've helped them to interact with those strangers whom they met whilst travelling. (Gugliotta, 2008). (Dillehay et al, 2015).

Either theory might be correct. Or it might be that we *followed our prey*.

Desmond Clark argues that our ancestors followed herds of wildebeest, whilst hunting them for food – going wherever *they* wandered. Such an event has parallels in the modern era: Some Frenchmen moved to the Americas in the seventeenth century, to hunt the animals they needed for pelts. And people from the Azores, in the mid-Atlantic, sailed to New England whilst chasing whales. (Shah, 2020).

Alternatively, it might be that *environmental* factors were at play.

A great drought occurred around the time our ancestors first left Africa. That might've forced those early humans to move wherever there was water. Cold snaps could've lowered the seas, opening up land bridges for them to cross. And climate change might've turned the deserts of North Africa into savannah-like corridors, which would've been easier to traverse than before. (Timmermann & Friedrich, 2016).

***

Whatever the cause, once they'd begun their onward march, our ancestors were hard to stop...

They began by following the coastline of Eastern Africa and Southern Asia – the route of least resistance. The fruits and shellfish which lined that route, would've been similar to the foods they'd always eaten. The climate and geography would've been similar to the places they'd always lived.

They arrived on the Indian continent within a few thousand years.

Archaeological evidence, discovered at Jwalapuram, suggests that an agricultural community already existed in the south of the subcontinent when the Toba volcano erupted, around 74,000 years ago. (Gugliotta, 2008). (Dillehay et al, 2015).

Our ancestors didn't stay still for long.

Those who headed north, arrived on the Tibetan plateau around 62,000 years ago. Others continued on through Indonesia and Papua New Guinea, before arriving on the Australian continent, at least 45,000 years before the present day.

That was a risky business.

Ben Finney, a Harvard anthropologist, estimates that over half-a-million people must've lost their lives whilst searching for Polynesian islands. But despite the death toll, those people continued to make that journey – compelled by an urge to explore. (Finney, 1991).

***

It took a little longer for *Homo sapiens* to arrive in Europe...

Perhaps our ancestors were discouraged by the inclement weather. Or perhaps they wished to steer clear of the Neanderthals who stood in their way. Whatever the case, they eventually made the trip, around forty-thousand years ago. Within five-thousand years, they'd spread across the continent – forcing the Neanderthals into the mountains. And within fifteen-thousand years, the Neanderthals were extinct. (Gugliotta, 2008). (Dillehay et al, 2015).

***

Just because our ancestors had spread across the globe, and settled in several locations, this didn't mean that they stayed put.

Modern Europeans don't share a single lineage – there's really no such thing as a "Purebred European". Over the millennia which followed, some people turned around, left Asia, and headed back west – joining up with their European peers. These new arrivals were a mixed bag – they included hunter-gatherers with darker skin, farmers with dark eyes but lighter complexions, and a second group of farmers who had lighter hair. They interbred with the people they met in Europe, creating a mongrel population – one which was part African, part Asian, and part European. (Reich, 2018).

***

That only left the New World...

Humans reached North America, either via the Bering Land Bridge or by boat, sometime within the last 25,000 years.

They made it to the southernmost tip of what is now Chile – a distance of 15,000 kilometres – in less than five millennia. (Gugliotta, 2008). (Dillehay et al, 2015).

Our ancestors had well and truly spread out across the globe.

THE BIRTH OF THE BORDER

The evidence is overwhelming: We humans have always sauntered about. *Homo erectus* migrated. Neanderthals migrated. Denisovans migrated. And *Homo sapiens* continue to migrate today.

So, what happened? When did we start erecting barriers – placing limits on who could move where, and when they could move?

You could point at the fact that some of us like to mark our territory, in much the same way that a dog might urinate on a post. Hunter-gatherers have been known to cut symbols into tree trunks, on the edges of their terrain. Some hang bones from the branches.

But it'd be wrong to compare these to the national borders that dominate the world today. A few wooden notches aren't going to deter an intrepid explorer. They're nothing like the militarised zone which separates North and South Korea.

***

Let's visit the Arctic Circle, to see what I mean...

In Siberia, Evenk clans mark their territory using hearths, tent frames, valuable objects, graves, coloured rags, sculptures, eyeballs and genitals. (It should be noted that they use *animal* genitals – not human ones).

The Evenk even display their dead – placing them in trees or on ledges. They have a clear idea of what is their territory, at any given time, and have gone as far as to kill people who've hunted on their land without seeking their permission.

But the fact remains that outsiders wouldn't be killed just for crossing a border. They'd be welcomed if they weren't hunting – plundering a precious resource.

Various Evenk clans share the *same* hunting grounds. And they subject themselves to collective agreements – to prevent over-hunting, and to ensure that each clan has equal access to their shared resources.

It should also be noted that there's an impermanence to it all, at least in the case of the Evenk: Their markers only define the area which is being used at a particular time. When the clan moves on, their markers decompose – vanishing from the face of the Earth. (Grøn, 2015).

***

It'd be wrong to read too much into a single society. Contemporary hunter-gatherers give us a view of what society *might* have looked like in prehistoric times, but their habits are influenced by the world at large. Groups like the Evenk are surrounded by nation-states, who'd like to claim their land. This has to affect their behaviour.

Still, we do have written accounts from colonial explorers, who encountered other tribal groups in the era *before* nation-states dominated the globe.

They give a nuanced view...

Such societies weren't all alike. They had different systems of governance, which evolved over time. But it's safe to say that their members *did* manage the land: So-called "Hunter-gatherers" were known to weed, coppice, fertilize, prune and burn. They terraced estuarine plots, built clam gardens, and created weirs to catch fish.

These peoples *did* restrict access to those weirs and terraces. But, like with the Evenk, this didn't require a hard border. Everyone was granted access to those resources, just at *different times*. Neighbouring groups agreed upon a set of rotas, which determined who could access the land on specific days, and what they could harvest. (Graeber & Wengrow, 2021).

***

So, what happened next?

It'd be easy to associate the emergence of controls on migration, with the rise of towns and cities – to think people must have erected barriers, to separate themselves from outsiders, just as soon as they began to live together *en masse*.

It'd be easy to think this, but it'd also be wrong. The first towns and cities were *temporary* affairs – short-lived camps, which were created when *nomads* came together, and destroyed when they dispersed.

At places like Dolní Věstonice (27,000 to 20,000 BCE), in the Czech Republic, the evidence suggests that people assembled to feast, perform rituals, complete artistic projects, and trade. Once they were sated, they went off on their merry way.

Similar archaeological sites can be found in Western Europe – at the French Périgord and alongside the Cantabrian coast.

In fact, almost *all* those Ice Age settlements which left archaeological remains – with monuments, architecture and burial sites that we can rediscover today – were created by people who were mobile for the larger part of the year.

***

The same can be said of the era that followed...

People gathered at the stone temples of Göbekli Tepe (9500 to 8000 BCE), in modern-day Turkey, during the late summer and early autumn. They hunted the gazelles which appeared at that time of year, processed nuts and cereals, built the world's oldest known megaliths, feasted, and then scattered in every direction.

The version of Stonehenge (3000 to 500 BCE) which exists today, is the latest in a long line of monuments which would've stood proudly at the centre of a temporary city. Pilgrims came from across the British Isles, to celebrate the solstices at Stonehenge. But when the festivities were done, they packed their possessions and left. (Graeber & Wengrow, 2021).

***

So, did the first controls on migration appear along with the first *permanent* city-states?

Perhaps.

If you were to visit the British Museum, you might come across a cream-coloured bollard. Covered in humanity's earliest-known writing, Sumerian cuneiform, it details the "Treaty of Mesilim" – a short-lived accord in which the rulers of Umma and Lagash, in modern-day Iraq, agreed to remain on either side of an earthy channel.

The peace didn't last for long. One side encroached upon the other's territory. The other side fought back. An even bigger canal was constructed, which was filled with water and surrounded by an exclusion zone – a literal *No Man's Land*. The first side felt aggrieved. They dried up the channel and launched another incursion. The border channel was enlarged for a *third* time. It extended for sixty kilometres, and probably featured several steles like the one on display in London.

It's the stuff of folklore as much as history. The fable refers to a deity who allocated the two towns to rival siblings, before commanding a third person to dig the channel. The stele's author clearly had an agenda: When the scribe writes of Shara, the god of Umma, the text becomes so pale and erratic, it's almost illegible. It's as though they're taunting the other side. The scribe portrays the people of Umma as a bunch of unrelenting meanies – menaces who don't appear to do anything other than burn temples, topple statues, plunder treasure, and spoil barley.

Perhaps it was one of the first examples of fake news. Or perhaps it shows us something more important: How taking two related peoples, and placing them on either side of a border, can create the sort of hostility which leaves a trail of blood in its wake. Such a tale must sound pretty familiar to anyone who lives in a disputed territory today.

But the Treaty of Mesilim has also been called the "First peace treaty" in human history. And it did mark out the world's first *known* border – a short-lived affair, which was created and destroyed around 4,500 years ago. (Crawford, 2023).

***

The message should be clear: The original borders were

contested. Some people attempted to rope off a section of territory, and say: "This is ours". But other people opposed them, saying: "No way! We also use this land. Learn to share, you greedy buggers!"

We had a *clash of cultures*...

On the one hand, there were these new, sedentary peoples – who constructed permanent settlements and dedicated themselves to farming full-time. These communities produced a surplus of food – meaning that some individuals could consume food which *others* had grown, whilst dedicating themselves to different pursuits – to construction, healthcare, or the production of items such as tools. In time, these societies expanded. They developed a political class – with priests, politicians and soldiers – people who drew borders and then attempted to defend them.

On the other hand, the majority of people were still nomadic: They lived in smallish communities, governed themselves, and moved whenever they chose. They practiced a little agriculture, but they didn't store much of a surplus. They didn't have fixed borders, and saw no need to recognise the borders which other people had invented.

State-based and nomadic societies both wanted to use the same tracts of land.

States wanted to expand into non-state spaces – irrigating the earth, erecting fences, and capturing slaves – forcing other people to become sedentary and practice their religions.

But stateless people wanted to continue to access the lands they'd always wandered, which were being consumed by these new and expanding states. (Scott, 1999).

***

This conflict – between nomadic and sedentary people – is summed up in the biblical story of Cain and Abel...

Cain was the first agriculturalist – a man who settled down on a fixed plot of land, to plant and grow his crops. Abel was more of a free-spirit – a pastoralist, who wandered about with his flock of sheep.

When the brothers made offerings to God, the Lord accepted Abel's sacrifice, but rejected Cain's. The farmer flew into a rage, and murdered his nomadic brother.

It's an allegorical tale, which demonstrates how townsfolk began to replace their more itinerant peers – not because they had the better way of life, and certainly not because they were more righteous – but because they were more *violent*. They obliterated their nomadic brethren.

***

It's best not to treat the scriptures as a factual source. And the transition from nomadism to sedentarism wasn't always so bloody.

Let's consider the Berber saying: "Raiding is our agriculture".

The Berbers *benefitted* from sedentarism, because it granted them the opportunity to harvest massive amounts of food – by *raiding* villages, gathering grains from the granaries, and leading the livestock away.

This might have inspired a violent reaction. But sedentary peoples were pretty helpless to resist. Their armies were able to ransack other *villages*. They could wage war on other *towns*. But they weren't much use when it came to combatting these small nomadic bands, who were agile enough to melt away into the surrounding hills, swamps, forests and grasslands. "Sea Nomads", such as pirates, could sail out into the great blue yonder. (Scott, 2017).

There was, however, only so much that those nomads could reasonably gather. If they took *all* the food, the villagers would perish. They'd kill the geese who lay the golden eggs.

It was in their own self-interest to only take a little – leaving enough for the sedentary community to survive. And so, these two unlikely bedfellows had an incentive to come to an arrangement – a kind of *protection racket*: The nomads would be granted a portion of the goods, grain and livestock that the townsfolk produced. In return, they promised to stop raiding, and they pledged to protect those communities from *other* potential raiders.

Sedentary societies were essentially bribing their nomadic neighbours, to grant them exclusive rights to the territories they'd claimed for themselves – paying their rivals to acknowledge their borders.

These arrangements could evolve over time: The raiders might be given the right to oversee a particular trade, police a certain trade route, or raid the state's enemies. They might settle down themselves, on a nearby patch of land – a territory with a border of its own. (Tilly, 1985).

***

We see this in Northern China...

When the Eastern Han Dynasty wished to establish their state, they faced a challenge from the Xiongnu – a tribal confederation of nomadic peoples, who were the ancestors of the modern-day Mongols. The Xiongnu were skilled raiders – able to empty the Han's stores, and retreat to the Asian steppes before anyone had noticed.

But the Xiongnu sensed an opportunity.

They sent envoys to negotiate with the Han – promising to stop their raiding, and usher in a period of peace – so long as they received a "Subsidy".

The Han acquiesced, both parties signed a treaty, and the Xiongnu pledged allegiance to the Han – recognising the Han's rights to their territory, and agreeing to respect their border. But this peace came with a hefty price-tag: The Han committed to pay what amounted to a "Reverse tribute". And it was massive – the equivalent of *one-third* of the government's annual budget.

***

Such a tale was hardly unique...

The Tang Dynasty did something similar – paying half-a-million bolts of silk a year to the Uighurs.

Further west, the Persian kings paid off the Cissians. In return, those mountain-folk promised not to raid the Persian's land, or threaten its trade.

Ramses the Third of Egypt appeased the Sea Nomads, by offering them land in Lower Canaan. They settled down, and became the "Philistines".

The Romans paid the Celts 450 kilograms of gold, to convince them to stop their raiding. They also paid tributes to the Huns and the Goths. (Barfield, 1991).

EGYPT, ATHENS AND ROME

For the vast majority of human history, borders didn't exist.

Then a few communities established permanent settlements. They had to bribe or attack their nomadic neighbours, to get them to respect the boundaries they'd invented.

Those communities became city-states, and then they became empires. Something akin to borders may have formed organically, as those empires began to expand – pressing up against their rivals' lands. It seems likely that a border would have formed between the Mesopotamian and Egyptian Empires, as they came into contact near Basra (Iraq), Abadan (Iran), and some other parts of the Fertile Crescent. But without sufficient archaeological evidence, it's hard to pinpoint that border's exact location.

Even if such a line did exist, it would've been very different to the borders we're familiar with today.

Those boundaries were in constant flux – they moved back and forth over time. Early civilisations didn't possess the manpower or technology required to police those tracts of land. Nor did they have the desire. Some ancient empires *did* discriminate between their citizens and their guests. But controls on movement were almost non-existent.

***

Let's begin by taking a look at ancient Egypt...

Egypt's status as the economic powerhouse of its age, and its convenient location – at the intersection of Africa, Asia and Europe – encouraged inward migration. The Papyrus Brooklyn documents a vast melting-pot of a nation, as far back as the Second Millennium BCE. The region was home to people from the Levant, Nubia, Libya, Delta and Nile Valleys. The records show people with non-Egyptian names at all levels of society – from the prisoners who were used for forced labour, to domestic servants, to high-ranking officials. Non-Egyptians worked as craftspeople, policemen and soldiers. They intermarried, and don't appear to have been treated any differently from the original population. (Priglinger, 2019).

The physical evidence supports the written records.

Archaeologists have studied the teeth, taken from thirty-six skeletons buried at Avaris. A person's teeth take in tiny amounts of strontium from the food they eat during their childhood. By analysing the isotopes within this strontium, and checking to see if they match the isotopes in the soil, scientists can determine if a person grew up in that specific area. In the case of the Avaris teeth, it turned out that twenty-four of the individuals had spent their childhoods somewhere else. *Two-thirds* of the people had moved after reaching adulthood. And this was no short-lived phenomenon. Those skeletons belonged to people who were alive at different times. They represented 350 years of migration.

The people at that site wouldn't have been regular Egyptians. Avaris was the capital city of the Hyksos people. And ancient artwork shows that the Hyksos were a little different: They wore multicoloured clothing, rather than the white robes which were worn by typical Egyptians. They don't appear to have assimilated. And they didn't have typical Egyptian names.

Yet the evidence shows that they came and went, living on Egyptian territory for several centuries, without causing much of a fuss. It has even been claimed that the Hyksos invented the Egyptian alphabet.

***

It'd be wrong to view the entire epoch through rose-tinted lenses. During a period of weak Egyptian rule, between 1630 and 1523 BCE, the Hyksos seized control of Northern Egypt. When the Pharaohs returned to power, they banished the Hyksos elite – an event which is thought to have inspired the Exodus story of the Old Testament. (Stantis et al, 2021).

That was one of the first documented cases of anti-immigrant policy. But it was an outlier. Foreigners remained welcome for the larger part of antiquity. Indeed, travel also played a crucial role in *Athenian* life...

Theseus, the mythical founder of Athens, travelled from place to place whilst establishing a name for himself – voyaging to Crete to slay the Minotaur. Hercules was just as famous for killing mythical beasts. He had to travel beyond the Peloponnese, to complete six of his "Twelve Labours".

Later generations of Athenian youths were also compelled to leave Athens' jurisdiction – to gain experience of the wider world. In a time before formal schooling, this kind of travel wasn't just a rite of passage, it was their main form of *education*.

Some youths appeared to have enjoyed the experience so much, they remained where they were – establishing expat communities abroad. (Bremmer, 2021).

***

Outsiders were welcomed in most of the city-states which made up Ancient Greece – so long as they could find a local who was willing to vouch for them. Indeed, between a third and a half of Athens's free inhabitants had been born elsewhere.

This isn't to say they were accorded equal status. The "Metics", as they were known, had to pay higher taxes. They were expected to fulfil all the responsibilities of full citizens, including military service, and yet they were denied the right to own property, marry or vote.

But the Metics were still protected by the law. They could earn their citizenship. And some of them, such as Aristotle, achieved a level of fame which has echoed down the ages. (Stefanopoulos, 2022).

***

The locals liked to have these new residents around. They were a boon: They served in the army, bolstered the economy, and paid a great deal of tax. The Delphic priests even argued that free movement should be considered one of the "Four Freedoms", which separated liberty from slavery. (Westermann, 1945).

Indeed, such was the clamour for immigrant labour, that the tax burden imposed upon the Metics was eventually reduced. The historian, Diodorus of Sicily, tells us that: "Themistocles persuaded the people... to remove the tax upon Metics and artisans, in order that great crowds of people might stream into the city from every quarter, and that the Athenians might easily procure labour for a greater number of crafts." (Siculus, 1946).

This *pro-migration* sentiment was summed up by Xenophon – the Greek military leader, philosopher and historian – who wrote: "The greater the number of people attracted to Athens, either as visitors or as residents, the greater the development of imports and exports. More goods will be sent out of the country, there will be more buying and selling, with a consequent influx of money in the shape of rents to individuals, and dues and customs to the state." (Xenophon, 2008).

***

This philosophy would prove contagious – fuelling the growth of Greece's neighbours: The Romans...

Legend has it that the city of Rome was established by twins, Romulus and Remus, who descended from a Trojan warrior – Aeneas – who headed west when Troy fell, made a home for himself, and gave birth to the Roman lineage.

If this tale is to be believed, then the Roman Empire owes its origin to the descendants of a foreign refugee – someone who moved to Rome from Greece.

Romulus and Remus didn't get off to the most auspicious of starts – they were orphaned and raised by a wolf! Romulus murdered his brother, established the city of Rome, and declared himself its leader. But he had a problem: He was a king, he had a kingdom, but he needed *subjects*.

And so, he declared Rome an asylum – a "Sanctuary or place of refuge and protection". He welcomed criminals, runaway slaves, the disposed, and the down-and-out.

As Mary Beard once put it: "The message about Rome's origins is clear: Rome was always foreign." It was founded by the descendants of a Trojan refugee, and it was built by people who moved there from other parts of the Italian peninsula. (Beard, 2016).

***

The empire which that city would go on to spawn was just as foreign – a multicultural, multilingual, "Empire of immigrants" – home to an array of Franks, Armenians, Vandals, Moors and Ethiopians. Tens-of-millions of these people were absorbed as Rome expanded. Others were enticed by the opportunities that Rome had to offer.

Whatever their story, such people remained free – so long as they weren't captured in war. They could move between Rome's provinces – each of which had a different culture, with different customs, a different climate, and different industries. (Boin, 2020). (Murphy, 2007).

There was a good chance they'd become citizens.

Whenever Rome incorporated a new territory, they granted full citizenship to the local elites – no questions asked. Those families didn't have to speak Latin, worship Roman Gods, or behave in a Roman fashion. It wasn't about *them*. It was about Rome. The imperial capital was buying the loyalty of would-be-enemies, by giving them a stake in the Roman system. (Beard, 2016a).

One of the most common ways to earn citizenship, was by working as a soldier for twenty-five years. There was a clear logic to the policy: Foreign soldiers assimilated on the job, whilst working alongside their Roman comrades. They received a formal education: Commanding officers oversaw lessons in geography, maths, engineering and Latin – preparing their charges for citizenship. And those foreign soldiers also ended up with a small slice of the empire for themselves: When soldiers retired from the Roman legions, they were rewarded with a portion of arable land – all the equipment, seeds and livestock they required to turn it into a going concern – as well as access to healthcare, legal rights, and tax exemptions. It was a good deal. And the citizenship they earned could be passed down the generations.

Other immigrants earned full citizenship by swapping the comforts of Rome, for a more hazardous existence near the empire's frontier. They could petition the emperor for citizenship. They could earn citizenship through marriage. Or they could get lucky: Rome extended citizenship to almost *every Roman resident*, on at least three occasions: During its Italian Wars, during its period of colonial expansion, and through Emperor Caracalla's reforms of 212. (Boin, 2020).

***

The Roman Empire did have a border. And it was extensive –

stretching on for eight-thousand kilometres. That's more than double the length of the border which separates the USA from Mexico. But Rome's borders weren't heavily patrolled. They weren't fixed. They were more like transitional zones. Many sections were defined by natural features – by mountains, seas or rivers. Only a few were marked by walls.

Hadrian's Wall, which divides England from Scotland, is one of the most famous. And at first sight, it might seem rather daunting – something which screams: "Oi, you nasty Scots, stay away from our lovely empire". But that wall was designed to be *permeable*. There were gateways every mile. Goods moved in both directions. Rome's frontiers were places where people *came together*, engaged in trade, and exchanged ideas. (Murphy, 2007).

Pretty much every soldier who patrolled that wall, had moved there from overseas. Some had come from afar afield as Syria and Ethiopia.

But it wasn't only soldiers who made that move. Traders were also in on the act. And the scale of their movement was extensive: Tooth enamel extracted from Roman-era skeletons found in Britain, tells us that more than one-in-five people had moved there *after* growing up overseas. (Beard, 2016a).

There were also occasions when *entire tribes* requested entry into the Roman Empire. They were welcomed. The Romans even had a procedure for dealing with these new arrivals: They had to surrender their weapons, renounce their previous allegiances, and supply men to the Roman armies. Their tribes were divided into smaller groups, and sent to live in sparsely populated regions.

This arrangement was mutually beneficial: The members of those tribes received land and protection. The Roman Empire benefitted from a stronger economy, with higher tax receipts and a larger army. (Heather, 2012). (Dyson, 1985).

***

Once again, it'd be wrong to paint *too* rosy a picture...

The Roman Empire never closed its borders. But as the centuries rolled by, so some Romans did begin to close their minds – judging outsiders for the way they dressed, spoke and behaved.

When a foreign-born soldier named Maximinus Thrax became emperor, in 235, senators nicknamed him "Cyclops". They quipped about his "Lowly origin", and implied that his ascent had as much to do with luck, as with talent. (Herodian, 1961).

These attitudes bubbled away for a couple of centuries – eroding Rome's liberal ethos, and setting in motion the events which would lead to its downfall.

There would be no repeat of Caracalla's reforms. People still came. They were still *required*. But they weren't accorded the rights of previous generations. (Boin, 2020).

A two-tier system emerged...

The first restrictions on movement were introduced in the third century. But it was under Constantine's legislation of 332 that things really transformed: The *coloni* – tenant farmers, who worked on estates which were owned by a new Roman elite – were downgraded to a slave-like status. They were bound to obey whatever rules their landlords imposed, and *forbidden from travelling* elsewhere – unless they were called upon to fight in a war.

Claiming that free movement was a threat to order, Rome's lawmakers even introduced the first ever *passport* – a certificate which requested that the bearer be granted safe passage. Anyone who didn't possess this document, was prevented from moving around *within* the Roman empire.

It was a turning point – the first step towards a system of serfdom. (Dowty, 1987). (Basta, 2017).

***

The Romans even turned their backs on the policy which had served them so well, when it came to integrating foreign *tribes*...

A few decades after Constantine's death, a Gothic tribe – the Thervingi – asked the leader of the Eastern Roman Empire to grant them admission. This request was accepted. But things turned sour when local military commanders withheld the Thervingi's food – selling it at inflated prices. The Thervingi became so desperate, they were forced to sell their children into slavery, just to get the money they needed to buy food.

Those local leaders even ignored their own rules – forgetting to take the Thervingi's weapons, and failing to split them into smaller groups.

When another Gothic tribe – the Greuthungi – arrived on the banks of the Danube, the emperor ignored protocol and rejected their request for admittance.

The Greuthungi crossed without permission. The Thervingi began to riot. Those tribes united with other Gothic tribes – launching a six-year war which left a trail of blood in its wake.

When that war ended, the Goths were granted an independent state within the Roman Empire – remaining a source of instability in the years which were to come. (Marcellinus, 1939).

***

Things spiralled out of control...

Foreign families were kidnapped and attacked in public, doors were slammed in the faces of starving immigrants, and a place of worship was burnt to the ground. One contemporary decried the foreign "Pestilence" which was ravaging the Roman way of life. (Claudian, 1922).

The Romans had become complacent.

They assumed that their foreign guests would be content with second-class status – tilling Roman fields, stocking Roman larders, and fighting in the Roman army – without receiving any of the rewards they'd been granted in previous times.

This attitude would prove to be catastrophic.

After many centuries of immigrant-friendly policy – in which the Roman nation had become an empire, expanded, and become prosperous – a two century period of intolerance, eventually culminated in a series of insurrections, which led to the fall of the Western Roman Empire. (Boin, 2020).

WALLING US IN

Hadrian's Wall wasn't the only border wall in the Roman Empire. It wasn't even the only wall which ran across Britain. The Antonine Wall was constructed a little to the north.

The Roman Empire was dotted with other walls, ditches and forts. But none of these could claim to be the *original* border wall.

That accolade probably belongs to the "Amorite Wall", which is thought to have covered a 160 kilometre stretch between the Tigris and Euphrates Rivers. The Sumerians erected that barrier to stop a nomadic people – the Amorites – from travelling across a portion of land they wished to keep for themselves. It failed to do its job, in a quite spectacular fashion: The Amorites and Elamites made it past that wall, ransacked Ur, and vanquished the Sumerians!

The Amorite Wall was built around four-thousand years ago. That's over two-thousand years before Hadrian's Wall, and 1,500 years before construction began on some portions of the Great Wall of China.

Mainly made from compressed earth, those walls were dispersed across various stretches of China's northern border. It was only when Qin Shi Huang united the Chinese nation, that those sections were connected. And that was in 220 CE – a century after work had begun on the Scottish border.

Over the generations which followed, Huang's wall was upgraded. Bricks, granite and marble took the place of wood and rammed earth. But it was only in 1368, when Zhu Yuanzhang founded the Ming Dynasty, that the wall began to take on the appearance we're familiar with today. All nine-thousand *kilometres* of it!

***

Along with the Treaty of Mesilim, and the trench which separated Umma from Lagash, these walls supply archaeological evidence which proves that some borders did exist, during the last few millennia.

As in the case of Rome, they may have been fairly permeable – welcoming a flow of people, goods and ideas. But their construction was often accompanied by an inhumane kind of rhetoric – this idea that the *insiders* needed to be "Protected" from the *outsiders* who lurked beyond: The Chinese built the Great Wall to keep tax-paying citizens within their territory. But they also wanted to keep the Huns away. The Sumerians built their wall to separate themselves from the Amorites.

Border walls would've been just as contentious back then, as they are today. The people who built them, might have approved of their construction. But the people on the other side weren't ever asked for their consent. Those walls might have marked a border, but we cannot say that those borders were *uncontested*. (Winchester, 2021). (Scott, 2017).

WHEN NATIONS BECAME NATION-STATES

After the fall of the Western Roman Empire, Roman landowners retained control over their estates. They became *feudal lords*. Their coloni became *serfs*.

Serfs worked on a small tract of land which was owned by a lord. They produced the food they needed to eat, as well as the materials they needed to build their homes and make their clothes. But they were never truly free. They had to secure their lord's permission before they could marry, change their occupation, or *leave their village*.

The majority of Europeans were denied the right to move, from the time of Constantine's reforms, in 332, up until the end of the Middle Ages. Similar arrangements began to appear in other parts of the world, throughout this period.

But it's hard to imagine that the serfs were especially happy with this state of affairs, and many did attempt to travel.

To prevent free movement, Thai lords tattooed their peasants – branding them as property. Those people still took flight, migrating to the forests, and bounty hunters had to be employed to track them down. In Russia, the majority of Czarist decrees focused on one issue:

How to deal with runaway serfs – those people who were determined to move around, despite it being illegal. Likewise, the Manchu emperors in China issued an outright ban on *emigration*, which remained in place until 1893. But people continued to move abroad, in defiance of that draconian law. (Scott, 1997). (Pan, 1994).

These are examples of *individuals* who rebelled in the name of freedom. It took quite a while for serfs to rebel *as a collective*. But this did happen, in the fourteenth and fifteenth centuries, in the wake of the Black Death.

That plague decimated the population – claiming up to 200 million lives. And that put the survivors in a stronger position than before: Craftspeople were in demand in different locations. And peasant farmers had a new incentive to move – to work on other tracts of land, where the soil was more fertile. (Khanna, 2021).

The system began to crack.

Some peasants were given permission to move. The others took matters into their own hands – staging a series of revolts which ended serfdom in Western Europe.

In England, these rebellions began with the Peasants' Revolt of 1381. And, by 1500, almost every English serf had been freed.

***

Nations had existed throughout the era of serfdom, but they were a little different from the nation-states we live in today.

The Kingdom of Wessex, in the south of Britain, can trace its roots back to 519 – just a couple of generations after the fall of Rome. It was one of Wessex's rulers, King Athelstan, who united the other Anglo-Saxon nations – establishing England, back in 927.

But at that time, most English people would've identified with their local areas, rather than their nation. Had you asked them who was in charge, they'd have pointed to their local lord, not their nation's monarch. Kings existed, but their power was limited. It was these lords who got things done.

The nation-state, with centralised control, didn't develop until much later: King Henry the Seventh began developing the English nation-state in the 1480s. Ferdinand and Isabella followed suit, in

Spain, the following decade. Ivan the Terrible unified Russia in the 1500s.

To shore up their grip on power, these monarchs encouraged a sense of *nationalism*. They wanted their subjects to feel a sense of loyalty to the *nation* – a portion of land encircled by a border.

***

After the system of serfdom was abolished, both immigration and internal migration were generally encouraged. Immigrants were even offered citizenship and tax incentives, because they were seen as *financial assets* – resources who produced wealth for the capital-owning classes. But emigration was usually discouraged. It represented a loss of these valuable assets. (Dowty, 1987).

Britain welcomed an influx of Italian musicians and German traders. Protestants from the Low Countries followed in their wake – bringing the trades which would spark the Industrial Revolution. Huguenot refugees arrived from France, and Christian refugees arrived from Greece. (Winder, 2010).

There was, however, a rather dark exception to the rule: To create a homogenous national identity, some ethnic-minorities were expelled en masse. By the end of the 1500s, most Jews had been forced out of central and Western Europe, around 175,000 Protestants had been banished from the Spanish Netherlands, and most Muslims had been removed from Spain. (Dowty, 1987).

***

Establishing nation-states with fixed borders, was no simple task. Different rulers laid claim to the same territories. Some groups desired independence from others.

Such disputes came to a head with the Thirty Years War – a collection of battles, which took place between 1618 and 1648 – and which plagued almost all of continental Europe.

That bloody conflict came to a close in the German province of Westphalia, when representatives from most European nations gathered to thrash out a deal.

The results were far-reaching: The member states of the Holy Roman Empire were granted full sovereignty, with independence from papal control. The Netherlands was granted independence from Spain, the Swiss Confederation became an independent republic, Sweden secured control of the Baltic, France expanded, and Spain lost its status as Europe's major power.

For the first time in history, the representatives from *several* nations, had agreed on an entire set of *undisputed* borders, which covered almost an entire continent. The "Settlement of Westphalia" created a community of sovereign states, each of which was defined by a fixed boundary which their neighbours – fellow signatories – had agreed to respect.

Within these borders, monarchs were granted a great deal of authority – with total control over religious matters, legislation, taxation and military policy. But they weren't granted absolute control when it came to their borders. As part of the agreement, the members of religious minorities and political dissidents were granted the *right to emigrate* – to flee from persecution, and find a safe haven abroad.

The right to migration had been enshrined in international law. (Crawford, 2023).

***

One thing should be evident by now: Centralised nation-states and internationally-recognized borders are incredibly recent inventions...

Humans have existed for two-million years. *Homo sapiens* have been walking the Earth for up to 300,000 years. But the first ever *internationally-recognised* border – which separated Andorra and France – was only defined in 1278. That's less than eight-hundred years ago. Modern nation-states have only existed for six-hundred years. And a system with multiple, international-recognised borders, has only been in place since 1648.

Even then, borders remained rather porous. As the Secretary of State once stated, in 1872: "By the existing law of Great Britain, all foreigners have the unrestricted right of entrance and residency in this country". (Goldin, 2011).

We may take international borders for granted. We may struggle to perceive a world in which they didn't exist – impinging upon our right to move. But borders didn't exist for 99.87% of our time on Earth. They're not a natural occurrence. They're an incredibly recent invention.

THE USA IS A NATION OF IMMIGRANTS

Borders create barriers to movement, but they don't outlaw it altogether. Even in this era of nation-states, some movement has been actively encouraged...

As European nations established their empires, they went to great lengths to move people around: From 1500 onwards, the European powers shipped over *65 million* people to the lands they'd recently conquered. Some individuals moved from one colony to another. Others, including eighty-million Brits, departed from the motherland.

Some of these people were fleeing from persecution – searching for religious freedom abroad. Among them were the Pilgrim Fathers, and the twenty-thousand Puritans – the people who established the Massachusetts Bay Colony.

Those who had a little capital, went in search of their fortune. There was money to be made in the New World.

Others fled from poverty – becoming indentured servants – agreeing to work for a fixed number of years, to repay the cost of their travel.

Whatever their background, these people were welcomed with open arms. And they continued to be welcomed, even after the USA declared its independence...

Landowners, such as George Washington, wanted to import more people, to create extra demand for the land they already owned – pushing up its price – thereby increasing the value of their portfolios. And the American government required an influx of new residents, to populate the territories it was acquiring as the nation expanded towards the Pacific. Just like in Ancient Rome, some pioneers were even given a parcel of land for free – a reward for heading west.

It wasn't hard for these new arrivals to become American.

The Naturalisation Act of 1790, granted citizenship to any free white person with "Good moral character", who lived in the United States for two years, and swore allegiance to the American Constitution. The act was discriminatory – it gave preference to people who were white. And it was open to abuse – anyone could challenge another person's "Moral character". But the act did offer a clear and straightforward route to inclusion. (Engel, 2021).

***

In the aftermath of the Napoleonic Wars (1815), the European powers became concerned with the prospect of overpopulation at home – believing it to be a cause of unemployment and social unrest. The British encouraged emigration, to alleviate the pressure, and their neighbours followed suit. Not to be outdone, the British went one step further: They shipped off their petty criminals to Australia, to punish them for their crimes. (Dowty, 1987).

Another wave of globetrotters left Europe to escape from *hunger*.

Almost half of those individuals who arrived in the USA, in the 1840s, were fleeing from the Irish Potato Famine. In total, around 4.5 million people travelled from the Emerald Isle to the States. They were only outdone by their German counterparts: five-million Germans moved to the American Midwest in the 1800s.

Around 27 million new arrivals made it to the USA between 1880 and 1930 – a number which included four-million Italians and two-million Jews. A record 1.7 million immigrants arrived in 1907 alone. (Emmer & Lucassen, 2012). (Massey et al, 1998).

Unlike the Western Europeans who'd arrived before, these individuals came from a multitude of nations. They practiced different religions, and spoke a variety of languages. (Nunn et al, 2017).

***

Despite claims from the anti-freedom lobby, rates of migration are actually lower today than they were back then...

These days, around three or four immigrants arrive in the USA each year, for every thousand people who already call that country their home. But between 1890 and 1914, during the "Great Migration", immigration was *double* that rate – about eight immigrants per year, for every thousand residents.

Of the 330 million people living in the States today, around 45 million were born abroad. That's about 13.6% of the population. Back in 1910, that figure was 14.7%. (Griswold, 2002).

In 1900, 77.7% of New Yorkers were either first or second-generation immigrants. That figure is considerably lower today. (Shah, 2020).

The country has *always* been international. And its demography has *always* been in flux: By the end of the 1900s, fewer than a third of Americans had any ancestors who'd been living in the country at the end of the 1700s. More than two-thirds descended from immigrants who'd arrived during the previous two-hundred years. (Gibson, 1992).

**

The USA was able to absorb each wave of new arrivals...

Overseas recruits were needed to *fight*: Both sides called upon foreigners during the American Civil War. The North recruited more than the South – around a quarter of its troops had been born abroad. And this might have even tipped the balance – propelling them on to victory. (Engel, 2021).

Overseas workers were also needed to *build* the USA: They established farms and businesses. They constructed highways, railroads, canals, public buildings and homes. When the States embarked on a process of industrialisation, it was these new residents who did a disproportionate amount of the dangerous work – in industries such as manufacturing and mining. (Hirschman & Mogford, 2009).

The sheer *quantity* of immigrants, enabled the USA to establish way more facilities than before, and to operate much larger factories. A small number of *quality* labourers – with specialist knowledge, skills and experience – enabled the nation to become more efficient. These people were the bedrock of the country's rise – propelling it onto superpower status.

And their contributions have trickled down through the ages: When economists at the Centre for Economic Policy Research crunched the numbers, they concluded that the mass migrations witnessed in *that era*, resulted in benefits which led to "Significantly higher incomes, less poverty, less unemployment, more urbanisation, and higher educational attainment *today.*" (Nunn et al, 2017).

***

During this period, plenty of other people were moving around the Old World...

The Irish didn't only head to the States, when the potato famine took hold. 400,000 of them headed to Britain. By the end of the 1900s, around forty-thousand Italians and fifty-thousand Germans were living in the UK. Many had intended to move to the States, but had settled down whilst midway through their journeys. They were joined by people from India and China, as well as 150,000 Jews – refugees on the run from the Tsarist pogroms. (Winder, 2010).

***

This isn't to suggest that these migrations were unequivocally good.

European colonisation resulted in an estimated 56 million deaths, in the Americas alone. Around 90% of the indigenous population died – succumbing to diseases which the Europeans imported, or coming to a bloody end on the battlefield.

As a consequence of the depopulation that followed, agricultural land was left unattended, fields became overgrown, the regrowth sucked up carbon dioxide, and Earth's temperature decreased. This brought about the "Little Ice Age". The Thames froze over, and snowstorms swept across Portugal. (Koch et al, 2019).

And the movement we witnessed in this era wasn't always *free*...

Between 1468 and 1694, around 1.75 million young men and women were captured by Tatar slave raiders in Eastern Europe, transferred to the Asian part of the Ottoman Empire, and forced to work as slaves. Another 200,000 slaves were sold to the Ottomans during the 1800s.

Other slaves were taken *to* Europe: Anywhere between a

hundred-thousand and a million African slaves were brought north – mainly to Portugal, Spain, Sicily and Northern Italy – where they were forced to work as domestics, craftspeople, and field hands.

The sugar plantations in Spain and Portugal struck upon a new model of operations: They were managed by white Europeans, but African slaves performed all the backbreaking work. This model was so profitable, that Spain and Portugal exported it to their new colonies in the mid-Atlantic. The British, French, Dutch and Danish soon followed suit – capturing between eight and twelve million Africans, and transporting them to the Americas. Millions died in transit. (Davies, 2003).

Having been subjected to a *forced migration*, these slaves were then denied the right to *internal migration*: In Guatemala, they had to wear clothes which featured their owners' unique patterns. In the USA, they were tattooed with their owner's brands. If they travelled without permission, they were returned to their masters and beaten until they bled.

But still, they longed for freedom.

Like the serfs who escaped from their lords, slaves continued to flee from their masters – travelling great distances, with blatant disregard for the law. Slaves in the USA headed for Canada or the "Free states" in the west. Tagalogs in the Philippines migrated to the hills, where they became free "Remontados". And slaves up and down the Americas became "Maroons" – establishing communities in secret locations. (Scott, 1997).

***

We're beginning to paint a nuanced picture...

European colonialism resulted in massive migrations. Some people did move of their own freewill. But others were pressured into moving because of circumstances which were beyond their control – because of things such as famine and poverty. And millions were taken *against* their will – as slaves or indentured labour.

The situation gets even more nuanced the more we look. That's because this period of mass migration, also gave rise to a new form of *anti-migration policy*.

The Spanish were never completely free to move about the Spanish Empire. They had to buy their right to travel – securing a licence which proved they were "Neither Jews nor Moors... Nor sons or grandsons of any that have been punished, condemned or burnt as heretics." Anyone who travelled without such a licence, and was caught, was made to forfeit their property and return to Spain at their own expense. From 1607 onwards, naval officers who helped such people to migrate, were captured and sentenced to *death*.

The Chinese Exclusion Act of 1882, banned Chinese labourers from entering the USA for a ten-year period. The Ellis Island Processing Centre opened its doors in 1890, to check that new arrivals were the "Right" sort of people – not anarchists, prostitutes or polygamists. Legislation passed in 1917, forced adults to take a literacy test upon arrival. And The Immigration Act of 1924, created a quota system – imposing limits on inward migration which favoured Europeans, and discriminated against Asians. (Crawford, 2023).

***

Passports were introduced during the 1700s, in an attempt to reduce emigration. By the end of that century, they'd become obligatory across most of Europe.

But passports fell out of use in the 1800s – when overpopulation had become an issue, and emigration was being encouraged.

During this era, those states which still used passports – the likes of Russia and the Ottoman Empire – were considered backwards and "Uncivilised". (Bregman, 2017).

Subjects moved around the British Empire, as though they were travelling between different parts of the same nation. Those pilgrims who moved to the New World, didn't carry any passports or papers. And where they did exist, passports were little more than a "Laissez Passer" – a request for safe passage. Benjamin Franklin even made his own passport, while working as an ambassador in France! (Khanna, 2021).

Travellers were met with bemusement, whenever they attempted to use such a document: When Phileas Fogg asks the consul of Suez for a stamp – in Jules Verne's novel, "Around the World in Eighty Days"

– he is told, "You know that a visa is useless, and that no passport is required?" (Bregman, 2017).

And they reacted with equal disdain, whenever officials asked *them* for documentation. A character in another novel, said this when he was asked for a passport in 1915: "I have no passport, nor have I any identification card, no immigration stamp, no customs house seal. I have no papers at all. Never in my life did I have any papers. Every age has its inquisition. Our age has the passport." (Goldin, 2011).

Passports were only reintroduced after World War One, in an attempt to control movement between rival nations – to keep soldiers at home, to keep spies at bay, and to control the flow of those people who'd become homeless during the war. (Bregman, 2017).

And again, it's interesting to note how recent this was: Just a little over a century ago, people were still moving from country to country *without any documentation*.

THE POST-COLONIAL ERA

The final position of the Mexican border was only drawn on a map in 1853. And even then, it was mostly ignored – people crossed that frontier without enduring any checks. When surveyors did eventually deposit some obelisks, to mark that frontier, ranchers repositioned them – grabbing a little extra land for themselves! (Washington, 2019).

The craze for nation-building kicked into gear soon after. And it reached a crescendo at the Paris Peace Conference, just after World War One: Between 1900 and 1920, an additional eighty-thousand *kilometres* of borders appeared out of thin air. That's a third of all the land borders which exist in the world today!

Additional exercises in boundary-making took place following the Second World War, the fall of the USSR, and the conflict in the Balkans. But the majority of the world's borders have been stable for around a century.

It might seem as though they've been in place forever. But in reality, they're an incredibly recent invention. (Winchester, 2021).

***

Still, plenty of people continued to travel throughout this period. Some trips were even *encouraged*...

The colonial powers recruited millions of foreign soldiers, to fight in the two world wars. Most came from their colonies – over four-million Indians packed their bags and travelled to the front. But several came from *other* nations. Between them, Britain and France recruited 140,000 Chinese soldiers, during World War One. Three-thousand of them remained in France, even after the fighting was over. (Wang, 2011).

***

Following the break-up of the European Empires, the tide began to turn, as people headed *from* the colonies, *to* their motherlands.

Civil servants returned to Europe, accompanied by their collaborators – by the Moluccan members of the colonial army, who moved from the Dutch East Indies to the Netherlands – by the Nepalese Gurkhas, who travelled to Britain – and by the middle classes in Vietnam, who abandoned communism for a life in the West. (Jordi, 2011).

Almost two-million loyalists arrived in Europe from French North Africa and Indochina, a million came from Portuguese Africa, and 300,000 made the journey from Indonesia. The vast majority of these people had never stepped foot in Europe before. (Maciel, 2011).

***

In 1951, their right to refuge was put on a legal footing by the *Geneva Convention*, "Relating to the Status of Refugees", in which signatories agreed not to return anyone to the countries from which they'd fled.

This right was supported by Article Thirteen of the *Universal Declaration of Human Rights*, which stated: "Everyone has the right to freedom of movement and residence within the borders of each state. Everyone has the right to leave any country, including his own, and to return to his country."

The USA also passed legislation, to allow refugees from Europe and the Soviet Union to make a home for themselves in the "Land of the Free". They welcomed hundreds-of-thousands of people from Cuba, following the Communist Revolution. And they eventually abolished their quota system, in 1965 – opening their doors to their Latin American and Asian peers.

**

Around 200,000 people moved to the UK from Britain's colonies in the West Indies, during the 1950s. Over 9% of Jamaica's population, and over 8% of Barbados's, made a home for themselves in Blighty. Those people – the "Windrush Generation" – were British citizens. They already had British passports. (Emmer, 2011).

These new residents would be outnumbered, the following decade, by those people who moved from India, Bangladesh and Pakistan. (Ballard, 2011).

But it wasn't until 1984, that the rate of immigration *into* Britain overtook the rate of emigration *out* of the island nation. Between 1961 and 1981, a million more people *left* the UK than arrived. Their roles changed: The missionaries and administrators of the colonial era, gave way to the entrepreneurs and employees of the free-market age. Hundreds-of-thousands of retirees headed for the Costa Del Sol, French Riviera and Algarve. But still we continued to travel. (Winder, 2010).

**

And it wasn't only Britain, that was welcoming subjects from their colonies. France was travelling a similar path...

When Algeria gained independence, in 1962, Algerians were granted the right to claim citizenship in France. A million made the transition. New suburbs, replete with housing and schools, were built to accommodate the new arrivals, who were a boon to the French economy: They introduced new machines to the agricultural sector, and helped to expand the fishing industry in the south of their adopted nation. (Mehlem, 2011).

THE END OF FREEDOM

By the end of the nineteenth century, *225 million* of the world's inhabitants were living outside the lands of their birth. These people represented around 14% of the world's population. (Khanna, 2021).

In 2020, around 280 million people were living abroad. But these individuals only represented 3.6% of the world's population. That's ten percentage points lower than before.

These days, *96.4% of people still live in the lands of their birth*. (Batalova, 2022).

Furthermore, most of those people who do move, tend to remain within the same *region*: The biggest group of international citizens – with around 25 million members – have moved about within the former Soviet bloc. The second largest group – comprising around twenty-million Latinos – have stuck to North and Central America. Fifteen-million Africans have moved around Africa, and twelve-million Europeans have moved around Europe. The largest group of people to have moved from one region to another, are the fifteen-million South Asians who've moved to the Gulf. But that's still a part of Asia. (Khanna, 2021).

***

Most people don't move abroad. And those who do, tend not to move too far. But that doesn't mean that many more people don't *wish* to relocate.

In 2021, Gallup interviewed nearly 127,000 people, in 122 countries. Based on this research, they estimated that almost *1.2 billion* people wanted to live abroad. But only 23.7% of these people had actually made the move. The other 76.3% were stuck in the lands of their birth.

Most of these individuals – and there's around 900 million of them in all – hadn't even made plans to move. A 2012 survey, also conducted by Gallup, found that just nineteen-million people were preparing to emigrate – buying tickets and applying for visas. Most of these were rich "Professionals" – three-fifths had a degree. For the majority, migration remained a pipe dream. Something was standing between them and their goal. (Pugliese & Ray, 2023). (Esipova, Pugliese & Ray, 2012).

***

So why has migration remained so low?

The *bureaucracy* has certainly become more complex...

In 1962, the British authorities made it necessary for people to hold a residence permit before moving to the UK – even if they already possessed a British passport. The Dutch copied this policy, in 1975, when they granted independence to Suriname. France, Portugal and Spain all followed suit. (Emmer, 2012).

Authoritarians have also been erecting *physical barriers*.

The fall of the Iron Curtain – that barrier which prevented free movement between Eastern and Western Europe – should've marked a shift towards a freer world. The fall of the Berlin Wall certainly ushered in a wave of optimism. As sections were toppled, so Berliners came together – dancing upon the wreckage – embracing those people who'd been trapped on either side. Tourists travelled from near and far, to grab a piece of the wall. One slab even ended up on display behind a urinal in Las Vegas. That border became an anti-border – dispersed across all six continents, never to divide us again.

But the number of border walls has *increased* during the years which followed – from a measly twelve, at the end of the Cold War, to *seventy-four* at the time of writing. (Crawford, 2023).

Today, more borders are blocked by walls, fences, watchtowers and gates – *than at any other time in history*.

Together, these fences have trapped over four-billion of our fellow human beings.

The longest wall, which separates Indians from Bangladeshis, is over three-thousand kilometres long. The fence between Hungary and Croatia, which was built by prisoners, electrocutes anyone who dares to touch it. Trenches filled with water, and a wall made of sandbanks, divide Tunisians from their neighbours in Libya. A fence cuts Austrians off from their Slovenian peers. A fortified border divides Norwegians and Russians. Saudi Arabia is attempting to fence off its *entire nation*.

(Shah, 2020).

***

These walls are an aberration...

For the vast majority of our time on Earth, we humans were free to go wherever we liked, whenever we chose. Even in the age of empire, most borders were blurry zones through which almost anyone could pass. These lines don't define who we are. They're not a fundamental feature of human culture.

The borders which divide Europe, were only formalised by the Treaty of Westphalia in 1648. Most of the borders which have appeared since then, only came about as the result of imperialistic horse-trading, wars of conquest, and agreements made by foreign statesmen – people who showed little concern for the communities they were dividing. The lines which divide India from Pakistan, were drawn by a British lawyer in the space of a few weeks. And the first sections of wall on the Mexican border, only appeared in the 1990s. (Washington, 2019).

Of course, some borders are dictated by nature: Chile and Argentina are separated by mountains. Island nations have boundaries that are defined by the seas. But other borders couldn't be *less* natural. Straight lines, drawn by distant bureaucrats, still divide great swathes of Africa. (Winchester, 2021).

***

This is the world we've created: One in which almost every last portion of land is wrapped inside a border – an imaginary line, drawn by a powerful minority, in service of their own vested interests. A world in which we're forced to apply for passports, permits and visas. A world in which a few border guards, with guns and ammunition, can say: "No! You shall not pass!"

But this wasn't always the case. It's a freakish abnormality – a drastic deviation from the norm. These things didn't exist in the past, and they don't have to exist in the future...

THE MOST "NATURAL" THING IN THE WORLD

"Those who do not move, do not notice their chains."
Rosa Luxemburg

So far, so good.

We've established that movement has been an eternal constant: Our planet, solar system and galaxy are on a journey through space. The tectonic plates are travelling beneath our feet. Animals migrate. Birds migrate. Even plants move around.

This has been the case since the beginning of time. And it continues to be the case *today*. That's because migration isn't only a historical event. It's a natural phenomenon – something that's happening right now, in an abundance of ways – some of which we're only just beginning to discover...

<u>NATURE IS ON THE MOVE</u>

Migrations come in several different forms...

The Arctic tern – a small bird with greyish wings, a black head and a pointed beak – practices something known as "Complete Migration". Each year, every member of this species flies from the Arctic Circle to the Antarctic and back again – a journey of around thirty-thousand kilometres. The American robin, however, only practices "Partial Migration". Some robins migrate, while others do not. American kestrels practice "Differential Migration". The females travel further than the males – visiting different places at different times. And blue jays practice "Interruptive Migration". They remain put for extended periods, but move on whenever their circumstances change.

Some migrations occur *underwater*: Zooplankton migrate vertically – travelling between the surface and the deepest depths of the ocean. Goby fish return to the places where they were born – leaving the Pacific, swimming against the current, and journeying *up* waterfalls – using suckers to climb the cliffs. Humpback whales make the journey from their summer feeding grounds in Alaska, to their winter home near Hawaii. Salmon swim up rivers, to spawn and lay their eggs.

The sheer *scale* of these migrations can be epic: The "Great Migration" features 1.5 million wildebeests, and hundreds-of-thousands of zebras, elephants and gazelles – who make a pilgrimage across the Serengeti, in search of water. Each year, 120 million red crabs leave the forests on Easter Island, to lay their eggs in the sea.

And some of these migrations cover a greater *distance* than we ever realised: One study found that a herd of Canadian caribou travelled 4,868 kilometres in the space of a single year. A khulan from Southeast Mongolia travelled 6,145 kilometres. But the champion migrator was a grey wolf from southwest Mongolia, who walked *7,247 kilometres*. (Joly et al, 2019).

***

The scientists who conducted that research were jumping on a trend, which began at the turn of the millennia. That was when the US Defence Department removed a stutter from the signals which were generated by their satellites – creating a constant stream of information. With this simple act, the GPS industry was born, and a raft of animal-tracking devices hit the shelves.

The data they generated was revealing.

Jaguars in the Amazon were found to migrate *ten times further* than scientists had previously supposed. There were crocodiles in Australia who we thought spent their lives near the land. It turned out that they paddled three-hundred kilometres out into the ocean. Tiger sharks didn't stick to the waters near Hawaii, as scientists had previously believed. They swam for thousands of kilometres. Even dragonflies migrated – heading from the USA to South America – flying hundreds of kilometres a day.

These animals have little respect for the borders which are supposed to contain them.

In Ethiopia, the authorities have created a nature park for giraffes. But those mammals pay scant regard to its border – spending the larger part of their time elsewhere. Turtles in the Chagos Islands show equal disdain – swimming free of their marine park, to explore the waters which lay beyond. The El Guácharo National Park in Venezuela is home to limestone caverns which are supposed to provide a habitat for birds. But 40% of the birds who reside in those caves, fly beyond the park's perimeter – foraging and roosting in other places.

And animals also disrespect *manmade borders*.

Elephants regularly cross back and forth between Kenya and Tanzania, without applying for any visas. A tracked leopard crossed three countries in Southern Africa – veering off course to avoid each settlement which stood in its way – and never possessed a passport. A wolf who was tagged in Trieste, galloped its way over the tops of frozen rivers, passed through head-high snow, and ascended a cloud-covered mountain pass – arriving in Austria, without notifying border control. (Shah, 2020).

***

We know it happens. But this begs a question: "Why?" Why do creatures embark on these epic expeditions?

A large part of the answer comes down to the environment in which they live: If an animal has everything it needs, it'll have little incentive to relocate. But if it were to find itself without food, water, a home or a mate – then it might feel compelled to move.

Birds who consume a fruit-based diet are far more likely to migrate than birds who eat insects. That's because fruit tends to be seasonal. Fruit-eating birds must travel to wherever it's growing, at different times of the year. But insects can usually be found on the forest floor. Insect-eating birds have fewer reasons to travel.

Bats who roost in trees are far more likely to migrate when the seasons turn – to escape from the rain and cold. Bats who sleep in caves, which protect them from the elements, are more likely to remain where they were.

Deer who live in smaller patches of woodland, which are more exposed to changing conditions, are more likely to migrate than deer who can hide within the deepest depths of a forest. Animals who live on the borders of a jungle, are far more likely to migrate than those who live in the interior. Arthropods who live in seasonal pools, must migrate each time those pools dry up.

In general, creatures who are affected by these changes are faced with two options: Hibernate or migrate. Those species which possess the ability to move, usually decide to travel.

***

The most prominent voice on this subject is Hugh Dingle – a professor based out of the University of California. Dingle hypothesises that rates of migration are related to a species' gestation period: If a mother can produce and raise a litter, before the environment around her begins to change, then she'll probably remain in that location. But if she resides in the sort of place which will change before her offspring mature – somewhere like a seasonal pond – then she'll probably migrate.

Such factors are clearly *external* – determined by the weather, the food supply, and the conditions of the world at large. But they manifest themselves *internally* – causing migratory creatures to experience *physical* change.

Migratory insects and birds will bulk up – accumulating reserves of fat which can amount to half their total mass. Rosy apple aphids, which tend not to have wings in the summer, will produce offspring which *do* possess the wings they'll need to fly to other orchards. Plants will produce seeds with a tougher outer coat, to prepare them for longer journeys. Young eels will become more transparent, and better suited to freshwater conditions. Salmon will produce an excess of prolactin and cortisol.

A restlessness will set in.

Migratory birds will become jumpy and almost frantic – ready for action – and then they'll take flight. They'll ascend at a much steeper angle, and reach loftier heights than at any other time of the year. They'll plough ahead – ignoring food in the forest below, and refusing to stop off to mate. They'll travel massive distances, before settling in a faraway land.

Their bodies *compel* them to act in such a way – to travel great distances, and find new homes. It's a natural phenomenon. The most natural thing in the world. (Dingle, 2014).

MIGRATION IMPROVES THE NATURAL WORLD

Animals, birds, fish and plants migrate because it's in their own self-interest: They move to places where there's a more abundant supply of food and a more appealing climate. They find new lands to inhabit, where they can increase their numbers and evolve.

But there's an unintended consequence to it all: When certain creatures migrate, it also benefits *others*...

***

Migratory species help *plants* to migrate.

Plants produce seeds covered in mucus, hooks, spines and barbs. These attach themselves to the fur of passing mammals, who carry them away, and deposit them in different locations. Plants also produce delicious fruits. Animals and birds are enticed by their fragrance and taste – they pick that fruit in one location, before eating and scattering its seeds somewhere else.

This can have a massive effect.

Over nine-in-ten of the tree species which can be found in our rainforests, owe their very existence to the creatures who disperse their seeds and pollen. Migratory birds and animals quite literally ensure that those forests survive – moving seeds to sunnier spots, where they're far more likely to grow. (Shah, 2020).

And that's a boon for humanity, because those rainforests play a vital role in our planet's water cycles – helping to create the clouds which carry rainwater to our farms and orchards. The trees in those forests also produce the oxygen we need to breathe. And they stabilise the Earth's climate, by removing carbon dioxide from the atmosphere.

***

Scientific research has also shown that migration can help *to improve the gene pool.*

When members of different populations come together and begin to breed, their offspring tend to be stronger, healthier and more intelligent – when compared to the offspring of similar parents, who both belonged to the *same* population. This phenomenon is known as "Heterosis" or "Hybrid vigour".

By the same dint of logic, those populations which remain isolated, and whose members *do not* breed with outsiders, tend to become *weaker*.

The Norwegian biologist, Jon Alfred Mjøen, conducted an experiment which supports this theory: In the beginning, he interbred several varieties of rabbits. Their offspring had a mortality rate of 11%. So around nine-in-ten of their kits survived.

Mjøen then bred that second generation, *without* introducing any outsiders. He repeated the process with their offspring, and with their offspring's offspring.

By the fifth generation, the mortality rate had risen to 38%. Barely six-in-ten of the kits survived past infancy. And those who did, were malformed. Several had mismatched ears.

Mjøen was forced to abandon his experiment, because those rabbits refused to mate! (Shah, 2020).

***

The theory should be intuitive enough: Isolated populations don't generate the genetic diversity they need to thrive. Some undesirable genes – which result in physical defects, or increase the probability of disease – will begin to multiply. The population will suffer.

We can see a real-world example of this over in the Great Lakes...

The winter of 1949 was so cold, that a section of Lake Michigan froze over. A pair of wolves strode across the icy surface, and made a home for themselves on an island within that lake – remaining there even after the ice had melted.

The couple reproduced. Their pups reproduced, and *their* pups followed suit.

The effects were stark: After sixty years of isolation, 58% of the wolves had deformed spines. Several had opaque eyes, and might've been blind.

Then something happened: An immigrant wolf arrived on the island's shores. That wolf bred with the locals, and its offspring also interbred. Within a generation, over half the island's wolves shared some of its DNA.

The wolves' health recovered, and their population increased.

Rolf Peterson, an ecologist who studied those wolves, concluded by saying: "(That single immigrant wolf) saved the population for another ten to fifteen years." (Mlot, 2013).

***

We see something similar in domestic dogs: When researchers analysed a dataset from the Royal Veterinary College – which included the records of over thirty-thousand dogs – they found that *mongrels had the highest life expectancy*, crossbreeds came in second place, and purebreds lived for the shortest amount of time. (Mata & Mata, 2023).

The Carnegie Institution found that mongrel mice were *more intelligent*: They took a group of white mice who had a diverse mix of parents, and another group who were "Purebred". They then challenged those mice to complete a maze. The mongrel mice completed the task in far less time than the purebreds. (Shah, 2020).

This is why farmers crossbreed – to produce stronger genetic strains. The standard meat chicken, the Cornish Cross, was created by crossbreeding White Cornish and White Rocks. The result was a bird that *puts on weight in record time*, in a predictable and efficient fashion.

Yields of corn, soybean, wheat and cotton – have all increased, after being crossbred with foreign strands. (Davis et al, 2011).

Grains and vegetables which have been crossbred, also tend to grow at a faster rate. They respond to fertilizer in a more efficient manner, and they're more resistant to drought.

***

We could even argue that something similar exists within humans, although this is controversial...

In recent decades, we've witnessed what's been dubbed the "Flynn Effect": In developed nations, IQs have been increasing by an average of about three points per decade. But until fairly recently, no-one could explain why. A person's IQ tends to be about the same as their parents'. It shouldn't be much higher or much lower. And it certainly shouldn't trend upwards over time.

Biologist Michael Mingroni, argues that the Flynn Effect can be explained by hybrid vigour: More people from different races and places have been starting families together, within these developed nations. Their offspring have inherited the *best* genes from each of their parents – becoming more intelligent than both their mothers *and* their fathers. (Mingroni, 2007).

And hybrid vigour hasn't only affected their intelligence: Mingroni argues that interbreeding is also to thank for the fact that we're now growing at a faster rate, becoming taller, and benefitting from lower rates of infant mortality. (Mingroni, 2004).

**

This can be seen as another argument in favour of the freedom of movement: Open borders would allow more people to move, form partnerships with people from other places, and create stronger, more intelligent offspring – improving humanity's capacity to achieve great things.

**

Perhaps this paints too rosy a picture. Interbreeding quite clearly leads to positive outcomes. But there can also be adverse effects – especially when populations *compete*.

Back in Britain, there are plenty of people who'll be happy to tell you about the grey squirrels, who were brought from abroad to live in the grounds of some stately homes. Those squirrels escaped, bred with *themselves* in the wild, and took over from the red squirrel – its more beautiful cousin. These days, red squirrels can only be found in a few remote locations, such as Anglesey and Scotland. (WildlifeTrusts.org).

This isn't an isolated case.

When Asian chestnut trees were introduced into the USA, they arrived with a parasitic fungus. This led to a wave of "Chestnut blight", which killed off a massive number of American trees. Likewise, when sea lamprey found their way into the Great Lakes, they annihilated most of the trout.

These things happened, and it'd be wrong to ignore them. But they're extreme examples. They shouldn't distract from the fact that the vast majority of new arrivals haven't affected their adopted ecosystems in any way whatsoever.

When the Suez Canal was completed, it created a channel which connected the Red Sea and the Mediterranean. Two-hundred and fifty species left the sea on one side and swam on through to the other side. A century later, scientists agree that this wiped out a certain variety of starfish – the starlet cushion – which can still be found elsewhere. But that was it: One lone casualty. Every other species survived.

Even this was more extreme than the norm.

When eighty marine species were introduced into the North Sea, every other creature continued on with its daily business. The same thing happened when seventy species were introduced into the Baltic. (Davis et al, 2001). (Mooney & Cleland, 2001).

We generally only witness these negative consequences within *closed ecosystems* – in lakes or on islands. The trout in the Great Lakes struggled, because they were stuck within the confines of those pools of water – they couldn't flee from the lamprey who attacked them. The creatures in the North Sea were fine, because that sea is massive. You could say it had *open* borders: Species who felt threatened by the new arrivals, were free to swim away – to move to another patch of sea, where they were safe.

***

We should avoid a common misnomer...

It's a false dichotomy to think of "Native" species and non-native or even "Invasive" ones. Most creatures move about in different ways, over various timeframes – calling one place their home at one point in time, but not at any other.

Let's take the camel as an example.

Where do you think camels belong?

Most people might associate them with the Middle East. They've become synonymous with that region. Others might think of the two-humped Bactrian camel, which can be found in south and central Asia.

But camels actually evolved in North America, around forty-million years ago! They spent longer there than anywhere else. These days, the most diverse selection of camels can be found in South America. The only place you'll find *wild* camels is in the Australian desert.

***

This isn't an isolated example. This is the *norm*...

"(Each) species has a characteristic distribution," explains Ken Thompson, a biologist and author. "Some have very wide ranges; others are confined to tiny areas such as single islands. But in every case, that distribution is in practice a single frame from a very long movie. Run the clock back only ten-thousand years, less than a blink of an eye in geological time, and nearly all of those distributions would be different." (Thompson, 2014).

***

Only 10% of immigrant species are able to establish communities in new locations. Only 1% flourish to such an extent that they might pose a threat to other species. And most of those don't do any actual harm. (Warren, 2007).

Even if we fall into the trap of discriminating between what we perceive to be "Native" and "Non-native", we still cannot pitch it as a battle between good and evil. Some so-called "Native" species, might wreak havoc on their ecosystems. The majority of species which we call "Invasive", still perform a useful function.

New species usually *increase biodiversity* in disharmonic environments – complementing the other species – such as in Hawaii's forest, where there hadn't been any amphibians, reptiles or ants.

Zebra mussels are considered "Invasive" in much of Europe and North America. But they provide a vital service – filtering the water, and providing food for fish and birds. (Thompson, 2014).

"Invasive" *plants* can provide food and pollen for local wildlife.

Many produce fruit when food is scarce – in early spring or late autumn – helping birds to survive the winter. Even Japanese knotweed, the scourge of so many gardeners, provides a source of sustenance for bees.

When a team of academics studied over sixteen-thousand small plots, spread across the globe, they found that the arrival of an "Invasive" plant resulted in a "Decline in species richness" in the short-run. But the areas which had been affected, then embarked on a "Post-disturbance succession", which resulted in "Increases in richness". (Vellend et al, 2013).

The lead researcher behind that paper, Mark Vellend, conducted another study in the States. He concluded that the arrival of new animals and plants, had caused an *18% increase in biodiversity*, during the previous four centuries. (Shah, 2020).

Their migration improved the natural world.

OUR GENES WANT US TO TRAVEL

We've established that some creatures have a biological impulse which compels them to migrate. They undergo physical changes when the time comes for them to move.

But what about us? Are humans also programmed to travel?

Why on Earth would we pack our bags and leave the lands of our birth, even if we weren't compelled to do so by some kind of political disturbance, natural catastrophe, or financial incentive? What possessed our ancestors to jump into rickety wooden vessels, and sail the seven seas – when they had plenty of resources on land? Why are billionaires like Elon Musk so hellbent on cramming themselves into tiny metal cans, and propelling themselves into space? Musk doesn't *need* to visit Mars. Christopher Columbus didn't *need* to sail across the Atlantic. So why did they bother?

Most other species don't behave in such a manner: Neanderthals were around for hundreds-of-thousands of years, and they didn't make it past Europe and Central Asia. Only a few other creatures – such as cockroaches and starlings – are as widespread as humans. Birds and mammals migrate for a reason – to find better climates, more food, or different partners. They don't relocate on a whim.

So why do we?

Does our genetic code push us to migrate? Is it a part of who we are? Or is it more of an individual thing? Is the impulse to travel hardwired into some people, but not others?

***

Back in 2019, ninety-three researchers came together to analyse the DNA of over a million subjects with European ancestry. It was one of the most extensive studies of its kind – using data which had been gathered by the ancestry company, 23andMe, as well as the UK Biobank.

Participants were asked about four "Risky behaviours" – their tendency to drive faster than the speed limit, the number of alcoholic drinks they consumed in an average week, the number of sexual partners they'd ever had, and whether or not they'd ever smoked. They were also asked to rank their "Risk tolerance", and to place themselves on a scale which ran from "Cautious" to "Adventurous".

The researchers then analysed the respondents' DNA, to see if any genetic markers were more common among the risk-takers.

The results were positive: It turned out that *124 single-nucleotide polymorphisms* ("SNPs") – the variations in the building blocks which make up our DNA – were related to risk-taking.

So, why is this relevant?

Well, leaving your homeland – waving goodbye to the people you love, turning your back on your society and your career – going to live somewhere else, with different people, and a different way of life – that seems like a mighty big "Risk" to me!

Even if you're only going backpacking – because you want to try some new activities, and experience foreign cultures – that might come from a penchant for "Adventure". And forty-nine SNPs also correlate with "Adventure".

This study suggests that such traits – for taking risks and seeking adventure – do have a genetic basis. People might move abroad, because they're compelled by a predilection for risk-taking which is written in their DNA.

Our genes encourage some of us to take risks, and these risks *might* include migrating. (Karlsson Linnér et al, 2019).

***

So, have scientists found a gene which isn't only related to risk in general, but to the *specific* risks which are involved with travel?

Well, sort of...

The gene in question is known as "DRD4-7R". It's a clunky name, which rather reminds me of the droid from the Star Wars movies: "C3PO". Fortunately for us, it has a more palatable nickname: "The Wanderlust Gene". And it could explain why some of us feel an urge to explore, whilst our peers remain at home – living in the same old place, sticking with the same old job, year after year, and decade after decade. It could explain why some people are happy to lay on a beach during their holidays, whilst others prefer to bungee jump, ski, or explore somewhere "Off the beaten track".

The DRD4 gene helps to control the amount of dopamine which is released into our brain. Most people are capable of triggering that pleasure response through simple things. They might eat a piece of chocolate, listen to some stand-up comedy, or stroke a cat. Some dopamine will be released, and they'll experience a fleeting sense of contentment.

But for the one-in-five people who possess the 2R or 7R variants of the Wanderlust Gene, these small things won't ever suffice. They need more! More chocolate. More thrills. More adrenaline. More adventure.

To satisfy their cravings, and feel the kind of dopamine rush that other people experience in their daily lives, these individuals have to take bigger risks. Compelled by curiosity, restlessness and passion – they might take drugs, gamble, or start a business. They might try new foods, immerse themselves in new cultures, or *visit new places*. They might embrace change, adventure and travel. And, having caught the travel bug, they might decide to relocate for good.

***

This is the theory. But does it happen in the real world? Do individuals or groups who have the Wanderlust Gene, actually move further afield?

One study suggests they do...

We've already mentioned that about one-in-five people have the Wanderlust Gene. But the gene is more prevalent in some populations than others. And these populations live in different places: Some can be found tens-of-thousands of kilometres from Africa – suggesting that their ancestors made massive migrations – whilst others still live on the mother continent.

Researchers from Harvard and Boston University, set out to see if there was a relationship between these two variables.

They started with the San – the African bushmen, who are thought to be one of the most ancient people on Earth. Then they measured the distances that the ancestors of *other* peoples would've travelled, when migrating from the San's homelands in Southern Africa, before arriving in the places where they settled.

The San had remained put – their ancestors were still living in the cradle of humankind. And *none* of the San who were tested, possessed either the R2 *or* the R7 variants. They didn't have the gene which encourages people to take risks. And they hadn't moved a jot.

The nearest group which was tested, the Bantu, lived 2,431 kilometres away. Among the Bantu, the summed frequency of the R2 and R7 variants was twenty-four (out of two-hundred). The Wanderlust Gene was more prevalent among the Bantu than the San, explaining why their ancestors had travelled a little further. But the alleles which encourage risk-taking were still less common than the global average – *forty* parts out of two-hundred.

There certainly wasn't a *perfect* correlation. The Mbuti and Biaka peoples live a little further from the San, and the Wanderlust Gene was less common among their members.

But the relationship was fairly strong.

The Columbians had ancestors who'd travelled around thirty-thousand kilometres – heading up out of Africa, into Asia or Europe, across into North America, and then down into South America. When they were tested, the R2 or R7 alleles appeared sixty-two times in every two-hundred samples – a rate which was just over 50% *higher* than the global average.

The Surui people, who live in the Brazilian Amazon, had moved further than anyone else in the study – just over thirty-two thousand kilometres. They also had the highest frequency of R2 and R7 alleles – over double the global average.

The study showed that there's a strong relationship between the two factors. The groups whose members were more likely to possess the Wanderlust Gene, also had ancestors who'd travelled the furthest distance from Africa.

The authors conclude that the presence of this gene, explains why our ancestors spread out so far, so quickly. It compelled carriers to take risks, explore new places, and live in new locations. This is why people sailed out into unchartered oceans, without knowing what was on the other side. It's why our contemporaries are launching rockets towards Mars. They're compelled by an impulse which is hardwired into their DNA. (Matthews & Butler, 2011).

Without this impulse to travel, we'd all still be living in Africa.

The Wanderlust Gene transformed our relationship with the world. It made us who we are today.

***

But just because a person has a gene which might compel them to migrate, this doesn't mean that they'll definitely move. Around one-in-five people have the Wanderlust Gene, but only 3.6% of us have gone to live abroad. (McAuliffe & Triandafyllidou, 2021).

Our *nature* might be encouraging us to move, but we're not slaves to our DNA. Other factors – such as *nurture* and *necessity* – might convince us to remain where we are.

There's also a "Psychopath Gene": MAOA-L. People who carry this gene, are more likely to engage in violent behaviour. But most of them *won't* become serial killers. And I'm not suggesting we legalise murder, just to placate those people who possess this DNA! (Sohrabi, 2015).

Of course, there's a big difference: Murder is a terrible thing for the victim and their loved ones. Migration can *help* a lot of people, as we'll see in the chapters which follow.

But what if restrictions on movement *did physically hurt* the people who wanted to move?

One study, conducted by a team of anthropologists and biologists, has looked into the effect...

The researchers studied the Ariaal people – a group of pastoralists, who live in Northern Kenya. The Ariaal were nomadic, for the vast majority of their history. But in the early 1970s, a number of their clans were encouraged to settle down.

Thirty-five years down the line, their members were tested.

Every group that was studied, was classified as "Underweight".

Those people who lived in *sedentary* communities, and who *didn't* possess the Wanderlust Gene, were the best-nourished – with a BMI of 18.2. They were healthier than their nomadic peers, who only had a BMI of 17.2.

But those people who lived in sedentary communities, and who *did* possess the Wanderlust Gene, were the *most malnourished*: They had BMIs which were almost an entire point short of the "Healthy" threshold. Carriers of the Wanderlust Gene who were still nomadic, were also underweight – but only by half a point. This suggests that when we restrict people's ability to move, they might lose weight and become undernourished, if they also happen to possess the Wanderlust Gene. (Eisenberg et al, 2008).

This can seriously affect a person's wellbeing. According to Healthline, "If you are underweight, you may be at greater risk of certain health conditions, including malnutrition, osteoporosis, decreased muscle strength, hypothermia, and lowered immunity. You are more likely to die at a younger age. Underweight women have less chance of becoming pregnant."

It's only one study, and it only looked at one group of people. More research is necessary. But if the effects are found to be widespread, then the consequences would be stark. It'd imply that stopping people with the Wanderlust Gene from migrating, would be a kind of physical abuse.

***

You might argue that this is an oversimplification – that we're not defined by a single gene, but by a much larger amount of genetic code, as well as our lived experiences.

This is true. But this genetic code comes together, to determine our overall personalities. And our *personalities* can also affect our propensity to migrate...

These days, scientists classify our characteristics according to the "Big Five" dimensions – extroversion, agreeableness, conscientiousness, neuroticism and intellect.

They're not *all* particularly relevant: There doesn't appear to be much of a relationship between migration and either conscientiousness and neuroticism. But the other "Dimensions" *can* help to cultivate a love of travel.

In the USA, people who are *less* agreeable, are *more* likely to relocate. But the two most significant factors, on a global scale, appear to be *extraversion* and *open-mindedness*.

Extroverts are more likely to move than introverts. Their outgoing personalities encourage them to go out into the world – to engage with people in different places. But they tend to move shorter distances. In the USA, extroverts are more likely to move about within their states, but they're *less* likely to move to another state. Extroverts like to be close to their social circle. They prefer not to move to places which have foreign languages and alien cultures – things which might make it harder for them to socialise.

Other factors can also come into play: Extroverts tend to gravitate towards urban locations, where they can find more types of social stimulation. And they're enticed by places with hotter climates, where people are more likely to mingle in public spaces.

Open-minded people are also more likely to move. And unlike the extroverts, they tend to move *further* away.

This makes sense on an intuitive level: The further you travel, the more likely you are to arrive somewhere which has a drastically different culture. That might excite you, if you're open-minded – eager to experience new ways of life. But it might scare you off, if you happen to be stuck in your ways. (Shuttleworth et al, 2021). (Jokela, 2009). (Fouarge et al, 2019).

And *emotional people* are also more likely to relocate, when compared to their less emotional peers. Although they tend to move shorter distances, as they can find long-distance moves a little overwhelming. (Jokela et al, 2008).

***

These are generalisations – there are plenty of exceptions to the rule.

I'm introverted, and I've spent my adult life moving from place to place. There are several reasons for introverts to migrate: To move *away* from prying neighbours, to search for places where people are less intrusive, and to find the peace and solitude they crave. In Bulgaria, we lived in a forest – we went for days without coming into contact with another living soul. That's an introvert's idea of paradise! But we had to move to a different country to find it.

HUMAN BODIES ARE MADE TO MOVE

Borders deny *some of us* the right to be ourselves.

If we have the Wanderlust Gene, or if we're extroverted, then those barriers can restrict our movement, and reduce our ability to achieve self-fulfilment. We feel a need to take risks, travel and meet new people. And borders say: "No! You can't be that sort of a person. You can't be yourself."

This is an argument in favour of free movement *for carriers of the Wanderlust Gene*, for extroverts and open-minded individuals. But what about everyone else? What about those people who *don't* possess the R2 or R7 alleles? What about those people who aren't extroverted, open-minded or emotional?

***

The aforementioned study showed that members of those groups who'd migrated the furthest, were more likely to possess the Wanderlust Gene. Among the Surui, the R2 and R7 alleles were found in eighty-three out of every two-hundred samples. But they were still *absent* almost 60% of the time.

So why did those Surui people, who *didn't* possess the

Wanderlust Gene, also make it to modern-day Brazil?

For the answer, we don't have to look at the molecular level – we only have to look at our bodies: We're clearly built to move. We have long legs which enable us to make grand expeditions, big brains which are good for imagining new worlds, and dexterous hands which help us to build the vehicles we use to travel.

Other large primates have legs which are shorter than ours, relative to their bodies. This helps them to balance, when they're fighting with their peers. Even the Australopithecus – the precursors to the first humans – were short and squat. They could hold their ground when they were shoved. But they weren't so proficient when it came to making long journeys.

Our long legs, narrow hips and lighter bodies – make us far more predisposed to walk and run, when compared to other primates. And our brains are bigger too. The average human brain weighs 1,352 grams. Our nearest living relatives, the chimpanzees, have brains which weigh 384 grams, on average. (Carrier, 2007).

Let's put these things together...

Our bigger brains encourage us to imagine other worlds – to ask ourselves: "What lies beyond those mountains?" – "I wonder what it'd be like to visit that place over there?" – "Wouldn't it be interesting to go and live on another planet?"

Our long legs and narrow hips allow us to get up, and walk great distances – helping us to discover some of the answers.

Our powerful brains encourage us to imagine new kinds of vehicles.

And our dexterous hands allow us to build those canoes, dinghies and yachts. They enable us to make the airplanes that shuttle people around today, and the rockets we'll need if we're to migrate to distant planets.

Moreover, we *all* have these long legs, narrow hips, dexterous hands and big brains. We're no longer talking about the one-in-five people who possess the Wanderlust Gene. We're no longer talking about extroverts and open-minded individuals. We're talking about *the entire human species.*

We were all born with the sort of curiosity which might encourage us to explore, and the bodies which allow us to travel. We've all been built to move. (Dobbs, 2013).

<u>NO-ONE IS INDIGENOUS</u>

Borders attempt to divide us – to say that we're all inherently different – that some people belong in certain places, whilst others belong elsewhere.

And yet our biology disagrees.

We all have longish legs, dexterous hands, and oversized brains. We all have lungs, kidneys and bladders.

This remains true, no matter where we were born – whether we're American or Mexican, British or Polish, Indian or Pakistani.

There's no such thing as a "British gene". Mexicans and Americans have the same DNA. Our genetics are universal...

***

It's a run-of-the-mill American chat show. Two guests are sitting on upholstered chairs, which have been arranged at a ninety-degree angle – half-facing their host, and half-facing the studio audience. The show's presenter, Trisha Goddard, is sitting on a matching chair – wearing a tight-fitting, blue-and-black ensemble.

Peering over the top of her glasses, Goddard reads from a golden certificate.

She's addressing her guest, Craig Cobb – a racial separatist who's attempting to establish a white-only enclave in North Dakota. Cobb is relatively handsome for a man his age, with flowing grey hair, and a tidy beard. Dressed in a regal-red shirt and tie, he exudes the confidence of a man who has total faith in his philosophy: That black and white people are like "Oil and water", and that "Oil and water don't mix".

"Craig Paul Cobb has undergone DNA testing," Goddard begins. "To determine his genetic ancestry. It is 86% European, and, err..."

Hahaha-hee-hah!

The second studio guest, a black woman who is wearing a colourful hat, leans back and emits a joyous chortle. It's contagious. As she slaps her thigh, the audience amplifies her response – hollering, clapping and stamping.

The second studio guest encourages Goddard to continue.

"Give it to him," she cheers. "Give it to him."

And Goddard is only too happy to oblige:

"14% *Sub-Saharan African*."

Cobb emits a nervous smile, as the audience continues to cheer.

"Wait a minute," he protests, as cheerily as he can. "Hold on…"

"Wah-ay!" Goddard cheers. "Ho!"

But Cobb remains defiant:

"This is called 'Statistical noise'."

Goddard leans forward, nodding furiously, whilst her eyes bulge out from their sockets:

"Sweetheart, you have a little black in you."

Cobb repeats his refrain:

"Listen. I tell you this: Oil and water don't mix."

But Goddard is already on her feet, leaning into Cobb's personal space, and offering him a fist pump:

"Hey… 'Bro'."

She offers another fist pump, and Cobb declines again. But it makes little difference. The science has spoken: This proud American is 86% European and 14% African. Oil and water *do* mix. They're mixed up within his DNA.

But there's another fact, implicit in these results, which goes unmentioned: Eighty-six and fourteen add up to a hundred. Cobb is *100%* European and African. *He's not even the slightest bit Native American*. He's the descendant of immigrants – a guest in another land.

***

There was nothing particularly unusual about Cobb's DNA…

A study conducted by genealogists from the Harvard Medical School, in collaboration with 23andMe, asked Americans to self-identify their ancestry. They were categorised as "European

Americans", for example, if they selected "Not Hispanic", if they also selected "White", and if they didn't select another category.

Of these self-identifying "European Americans" – which would've included the likes of Craig Cobb – 3.5% were shown to have at least 1% Sub-Saharan African ancestry. In the south, one-in-ten people who self-identified as white, had some African ancestry. But very few had any *American* DNA. On average, only 0.18% of their DNA was Native American. The other 99.82% had come from immigrants.

It was actually those people who self-identified as "Latinos", and only as "Latinos", who had the highest proportion of local DNA. *18%* of their genetic makeup was Native American. They were a hundred-times *more* American than people like Craig Cobb.

Let that sink in for a moment: The people trying to cross over from Mexico into the USA, were over a hundred-times *more* American than the likes of Donald Trump – the people who were trying to stop them. The descendants of immigrants, with massive amounts of foreign DNA, were pointing their fingers at people who *did* have some American DNA, and saying "You're too foreign. You can't come in."

The science would beg to differ. (Bryc et al, 2015).

***

In reality, even "Native" Americans have international heritage – they descend from the first people who stepped foot on that continent, up to twenty-thousand years ago. No-one in the Americas is truly indigenous.

We see a similar picture over in the land of my birth...

No-one in Britain is really indigenous. The very first Britons didn't evolve in the British Isles. They moved there from Europe.

Scientists spent twenty years, analysing the DNA of people in different British regions, applying two simple caveats: All the people had to be white, and they all had to have four grandparents who lived within eighty kilometres. This excluded recent arrivals. It created a snapshot of different British peoples, who might consider themselves to be "Native".

The team then compared the DNA they'd gathered, with DNA from people who lived across Northern and Western Europe.

What they found, surprised them: Within their regions, British people had a remarkably similar ancestry. But people from different parts of the nation, had different DNA.

The three Welsh clusters were dominated by genes which originated in the places we'd now call Western Germany and Northwestern France – DNA which is thought to have been inherited from the original Britons. The people in these clusters didn't possess *any* DNA which originated from the *north-central* area of modern-day France, even though DNA from that area *did* feature heavily in other parts of Britain. Up to two-fifths of the DNA found in Cornwall, can be traced back to people who migrated from that region.

When we look at the islands to the northeast of Scotland, we find a heavy Viking influence. More of the DNA in that region comes from modern-day Norway, than from anywhere else.

Anglo-Saxon DNA – originating in the north and northwest of contemporary Germany – has been passed down the generations in *some* places. It has a heavy presence in Southern and Central England. But it's absent in Wales and Scotland.

This isn't to say there's *no* commonality. That same DNA which was so dominant in Wales – which was brought over by the Britons – can also be found in the genetic makeup of *every British region*. A tiny amount of DNA from the places we now call Norway, Belgium and Western Germany – can also be found all across the UK. But the *proportions* are completely different.

There's no single British genetic identity.

There are several *regional* identities. And each of these can trace their roots back to a variety of places in Europe. The entire British genome was brought to Britain by different groups of travellers, who arrived at different times, made homes for themselves in different places, and preceded to interbreed with the locals – combining their DNA. (Leslie et al, 2015).

It makes very little sense to put up a border between Britain and the rest of Europe, when we share such a common ancestry. It'd make as much sense to place borders between each British *region*. And yet, to most people, that would seem absurd.

DNA HAS NO RESPECT FOR BORDERS

We're clearly not a bunch of clones. We have different physiques, appearances, attributes and characteristics. Some of us are inclined to take risks, whilst others are not. And geography *does* make a difference – people who live further from Africa, are more likely to possess the Wanderlust Gene.

This isn't an anomaly.

Movements in the past, forced people to adapt – to survive in their new surroundings.

When humans arrived in the cold dark lands of Europe, their bodies evolved – their metabolism found ways to digest new kinds of food, and their immune systems evolved to resist European pathogens. (Hunter, 2012).

People who live further from the equator, where there's less sunlight, have evolved paler skin – allowing them to absorb the UV light they need to generate vitamin D. People who live in particularly cold places, such as the Arctic, have developed stockier bodies which help them to retain heat. People who reside in malarial zones, have developed genetic strains which protect them from that illness. And people who live near the Ganges, have developed a resistance to cholera. (Yuen & Jablonski, 2010). (Foster & Collard, 2013). (Harris et al, 2009).

In large parts of the world, the gene which allows us to consume milk "Switches off" in adolescence. But the members of some cattle-herding societies have developed a mutation that allows them to consume that drink as adults. This happened in *different places* – among the Bedouins of Northern Africa and the Middle East, the Dinka of Southern Sudan, and the Caucasians of Europe.

So, a tiny number of our genes *can* be traced back to a few particular locations. This enables us to perform ancestry tests, which show us the regions where our ancestors might've lived.

But, as this last example shows, different genes can be found in a *variety* of locations, dispersed throughout the world.

When white supremacists began chugging milk, and telling African Americans – "If you can't drink milk... you have to go back (to Africa)" – the response was obvious: People from Africa have also developed the ability to consume milk. That genetic trait wasn't uniquely European. (Harmon, 2018).

People with the Wanderlust Gene were more likely to have travelled further from Africa. But they spread out in every direction – ending up in a variety of places, all across the globe.

Paler people inhabit the more northerly parts of our planet *and* the more southerly parts.

Barely anyone has homogenous DNA. It's all mixed up. Even white separatists, like Craig Cobb, have African DNA.

When we crunch the numbers, the results are clear: DNA has no respect for borders.

***

Let's go back to the beginning...

The most recent estimates suggest that the human body contains around 37 trillion cells. Inside the membrane of each cell, you'll find an array of things with far-out names like "Golgi apparatus" and "Cytoplasm". Most significantly, you'll also find the "Nucleus". Within the nucleus, there are twenty-three pairs of "Chromosomes" – so there are forty-six chromosomes in total. Each of these chromosomes contains a long DNA molecule. These strands of DNA contain between 50 and 250 million "Nucleotides". And each of these contains a "Base pair" – which could either be adenine (A), cytosine (C), guanine (G) or thymine (T). These are the building blocks of our genetic code. (Roy & Conroy, 2018). (Bianconi et al, 2013).

Have you got all that?

If not, don't worry. Here's the point to take away: We all have approximately 3.3 billion "Base pairs" in each of our cells. These define everything about us – from the size of our foreheads, to the very fact that we each have a liver.

In 2015, the 1000 Genomes Project sequenced the genomes of 2,500 people, across twenty-seven parts of the globe – in Africa, East Asia, Europe, South Asia and the Americas. They found that the vast majority of their base pairs were *identical.* Only twenty-million pairs showed *any* variation whatsoever.

That may sound like a lot. But it only represents a tiny portion, when you consider that we have *3.2 billion* base pairs in total.

Let's break this down...

Twenty-million minutes is the equivalent of about 38 years. I was alive 38 years ago! Even if you weren't, I bet you know plenty of people who were.

3.2 billion minutes is a little over six-thousand years. I bet you've never met anyone who was alive six-thousand years ago! It was still the Stone Age. Civilizations were starting to form, but there weren't any empires, and most people were still nomadic.

The proportion of our DNA which differentiates us from each other, is tiny when compared to the amount of DNA which we hold in common. Almost all our base pairs are identical, regardless of where we were born, or where our ancestors happened to live. Just 0.6% of our base pairs show any sort of differentiation. And over 99.9% of these differences are so small, that they barely make a difference. (Auton et al, 2015).

Furthermore, just because 0.6% of our base pairs *could* be different, this doesn't mean that they *will* be different. More often than not, you'll find that they're mostly the same.

If we were to choose a random base pair from the corresponding sites in two people, from anywhere in the world – they'll be identical *99.9%* of the time. It's really only *0.1%* of our DNA which differentiates us from our peers. (Crow, 2002).

Please take a moment to allow that to sink in: *At least 99.4% of our DNA is held in common*, no matter where we were born, where our family lives, or where our ancestors happened to roam. If you were to pick two people at random, the chances are that they'll *share around 99.9% of each other's DNA* – no matter if they came from Los Angeles, Lagos or Laos.

***

This is a uniquely human trait...

Take a couple of people from any two nations on the planet –

people who look and behave in a completely different fashion. And then take a pair of rhesus monkeys, who look identical, and who behave in a similar manner. If you were to test their DNA, you'd find more genetic variation between the rhesus monkeys, than between the so-called "Foreigners". That's because rhesus monkeys have 2.5 times more genetic diversity than humans. And *they* don't split themselves into nations, create artificial borders, or construct border walls! (Xue, 2016).

But we don't only have to compare ourselves to monkeys. We reach a similar conclusion when we analyse the common chimpanzee. Along with bonobos, these animals are our closest living relatives – our lineages split apart somewhere between four-million and seven-million years ago.

Henrik Kaessmann sequenced a stretch of DNA on the X chromosome in a sample of these chimpanzees. And he repeated the process – sampling the same stretch of DNA in a group of humans.

His results were revealing: Kaessmann found between three and four times the amount of variation within the chimpanzees' DNA.

This is all the more remarkable, when you consider the two populations: There are only around 200,000 chimpanzees in the world today. They all live in the same tract of land – in equatorial Africa, between Tanzania and Guinea – in forests or on the savannah. You might think they'd become inbred, and hold a great deal of DNA in common.

In contrast, there are over *eight-billion* human beings. We've populated every part of the map – living in places with completely different environments. You might think this would create mutations – that we'd evolve differently in each location.

A few minor differences have emerged. But Kaessmann found way more variation among the much smaller population of chimpanzees. And he found even more genetic variation when he went on to test gorillas and orangutans.

***

This study wasn't unique.

When Allan Wilson studied mitochondrial DNA, he found far less variation among the samples he took from humans, than in the samples he'd gathered from apes.

This supports the theory that we all descend from the same mitochondrial "Eve". We're all members of the same human family – no matter where we were born. (Pääbo, 2014).

***

This point cannot be emphasised enough.

Let's look at our *genes* rather than our *base pairs*...

Each gene is comprised of anywhere between a few hundred and a few million base pairs. So we don't have nearly as many genes – just twenty-thousand in all. (Grishkevich & Yanai, 2014).

To put that in context, we don't have to compare ourselves to our nearest living relations – the bonobo or the common chimpanzee. We can compare ourselves to the nematode worm – a tiny creature, you might not have heard of before. It was certainly new to me! They're minuscule things. Most of them are between 0.1 and 2.5 millimetres long. And these worms also possess twenty-thousand genes!

So, we humans have around twenty-thousand genes. These determine everything about us – as we develop from an embryo, to a foetus, to a fully-grown human being. They provide a code which determines the fate of over thirty-trillion cells.

And a microscopic worm, with far fewer cells, and much less complexity – *also* has twenty-thousand genes.

We humans are just as diverse as a microscopic worm! That's it. We really are incredibly similar – no matter what the nationalists would have you believe. (Rose, 2016).

***

It might not seem that way at first glance.

People from different regions *can* have a distinctive appearance. Someone who has brown skin, might look completely different from a person who has black skin. These differences *are* determined by our genes: Our skin tone is determined by eight genetic variants, which regulate the amount of pigment our skin cells produce. But these genes have very little to do with geography.

The gene for brown skin didn't develop in Asia. The gene for white skin didn't evolve in Europe. These variants *all originated in Africa*. They existed in our ancestors, before they evolved to become *Homo sapiens*. One variant for light skin is almost a *million* years old! And these genes can be found in every corner of the planet – within people who have lighter skin, and those who have darker complexions. (Crawford et al, 2017).

***

Now let's consider our eyes...

Our eyes are always placed on the fronts of our heads, where they are protected by eyebrows and lashes. It doesn't matter if we were born in Britain or Poland – we all possess a genetic code, which ensures we have a pair of eyes, each of which has a pupil, iris and lens.

Now, of course there are differences. Some of us may have bulbous eyes, whilst others may have narrow ones. Our iris might be turquoise or brown.

But only a tiny number of our genes determine such characteristics: As things stand, scientists have identified sixty-one genes which code for eye colour. They've discovered around *450 genes* which code for short-sightedness. This means that an Indian who has brown eyes, but who is also short-sighted – will probably share more of their genetic code with a blue-eyed short-sighted Norwegian, than with a brown-eyed Indian who isn't short-sighted. (Simcoe et al, 2021). (Hysi et al, 2020). (Chen, 2008).

***

People from different places may very well have different hair colour, hair texture, eye colour and eye shape. These minor differences explain why ancestry tests do work. They can be used to check for genetic markers, which link a person's ancestors to a specific part of the globe.

But these markers only represent about 15% of our molecular diversity. And that diversity, as we showed above, is rather small: We hold 99.4% of our genetic makeup in common, so we're only talking about 15% of the *other* 0.6% – about 0.09% of our DNA. (Crow, 2002).

That figure goes down to *10%*, when we compare the inhabitants of different *continents* rather than different *regions*. Being from a different continent can only explain a tenth of a person's genetic diversity – just 0.06% of their DNA.

Individual diversity – the genetic differences between people who live in the *same* country – is way more significant than *regional diversity*. It explains the other *85%* of the things which set us apart. So you'd expect to find way more diversity when comparing a group of Americans to each other, than when comparing the average American to the average Mexican. (Jorde et al, 2000) (Barbujani et al, 1997).

There really is no scientific justification for creating borders, and pretending that people are different on either side. It doesn't matter where you draw the lines – you're still going to share the vast majority of your genetic code with whomever you decide is "Foreign". Some differences will exist. But they'll be outweighed by the differences which exist between you and your compatriots.

There's no genetic case for borders.

There's no scientific reason to deny us our freedom to move.

THE SOCIETIES WHICH "NURTURE" MOVEMENT

"The horse is the wings of the rider."
Kazakh expression

"When the man mounts his horse, and travels at great speeds, he becomes a Kazakh. He becomes a horseman. He merges with his horse, and with the clouds, and with the distant horizon. He feels that this is the new speed of life."

You could say that the Kazakhs have an ancient bond with their horses: Horse remains and artefacts, unearthed in Northern Kazakhstan, are thought to be almost six-thousand years old. We're yet to discover the remains of any other domesticated horses, which are older than that. This means that the Kazakhs were probably the first people to domesticate those creatures.

And horses continue to be an integral part of Kazakh culture today...

This nomadic people mainly live in Mongolia. It's a ruggedly beautiful place – filled with jagged terrain, barren steppes, snowy peaks, dusty valleys, and a landscape which undulates in melodic waves. But it's desolate – a vast expanse, much of which is inaccessible by car. Roads are scarce. Electricity is rare. You'll struggle to find a 7-Eleven or an iStore.

Movement is the lifeblood of this society. The Kazakhs *need* to move, to find food for their goats, sheep, yaks and camels. And it's their horses who enable that movement.

Riding atop their stallions and mares, they move from pasture to pasture – finding grounds where they can graze their livestock. In return, those animals supply the Kazakhs with almost everything they need – their income, food and fabric.

During the summer months, these nomads move to the highlands, where the air is cool. They erect the same sorts of "Gers" they've used for three-thousand years – circular tents, made from felt or skins, which they decorate with jazzy hangings. These are sturdy, comfortable abodes. But they can be packed down in a couple of hours

– allowing their members to move on whenever it takes their fancy.

As the weather closes in, the Kazakhs head for the valleys – taking up residence in dwellings they've built from earth, dung and stone.

Some things change. Some things remain the same.

These homes are smaller, and therefore easier to heat. But, like the yurts, they're also decorated with a dizzying array of colourful material: All cherry red, mustard yellow and aquamarine.

The Kazakhs move up to 150 kilometres at a time. They settle down. And then they move again.

But it's not only a matter of *necessity* – a need to escape the cold, or find better pastures. They could always live a sedentary life in a city. For these people, it's a matter of *culture*. Movement makes the Kazakhs feel alive.

***

The Kazakhs also travel great distances to attend *weddings*. They have little choice. In Kazakh culture, a person isn't allowed to marry within seven generations. If you share a great-great-great-great-grandparent – and everyone has sixty-four of these relations – then you're not allowed to wed. In a sparsely populated part of the world, this means you'll have to cover a fair distance, to find a suitable spouse. And the guests at your wedding will have to travel a fair old way to attend.

They don't stop moving, even *after* they've arrived.

Kazakh weddings are energetic affairs. People would feel shortchanged if they attended such a ceremony, and didn't witness a group of grown men wrestling in the dust, wearing little more than a turquoise thong. And they'd feel hard-done-by if they didn't witness a horse race. But not just *any* race. The sort of race which covers eighteen or twenty kilometres – starting in the distance, proceeding through rain and shine, lasting for over an hour. The sort of horse race which isn't contested by adults, but by *children*.

Yes, that's correct: They start them young in this culture. It's as though they're born in motion – eager to emerge from the womb, climb atop a horse, and move from place to place.

It's their culture. And it's also their *philosophy*.

The Kazakhs believe in finding a balance between them, as individuals, and the universe which surrounds us all. This manifests itself in the way they move: They travel from one spot to the next, whenever *nature* calls – changing homes in accordance with the seasons – flowing back and forth like the tide, or the wind, or the coming of night and day. (DeCocker, 2023). (Portnoy, 2017). (Pearson, 2021).

***

Such a philosophy has always been central to the nomadic mindset...

The word "Nomad" comes from the Greek word "Nomós", which means "Pasture" – and from its derivative, "Nomás", which means "To roam about for pasture". It does mean to *move*. But that movement is tied to a specific area of *land* – the pasture upon which this "Roaming" occurs.

Sedentary peoples might feel an affinity for the small plot of land beneath their house, or to the territory which makes up their nation. These pastoralists feel that very same affinity with the grasslands which sustain their herds. They live in harmony with that terrain, as it transforms throughout the seasons – visiting a similar set of places each year. (Marquardt, 2021).

***

There was a time when the Kazakhs were *forced* to migrate...

They couldn't help but notice the Russian outposts which were pockmarking the landscape they'd always roamed, or the Russian settlers who arrived soon after – grabbing the best plots – imposing their customs and culture. Some Kazakhs did rise up in defiance. But their rebellions were crushed. And, in 1920, Kazakhstan was absorbed by its larger neighbour.

Several Kazakhs moved to Mongolia.

But it'd be wrong to say they "Emigrated", or even that they were "Refugees". Nomads are always on the move. The Kazakhs had been crossing back and forth – leaving Kazakhstan, traversing a corridor of Chinese land, and continuing into Mongolia – for as long as anyone could recall. Nomads don't have much respect for the concept of a

"Border".

These days, the Kazakhs are the largest ethnic group in Western Mongolia. It's such a large, underpopulated region, that they've tended to be left alone – even when Mongolia aligned itself with Moscow – and even though they haven't attempted to assimilate.

Some were enticed back to Kazakhstan, in 1991, following the fall of the Soviet Union. But the country had changed beyond recognition. Its new leader had grand, materialistic ambitions – filling the cities with skyscrapers, and filling the roads with cars. He seemed to have forgotten the simple, Kazakh way of life.

Many who made the journey, gave up and returned to Mongolia. It wasn't their historic land. The locals practiced Buddhism, rather than Islam. They looked a little different. They spoke another language. But the Mongolians also lived close to nature – riding horses across the plains, living in yurts and gers.

Mongolia might not have been the Kazakhs' original *homeland*. But it'd become their *home*. (DeCocker, 2023). (Portnoy, 2017). (Pearson, 2021).

TRADITIONAL NOMADIC SOCIETIES

So, why mention the Kazakhs?

They have a lifestyle which must seem pretty detached from the world most readers will live in today. Kazakh horsemen haven't ever caused an issue at the Mexican border. They're not planning to cross the British channel.

But the Kazakhs aren't alone. Other groups are also trying to preserve a nomadic culture. These include the Sámi of Northern Europe, the Kochi people of Eastern Afghanistan, the Gaddi of India, the Maasai of East Africa, the Bedouin, the Mongols, the Irish Travellers, and the Romani – whose diaspora has spread across the globe.

There are thought to be somewhere between thirty-million and forty-million nomads today. That's akin to the population of Canada.

(Sattin, 2022).

These nomads offer a kind of bridge.

In the first chapter, we discussed the history of human movement – showing how people have been moving around for tens-of-thousands of years. Now we're saying that this prehistoric culture is still alive. It hasn't been abandoned. Some peoples still maintain this traditional way of life – although their lifestyles do vary quite considerably.

Many hunter-gatherers have become *temporary* nomads. The Nambikwara of Brazil, for example, settle down in hilltop villages during the rainy season. But they split into foraging bands and go on "Nomadic adventures" as soon as the rains subside. (Lévi-Strauss, 1967).

Like the Kazakhs, several other groups have become *pastoralists* – people who travel around to find new pastures.

And others have become *peripatetic nomads* – moving around for *work*. You may have encountered some of these people yourself: The fruit pickers who move from one farm to another, whilst working abroad each summer – living alongside their fellow pickers, in makeshift camps – bonding over their communal dinners. The people who live in mobile homes, driving from job to job – forming communities in the trailer parks they establish along the way. And the ski instructors who flip between hemispheres, so they can teach for eight months a year.

These nomadic communities haven't disappeared.

But, unlike the common perception – that the nomads are imposing themselves on us – the truth is that it's *their* cultures which are under threat.

We mentioned this in the second chapter: When people first began to lead sedentary existences, they tried to monopolise the land for themselves. Of course, the nomads resisted – raiding their stores, and leading their livestock away. But the sedentary populations grew at a faster rate than the nomads. Their villages expanded – becoming city-states, nations, and empires. They took more territory, and left less for the nomads. These days, almost all the land on Earth has been claimed by a nation-state. Almost nothing has been left aside for the travellers.

Some nomadic peoples have been forced to abandon their culture. Some have been pushed to the periphery, in places like Mongolia. Others have been eradicated.

***

Back in Britain, we're home to a handful of nomadic groups...

The Romani Gypsies first emerged in India, before spreading across the world. The Travellers came over from Ireland. Show People have been putting on fairs and circuses for several generations. The New Age Travellers emerged with the Hippy movement of the 1960s. The Barge Travellers traverse Britain's waterways by boat.

A few campsites are still reserved for traveller communities. But there are far fewer than are required. Between them, they only supply pitches for around eight-thousand caravans. That's less than twenty-five spots per local authority. (Commission For Racial Equality, 2006).

And yet, according to the most recent national census, there are almost sixty-thousand Gypsies, Roma and Travellers in the UK. The Traveller Movement claims that there are five-times this amount. (TravellerMovement.org.uk)

So we're trying to squeeze anywhere up to 300,000 people, into around 8,000 pitches. The numbers don't add up.

Travellers have been left with little choice but to set up camp in unauthorised locations. Such "Illegal" encampments have been reported by 94% of local authorities. And this has led to conflicts. Around two-thirds of local authorities have reported tensions between travellers and sedentary people. (Commission For Racial Equality, 2006).

We clearly don't put enough land aside for migratory peoples. The land we do put aside, only takes up a tiny proportion of the British Isles. And there are no expanses of pasture, where these people can roam, as is the case in Mongolia.

Yet these people aren't immigrants. They're British citizens, with long-standing roots in the nation. The Roma have been in Britain for over five-hundred years. That's about fifty years *longer* than the potato!

They arrived before England and Scotland combined, to form "Great Britain". They arrived before William Shakespeare wrote "Hamlet", and well before football was invented in a pub near Covent Garden.

The Irish Travellers moved to Britain around two-hundred years ago. They mixed with Scottish, English and Welsh Travellers – who existed long before that. (TravellerMovement.org.uk)

Between them, these people are helping to preserve a lifestyle that goes back *thousands of years* – to the Britons who first spread across the British Isles, and the Pagans who crisscrossed the land whilst making their pilgrimages to Stonehenge.

Despite this, there's a perception that *they're* the outsiders.

A study, conducted by the University of Birmingham, found that 44.6% of British people had negative views about nomadic people. That's way more than any other group: Only 25.9% of Brits were prejudiced against Muslims. Just 8.5% had an unfavourable opinion of Jews.

Romani Gypsies and Irish Travellers are recognised as ethnic minorities in Britain. They're supposed to be protected by the Race Relations Act and the Human Rights Act. But the few traveller sites which still exist, are under constant threat. The "Police, Crime, Sentencing and Courts Bill", is being debated as I write. If it passes, it might threaten the very existence of traveller culture. And travellers are subjected to a constant stream of harassment.

One Roma woman told Sky News: "You tend to find things like, 'Oh, let's blow them up in their caravans, or let's blow up their gas bottles while they're inside'. Death threats, to us, is like a way of life." (Dowd, 2022).

The effects can be catastrophic.

In Britain, life expectancy for nomadic people is ten years lower than the norm. Mothers are twenty times more likely to witness the death of a child. (Abdalla et al, 2010). (Commission For Racial Equality, 2006).

Even if you support the existence of borders, and even if you're concerned about immigration, you still have to feel for people like these. They've lived *within* our borders, as members of our nations, for generations and sometimes for centuries. These people practice a migratory lifestyle which predates our nation-states – with their passports, visas and walls. They're not trying to impose a new culture onto us. They're trying to preserve a traditional way of life.

THE NOMADS OF THE DIGITAL AGE

So, what would we need, to enjoy such a way of life?

According to Anthony Sattin, it requires three things: Firstly, nomadic peoples must recognise their dependence on the natural world. Pastoralists, in particular, need to find fresh pasture. Secondly, nomads must live lightly. They have to be able to carry their possessions around. And thirdly, they need to be flexible – to adapt to a changing world. (Sattin, 2022).

You might argue that something is missing from this list: They need to have been born into a nomadic culture. But this is no longer the case. People who've caught the travel bug, who possess that Wanderlust Gene, can also form *new* nomadic societies.

We already mentioned the New Age Travellers, who emerged in the 1960s, and those seasonal workers who form new communities whilst they're on the road. To this, we should add a much larger, more global group, who've emerged in recent years: The "Digital Nomads" – people who work online, whilst moving from place to place.

They come in different forms.

They might have decided to take a short "Workcation" abroad. They might be serious backpackers, who are constantly on the move – only stopping to open their laptops and render a little work. They could be "VanLifers", travelling about in a mobile home, perhaps with their partners, pets or children. Or they might choose to bed down in a single place for a while – a process known as "Slow travel".

What unites such people, is a sense of being "Location independent" – able to work from whatever location they choose, and to move whenever it takes their fancy.

According to the *State of Independence Study*, in 2022 there were almost seventeen-million American digital nomads. This number had surged by 131% in the previous three years. Almost half of these people had moved abroad. Over two-thirds intended to stay on the road for at least another two years. And plenty of their peers were thinking of joining them: According to that study, a whopping *72 million* Americans had aspirations to work remotely in different locations. That's over a third of the working-age population! Although, it should be noted, that the vast majority hadn't made any actual plans.

This new traveller community is a varied bunch, but they tend to share a few characteristics: The study found that three-quarters were self-employed. They were more likely to be male, white, Democrats, and relatively young. 47% were Millennials. But there were plenty of older nomads – a quarter were over forty-five, and 10% were over sixty. Digital nomads were more likely to be highly educated, and the types of people who were early to adopt new technology. 21% worked in IT, 12% were creatives, and 11% were educators. Others worked in marketing, sales, public relations, finance, accounting, consulting and research.

Digital nomads were found to be far more satisfied with their incomes, when compared to their sedentary peers – in part because they lived in countries where the cost of living was lower, and in part because they cared less about material possessions and cold hard cash, and more about things such as flexibility and travel. A different survey found that 70% of digital nomads in Mexico, wouldn't return to an office job, no matter how much money they were offered.

This isn't to say that nomadic life is perfect.

Digital nomads have been the subject of hostility in some locations, such as Mexico City, where they've been accused of "Gentrification" – pricing the locals out of the market for accommodation. 34% of nomads have expressed concerns for their safety, 32% miss their families, and 30% struggle to deal with the differences between time zones. (Everson, King & Cockles, 2022). (Frydman, 2022).

There certainly seem to be a lot of people who judge digital nomads differently from the other nomads – accusing them of being privileged and spoilt. The majority *have* benefitted from a university education. Most come from wealthy nations – they possess powerful passports, which put them at an advantage.

But there's no need to be snobbish. Before we met, my wife worked in Saudi Arabia (as a nanny) and Thailand (as a teacher) – all with a Filipino passport. She worked online, in the "Digital domain", while we lived in Bulgaria. (She taught English to Japanese students).

Just because digital nomads are more likely to come from certain nations, doesn't mean they cannot come from others. Let's keep an open mind!

***

So, why mention such people in a section about *nurture*?

It might seem that these people are acting of their own accord – going off to work in other places, because *they* fancy it. But if that were the case, their numbers would be steady. They wouldn't be on the rise.

In reality, more people are becoming digital nomads, because of a variety of *external* pulls, which have encouraged them to migrate...

***

The first factor is *technology*: You couldn't have digital nomads without the "Digital" infrastructure which has appeared in recent times – enabling us to send content by email, communicate via video call, and sell products online. Technology has freed some of us from the office.

***

The second factor is *culture*: A new nomadic culture is emerging, as digital nomads begin to congregate in popular spots – forming new communities, offering each other support, providing companionship, and encouraging their peers to visit new destinations.

I witnessed this myself, when I arrived in Bulgaria. Back then, I'd never heard of a "Digital Nomad". That changed when I discovered a chain of "Coworking spaces" – offices and lounges where digital nomads could work, collaborate and socialise. They offered hot desks, a WIFI connection, coffee, organised outings, movie nights, board-game nights, and a "Coliving" service – arranging shared accommodation for their members.

I never joined myself. I'm far too reclusive! And I didn't see the point in paying the fees, when I could work at home for free. But I did meet some of the coworkers.

Once or twice a week, they turned up in their bright orange shirts, and challenged us – a regular bunch of expats – to a game of football. They seemed to improve as time rolled by. I think they trained in secret behind our backs!

I soon noticed a pattern: A fair few of these digital nomads only came for the summer – to trek and cycle in the Pirin mountains. They spent their winters in Thailand. It was as though they were encouraging each other on – enjoying the same two locations, at the best times of the year – escaping from the frigid Bulgarian winters, and the sweltering Thai summers, in a fashion which was reminiscent of the Kazakh horsemen.

So it wasn't just a matter of technology. A *community* had formed, which was nurturing these nomadic workers. And it certainly wasn't unique: Other communities exist in different locations. And they also exist online – on sites such as Nomad List, and on social media.

***

Employers can be a third factor.

While most digital nomads are freelancers, the boom in the last few years has been driven by those *companies* that've allowed their workers to work remotely. It's in their own self-interest: They get happy, productive staff – people who've been reinvigorated by life on the road. They save money on office expenses. And they get to recruit from a global talent pool.

When Flex Jobs looked into the companies that only posted listings for jobs with "Zero time in the office", the Wikimedia Foundation topped the charts. They were joined by the likes of GitHub, Quora and Study.com. (Bloom, 2022).

Flex Jobs also listed plenty of other famous names who recruited digital nomads for *some* positions. These included Ancestry.com, Coinbase, Dropbox, Google, Lyft, Reddit and Skillshare. (Howington, 2022).

Spotify believes that, "Work isn't somewhere you go, it's something you do". It's an ethos which is paying dividends: Quit-rates at Spotify have fallen by 15%, since they embraced this flexible approach.

And Airbnb has also announced that their workers can work wherever they like. When they went public with the news, *800,000 people* logged on, and viewed the company's careers page! (Frydman, 2022).

***

It's not just the business community that's nurturing these nomads. Certain *governments* are in on the act...

At the time of writing, fifty-four countries had introduced (or were about to introduce) some kind of visa for digital nomads. That's around a quarter of all the nations on Earth.

This number is on the rise – up from forty-six the previous year. Perhaps more will have followed suit, by the time you read this book. You can check out the "Nomad Girl" website, to keep track of the current situation.

The authors of that site seem to think that Georgia is the best location for digital nomads – with visa-free entry for up to a year, and a 1% rate of tax.

Estonia wins the prize for being the first country to have introduced a visa designed specifically for nomads. It's also developing a cloud-based pension, which nomads can access no matter where they wander. And it offers wayfaring entrepreneurs a virtual residency, which grants them access to all the EU's markets, and all the country's online services.

Goa is about to introduce a digital nomad visa – even though no such visa exists in the rest of India. The likes of Croatia prefer to offer a kind of temporary residence permit. And Indonesia has plans to introduce the longest nomad visa to date – one which will be valid for *five years*. They wish to capitalise on the tropical lure of Bali – a haven for digital nomads.

These are hardly examples of free movement in a borderless world. Many require nomads to prove that they have a certain monthly income, private health insurance, or a master's degree. (Johnson, 2023). (Castrillon, 2022). (Khanna, 2021).

Still, the fact that *some* people are being welcomed, *nurtured* even, does provide reason for hope.

THE NATIONS WHICH ENTICE IMMIGRANTS

Other nations are encouraging *permanent* immigration...

Canada is a prime example: 15% of its parliamentarians have foreign heritage. A fifth of its residents were born abroad. By 2036, half of its population will be immigrants or the children of immigrants.

But the Canadians haven't turned on their guests – making them scapegoats for society's ills. They *celebrate* newcomers, by hosting ceremonies in large arenas – cheering their new compatriots, as they're bestowed with Canadian citizenship. (Khanna, 2021).

The Canadians are even *luring* people from abroad.

In November 2022, Sean Fraser – Canada's Immigration Minister – laid out ambitious plans to entice just under half-a-million foreign nationals a year.

Almost six-in-ten were to be members of what Fraser called the "Economic Class" – a fancy way of saying "Workers". Canada has an ageing population, with relatively low birth rates. As Baby Boomers leave the workplace, the country is having to attract workers from abroad to fill the gaps. It also requires healthcare professionals, to care for its ageing population. It needs people to rejuvenate its eastern provinces – working in industries such as IT and hydropower. And, as Canada's ice-lands begin to thaw, creating more habitable territory, so the country will have to find more workers to fill that terrain – building infrastructure, such as railways and pipelines – establishing new firms, farms and factories.

The nation is even cashing in on the USA's hostility towards immigration – enticing the overseas workers who might've headed to the States in the past. When Donald Trump passed an executive order, banning the issuance of H-1B visas, their northern neighbours rejoiced – calling it the "Canadian Job Creation Act". The Canadians have even created an "Express Lane" for people who work in healthcare, manufacturing, construction and the STEM professions. They're making allowances for these workers to bring a hundred-thousand family members each year. And they plan to welcome almost as many refugees. (Khanna, 2021). (Singer, 2022).

It's not perfect: The system discriminates in favour of educated individuals. And it seems to be set up for the benefit of Canadian employers, rather than everyday folk. If you wish to migrate to work, there's a good chance you'll be welcome. If your goal is to live off-grid and be self-sufficient – like me – then it's hard to see which box you'd have to tick.

Indeed, I've only ever been refused entry into one country. And yeah, you guessed it – that country was Canada. When applying for a tourist visa, I was asked if I'd ever been arrested. I ticked the "Yes" box – I'd been arrested at a political protest, although all the charges were soon dropped. I never heard back from the Canadian authorities, no clearance was issued, and I was denied entry onto the plane when I arrived at the airport.

No country is perfect.

***

So, what is Canada doing to nurture its cosmopolitan culture?

Well, they're stepping out into the world – wooing people in their "Immigration Operation Centres" – in places such as Delhi, Chandigarh and Islamabad.

Their office in Manila, is run by thirty-seven members of staff, who help potential movers to process their paperwork and book their transportation. That outpost has welcomed delegates from different Canadian provinces, who've made job offers to hundreds of Filipinos – mostly healthcare professionals. It plans to introduce a scholarship – enabling Filipino nurses to complete their studies in the North American nation. And it also seems to have recruited several local agents. The Facebook groups in my town, are inundated with posts which advertise job opportunities in Canada.

There are financial incentives too: A Filipino nurse can increase their salary almost six-fold, simply by moving to Canada. The Facebook posts I keep seeing, advertise wages which are considerably higher than those which are available in my district.

And the Canadians are also offering *permanent* residency to their international residents.

So we have a system in which Canadian officials are travelling to the Philippines, reaching out to Filipinos, luring them with a massive pay rise, and offering them residency. (Dawson, 2023).

It's a long cry from the anti-immigrant policies that have become so ubiquitous elsewhere.

***

Japan finds itself in a similar predicament...

Back in 2014, Japanese companies were offering 1.09 jobs for every person who was seeking employment. Five years later, there were more vacancies than job-seekers in *every single prefecture*, for the first time in the nation's history. (De Meyer, 2017)

To fill the gap, Japan is having to entice a large number of workers from abroad. Research from the Value Management Institute, has concluded that it'll need almost seven-million foreign workers by 2040 – a fourfold increase in just seventeen years. If technology doesn't develop at the predicted rate, the Japanese will have to entice even *more*. (Obe, 2022).

The Japanese authorities are working hard to find new residents.

In 2013, they expanded their trainee schemes, which attracted hundreds-of-thousands of apprentices. And in 2019, they passed a new bill, to entice another seventy-thousand employees per year – offering them long-term work permits and permanent residency. The government has also drafted bilateral agreements with the likes of Indonesia and the Philippines – encouraging those nations to send more caregivers.

Japan is focused. It's attempting to attract the professionals it needs the most. But it's not snobbish. It's seeking both white-collar *and* blue-collar workers – including a mixture of shipbuilders, nurses, mechanics, farmers, fishermen and builders.

Its policies are already having an effect: The number of immigrants in Japan, has tripled in the three decades since 1990.

And these foreigners are being welcomed: A survey conducted by Nikkei, found that 69% of Japanese people believed that immigration was "Good" for Japan. Only 26% said it was a "Bad" thing. Anti-immigration groups do exist, but they've only won the support of one or 2% of the population.

Japan is far from an immigrant's haven. Foreign workers are more likely to suffer an injury while on the job. They're more likely to experience physical and verbal attacks. Many have been subjected to racial slurs.

But Japan has shown that countries can change. And most Japanese people *support* their nation's transition. (Gelin, 2020).

***

Canada and Japan are hardly alike: Canada, like America, was built by immigrants. Japan had a closed-door policy, until the relatively recent past. Canada is trying to attract *more* people from overseas. Japan is trying to establish a whole new demographic. Canada is sending ambassadors across the world. Japan is tinkering with a few of its rules. But both are doing their bit to *nurture* a migratory culture, because they need foreign workers to help sustain their economies.

Other nations are being more proactive – enticing those people who'll help their economies *grow*.

The Gulf states are famous for this: A couple of generations ago, the Arabian Peninsula was a vast expanse of desert, with a tiny population. These days, its nations are among the richest on Earth – filled with booming towns, luxury hotels, swanky shops and futuristic towers. The discovery of oil has certainly helped. But so did inward migration: Immigrants make up three-quarters of the population of Kuwait, and almost nine-tenths of the population of the United Arab Emirates. It was immigrants who turned the region's oil into tangible wealth. It was immigrants who built those nations. (Caplan, 2019).

The Gulf states shouldn't be held up as paragons of virtue.

These countries have a reputation for mistreating their international guests – forcing them to toil beneath the midday sun, and endure slave-like conditions. The last time my wife worked in the region, her passport was confiscated, and she struggled to leave. But they do give a fine example of how nations can reap the rewards, when they *encourage* immigration.

***

A raft of nations are encouraging immigration in other ways...

Several are enticing *wealthy* individuals: Tax havens have been luring the rich for decades – saying, "Come here and save a fortune on your tax bill". Saint Lucia is even advertising on my Facebook feed right now. I think they've got me confused with someone else!

Other nations offer a "Golden visa" – granting passports to anyone who invests a hefty sum: Spain issues them to anyone who pays €500,000. In Malta, one will cost you €750,000. And in Ireland, one will set you back a cool €1,000,000.

It's big business: Portugal has made $2b, just by selling these visas.

And it's a growth industry: Back in 2017, only five-thousand people purchased their citizenships. *Twenty-thousand* were bought in the first *half* of 2020. (Khanna, 2021). (Springer, 2020).

***

Other countries are doing their bit to attract *retirees* – so long as they have a sizeable pension and private healthcare. There's even a "Global Retirement Index" – a league table that helps pensioners to choose a country that's right for them. Portugal, Mexico and Panama topped the charts in 2023. (Donaldson et al, 2023).

Some nations are enticing new residents – *unintentionally* – whether they like it or not! Each time the Americans release a movie or TV show that portrays the country in a positive light, it's essentially advertising itself, saying: "Look at this fabulous place. Wouldn't you like to live here?" People see those shows. And they think, "Yeah, okay then". And they buy themselves a ticket.

And some governments are encouraging *students* to migrate. It's hardly surprising. International students tend to pay higher tuition fees – helping to generate the income that universities need: They contributed just over £28b to the United Kingdom's economy in 2021 alone. They did use almost £3b worth of public services. But the net benefit still amounted to around £380 per British citizen. And these benefits were felt in every part of the nation. As a result, the British government is actually working to *increase* the number of international students in the country – even as it attempts to create a hostile environment for other groups of people. (Hillman & Stern, 2021).

THE RETURNEES: A CASE OF CIRCULAR MIGRATION

We tend to think of migration as one-way traffic. A family might move from Mexico to the States. But then we might expect them to settle, and never move on again.

I'd like to think we put that misnomer to bed, when we discussed the modern nomads. But there's a third type of international citizen, who we haven't encountered so far – those people who move around a little, before *returning* to the lands of their birth.

These "Returnees" now find themselves back in their original location. But they have more skills and experience than their countryfolk. And this puts them at an advantage.

Let's consider a couple of examples...

When IBM learned that one of their leading engineers – Dov Frohman – was going to return to Jerusalem (in 1974), they decided it'd be better to open up a new design centre in nearby Haifa, than to lose out on his expertise altogether. This one act, inspired by a single returnee, helped to transform Frohman's country into an international leader, in the design and manufacture of integrated circuits.

Ten years later, six Chinese engineers followed Frohman's lead. They quit their jobs in Silicon Valley, returned home, and established Taiwan's first three semiconductor-producing firms. One went bust, and the other two merged. But they were an inspiration – kick-starting Taiwan's technological revolution.

By the 1990s, the IT sectors in these two small countries were bigger than those in Germany and France. The growth had been phenomenal. And it can all be traced back to these "New Argonauts" – these globetrotters who turned around and headed home. (Saxenian, 2007).

***

Returnees are such a boon, that some countries – such as Vietnam, Portugal, India and China – are actively *enticing* their diasporas.

This form of migration can take a couple of forms.

"Heritage Migration" is where a person who was born abroad, is enticed back to their ancestral homeland. They might have a parent or a grandparent from that land, but they've never actually lived there themselves.

"Frontier Migration" occurs when a person who left for a life abroad, is persuaded to come back – usually with new skills, contacts and perspectives. They may not have intended to return. It used to be the case that if a Chinese person went to study in the United States, they stayed in the States to work – especially if they'd completed a degree in one of the STEM subjects (science, technology, engineering or mathematics). But an increase in anti-migrant sentiment, following the attacks on the Twin Towers, has encouraged a growing number of foreign graduates to leave. According to the Chinese Ministry of Education, 353,500 returned to China in 2013 alone. (Myambo, 2017).

***

Those young professionals are being *enticed* by their compatriots...

Alibaba – a "Scrappy cross between Amazon and eBay" – is Chinese to the core: It was established by Chinese entrepreneurs, in China, and most of its staff have a Chinese heritage. But its outlook is international. Its headquarters look like a feng-shui-compliant version of a campus in Silicon Valley – replete with table-tennis tables, free massages, and a statue of a naked man.

Jack Ma, one of Alibaba's cofounders, is Chinese himself. But he's never been a nerd. He readily admits that he didn't have a clue what he was doing, back when he started out. Ma needed help. And he got it from China's *diaspora*.

Ma partnered with Joe Tsai, who'd been a senior executive at Rosecliff Venture Management – a private equity firm, based out of New York. Tsai supplied the financial smarts which the fledgling firm required – bringing experience and contacts – securing investment from the likes of Yahoo and Softbank. A person who'd spent their entire life in China, might've struggled to attract that sort of foreign funding.

Tsai also brought a fellow Chinese American on board – recruiting Brian Wong, who'd go on to become Alibaba's head of global sales.

Together with Ma, they employed a "Disproportionate" number of staff who'd lived, worked and studied abroad. These people understood foreign cultures – they were well-positioned to build relationships with professionals in other lands. And they possessed the kind of skills which were in short supply, back in China.

It was these returnees who built Alibaba's website – writing the code, designing the user interface, and bringing their e-commerce expertise to the table. It was these returnees who created a company which employed over 250,000 people, in 2022 – generating revenues of more than a hundred-billion dollars a year. (Guest, 2011).

***

But it's not only entrepreneurs who're wooing China's diaspora. Chinese *states* are also in on the act.

The authorities in Shanghai have encouraged twenty-thousand people to return from abroad. Between them, these returnees have established four-thousand firms.

Jiangsu province offers up to a million yuan – around $140,000 – to support entrepreneurs who return to China. They've implemented policies to ensure that these individuals can access good housing, find a job for their spouse, and get their children into the best schools. To spread the word, they've opened liaison offices in eight developed nations – in places such as Australia, Japan and the States.

Beijing has also established overseas offices, to woo potential residents. It's created the "Chinese Silicon Valley" – a technology hub which was already home to twelve-thousand entrepreneurs, by 2012. Almost half of those people had arrived with patents for new merchandise. They were ready to go. They just needed a little support. (De Meyer, 2017). (Wang & Bao, 2015).

***

So, we can see a clear distinction between the Chinese and Canadian models: Canada is enticing employees *to take jobs*. China is enticing entrepreneurs *to create jobs*.

But this is an oversimplification.

The Chinese are also attracting *brides* from Korea, Vietnam and Myanmar – not only to marry its male youth, who outnumber their female counterparts, but also to act as caregivers. The Chinese are suffering from what they dub the "Four Two One" dilemma – whereby *one* adult is expected to provide for *two* parents and *four* grandparents. Immigrant spouses can help to lighten their load.

And the Chinese are also enticing *students*. In 2019, their country provided a temporary home for half-a-million foreign pupils. They're providing vocational training to *young professionals* from afar afield as Nigeria and Pakistan. And they're welcoming *scientists*: eight-thousand Japanese academics are employed at Chinese universities – teaching everything from zoology to engineering. (Khanna, 2021).

***

India is also benefitting from its returnees...

Shivinder Singh established Fortis – a chain of private hospitals – after witnessing the quality of treatment his father received at an American hospital.

He decided to return to India and open a hospital that maintained those exacting standards:

"If you only live in India, you naturally measure yourself against Indian standards. If you have lived abroad, you measure yourself against the best standards in the world."

These days, Fortis recruits Indian doctors who've studied or worked in another country. Some have *specialist expertise*, the likes of which can be hard to find in India. And most return with a network of *contacts* – doctors in other lands, whom they can call for advice.

But the company supports those staff with *local* secretaries and cleaners, who can be employed at a lower cost than in other countries. These assistants do *all* the administration – including paperwork which the doctors in the West often have to complete themselves. Fortis's doctors don't even make their own coffee. And this frees them up – allowing them to perform more operations than their foreign-based peers.

The results are there for all to see: A kidney operation that'd cost around $100,000 in the States, might only cost around $10,000 at a Fortis hospital. The quality will be about the same. And the doctors will still receive a similar wage. (Guest, 2011).

***

These anecdotes paint a fairly narrow picture: We've only spoken about the high-tech sector, and about a person who was rich enough to open a hospital.

In reality, there are a vast array of opportunities in the developing world, because it's still *developing*. If you wanted to establish a fast-food empire in the United States, you'd have your work cut out – going up against the likes of KFC and Burger King. But in other lands, where the markets aren't so saturated, there are many more niches left to exploit.

The numbers speak for themselves.

The OECD has ranked thirty-three of their member states according to what they call the "Employer enterprise birth rate". This measures the rate at which new firms appear, *relative* to the number of firms that already exist in a nation.

The United States and Canada both came in the bottom five of the OECD's rankings. Hungary and Poland topped the charts. And that's hardly surprising. These are less developed nations, where there's far less competition, and a much clearer route to growth. (Suchodolska et al, 2017).

Put these things together...

You have these highly motivated, highly educated entrepreneurs in developed nations. But there aren't many opportunities for them to exploit, because there's so much competition. Now, some of these people have links to a developing nation – either because they lived there as children, or because their parents had lived there before. If such a person were to return to those nations, they could make a real difference.

This sort of thing *does* happen.

Take Yasser Ali as an example: Yasser's parents moved from India to Cleveland and then onto Los Angeles, where Yasser was born. Yasser didn't vibe with India the first time he visited his ancestral homeland. He found it dirty, and couldn't understand how people could live without running water. But he visited India again, while he was at university, and something clicked:

"It felt like I was coming home... I suddenly felt awake and connected to the entire universe. It was like not knowing you can't see properly until you put on glasses. Everything came into clarity. I suddenly understood where I came from and where I wanted to go."

Yasser wanted to "Go" to India.

But first, he had to return to California, where he got a job at a gelato emporium. He loved it. And then he had a brainwave: There was nothing like this in India. Yeah, you could get kulfi and some basic ice-cream. But you'd struggle to find any real gelato.

Yasser got some more hands-on experience at the Marriott Hotel in Mumbai – "They were doing everything wrong. It was like McDonald's for ice cream". He studied Baskin Robins, to understand customer flow. And he travelled to Italy, to find a partner – Costanzo Malatto – the boss at an award-winning gelateria.

The rest, as they say, is history.

Yasser didn't do anything particularly original. He just imported a foreign product, and recruited an Italian mentor. But it was never about *what* he did. It was about *where* he did it: Yasser set up shop in India – a nation where there was a gap in the market. And then things began to explode:

"We were the first of our kind in Mumbai. Within six months, we had forty branches. By the end of the year, seventy." (Marquardt, 2021).

***

These are just a handful of anecdotes. But they're exemplars of a broader trend.

It's impossible to say how many emigrants return to the lands of their birth, because nations tend not to keep track of emigration. Departing citizens can waltz back through the border at any time, as though they'd never left. But some incomplete estimates do exist: A club for Indian expats – the Indus Entrepreneurs – reckons that sixty-thousand IT workers had returned to India by 2007. Between fifteen and twenty-thousand returned in 2003 alone. And that's just in a single industry. (Guest, 2011).

Then again, this is hardly surprising when you consider that over eighteen-million Indian citizens live abroad – mainly in the Arab world. That's the largest expat community of any nation, anywhere on the planet.

Even if only a small proportion of these people returned in any given year, the numbers are still going to add up.

Several are certainly heading back from the Middle East. As of March 2021, *3.25 million workers* had been repatriated from the Gulf states alone. That number is similar to the entire population of a country like Puerto Rico! (Khan & Arokkiaraj, 2021).

We should be careful not to imply there are no downsides. A lot of those people were construction workers, who were subjected to appalling conditions while they were abroad. Repatriating so many people at once, can bring challenges of its own. (Naudé et al, 2017).

Still, these globetrotters do maintain an advantage over their sedentary peers – both because of the *experience* they've accrued abroad, and also because they remain in *contact* with the people they've met.

Research into returnee businesspeople from India and China, has found that well over half of them communicate with their former *colleagues*, at least once a month. Over a third make monthly contact with a *professional association* that is based overseas. A third of Chinese returnees, and a sixth of Indians, reach out to staff at foreign *universities*. And they also make trips in person – meeting up with old acquaintances.

They share vital information.

Over three-in-five of these returnees talk to their contacts about their customers and markets. Almost as many chat about "Technical information". And over half of Chinese returnees speak about funding.

By maintaining regular contact, they're able to get information as soon as it emerges. They can jump on new trends, and adopt new techniques – staying one step ahead of their peers.

This means they can expand, and create more jobs: Around one-in-six of the returnees interviewed in the study, already employed over a hundred workers. And that's all the more impressive, when you consider that over half of their firms were less than five-years-old. (Wadhwa et al, 2011).

WHEN EMIGRATION IS ENCOURAGED

We've shown how nations encourage immigration and reverse migration. But what about *emigration*?

We know it's significant. Large numbers of people leave home each year. But are there any cultures which actively encourage their citizens to leave? And why would they do such a thing?

***

Some nations encourage their *students* to move abroad – to access better courses. I can't help but think of the Norwegians I met at university. Their government paid their fees, because it wanted them to study at a top university, and experience another culture.

Some *employees* are also asked to relocate. Most governments send diplomats to outposts around the world. My cousin's firm once sent him to Prague, to open a new office.

But what about those people who move of their own accord?

I may be biased, but when it comes to the subject, I can't help but think of the Philippines.

We've already mentioned this place a couple of times – noting that Canada has been sending envoys to woo the locals, and that the Japanese have been working on a bilateral agreement. The numbers don't lie: According to the International Labour Organisation, "Ten-million Filipinos live abroad, and more than a million Filipinos leave the country each year". (www.ilo.org).

There's clearly a lot of emigration. But is there a *culture* of emigration? And is it being encouraged?

It'd be fair to say that some people leave more because of *necessity* than *nurture*. The Philippine population is growing at a faster rate than its job market. Some people *have* to move to find work. Other Filipinos might emigrate to escape from poverty or debt. (Yeung & Bacani, 2020).

But there's clearly support from the top.

This is a quote from the former president – Rodrigo Duterte – who was addressing a crowd of Filipino emigrants:

"Let me take this opportunity to acknowledge your impact on our country's progress, not only in terms of your invaluable contribution to the economy, but also (in showcasing) the skills and talents of the Filipino to the international (community)... Now, more than ever, we need you, the *Oversees Foreign Workers*... to take part in our nation-building efforts. I thus call on you... to make our country proud." (Gita-Carlos, 2019).

Duterte was celebrating emigrants for two reasons: Because they acted as *ambassadors* – earning the Philippines an international reputation. And because they benefitted the Philippine *economy* – by wiring money back to their families.

***

When I raised the subject with my wife, she looked at my phone – which had just begun to record – and proceeded to laugh for the best part of a minute:

"Why are you recording me?... You're recording me! You're recording me! This is so creepy. Don't do that."

She only realised that I was serious, when I repeated my original question:

"What gave you the idea to move abroad?"

"I think it's always been like that for Filipinos. It's been instilled in our mind at an early age... Like, we've seen our neighbours or some people, like my classmates, whose parents were working abroad. They had a better life than those of us who didn't have family working abroad... My best friend in high school – Kate – her mother was working abroad. I think she was working in Kuwait, during our high school days. And she got an MP3, stuff like that, which I couldn't afford. They had better dishes, compared to us. We were just happy to have sardines and egg. They had nice pork stews... Actually, I have two best friends. (The other one), her mother was working in Hong Kong. And she had nice clothes. My parents couldn't afford that. I always borrowed clothes from her."

But it wasn't selfishness that inspired my wife to emigrate. She didn't move abroad to secure a better life for *herself*. She saw the sacrifices her parents had made, and felt a duty to do something *for them*:

"Papa used to wake up at three in the morning, to start work, and he worked until six in the evening... Mama's the same. She worked as a maid for quite some time."

They got little in return:

"Like, for our dish, we maybe only had three fishes. And that was very expensive. We couldn't even afford that, back in my elementary days... We'd have three fishes, and during that time there were six in the family. So instead of my parents having a big part of the fish, Mama would cut it in two... I mean the small tiny fish, like the ones you feed to our dogs. And Mama divided that... And that half is Boyet, that half is for Noonoy, that half is for me. Mama and Papa would just take a small fish head for themselves."

"(At school) you had to pay for the extracurricular activities. You had to pay for the computer subjects... I wanted to be a majorette. And so do you know what Papa did? He sold his caribou, so I can become a majorette!"

I asked my wife if her parents encouraged her to move abroad:

"No, they pushed us to get an education... Papa's mindset was like, if you have a better education, you're gonna have a better life... (Although) my brother *was* forced to take a marine engineer course. Because if that's the case, he can be a seaman and work abroad. One of my cousins – Riza – she wanted to study nursing, so she could follow her auntie in the US.

"For me, I wasn't really planning to (move abroad). Because I thought that if I have a degree, I'll be able to have a better salary (in the Philippines). But then, when I graduated, I went to Manila. I was so excited. And when I went to Manila, and the reality hit, you know? That life is not going to be easy for me, just because I have this piece of paper. And then you see that your salary is like twelve-thousand pesos ($220 a month). You still have to pay for your rent. And you can't even afford to get your own room. And then this reality hit like, oh no! I don't care if I'm just going to clean someone else's house abroad, as long as I'll be able to earn twenty-thousand pesos ($360 a month). And you know, when I worked abroad in Saudi Arabia, that twenty-thousand pesos is already the net, because they provide everything – your uniform, your underwear, your shampoo, everything... twenty-thousand net was a huge help to my family. Like, I was able to help them to *finish their house.*"

When she was a child, my wife's family lived in a bamboo shelter, which they'd built themselves. But they hadn't owned the ground on which it stood. Then the government issued them with a small plot of land. They had the right to build a home, but they needed money. My wife's aunt provided a little, to get things started. And my wife moved abroad, to secure the funds they needed to finish the job:

"I wanted to finish my bachelor's degree, so I could give something to my parents. It's not like in the US or in Europe, where kids have a dream since they were young, because that's what *they* want to do. For us, it's usually connected to our love for *someone else.* You know, we do stuff for someone else... We do stuff for someone else, because it's a service. We feel valued, we feel like we are a better person, we feel validated... So, growing up, I wanted to finish this, and do like this, so I could give my parents a better life... When I finished my degree, and the reality hit, it's like yeah – you don't have any other option but to go abroad."

***

I think there's a bit of everything in my wife's story. There's a bit of *necessity*. She felt a *need* to go abroad, to receive the sort of wages she couldn't secure at home. I think her *nature* also played a part – not that she mentioned it. My wife is an explorer: She's zipped about between places like Saudi Arabia, Thailand, Vietnam and Bulgaria. But, more than anything, there's this overwhelming sense of *nurture*. Her society nurtured a sense of duty – this idea that she was expected to help her parents. Her peers had already moved abroad – sending money home to their families – setting an example for her to follow. This kind of thing was the norm.

No-one that I know in Britain has ever behaved like this. None of my classmates moved abroad, to get money to send home to their parents. But it's a part of the Philippine *culture*. If you were born there, you might do the same.

***

Filipinas emigrate for other reasons too: Some move for love – to live with a foreign spouse. Others join up with family members who emigrated in the past. Some go to earn the money they need to pay for their children's education.

But I think that their willingness to make the plunge has a lot to do with culture – with this idea that it's okay to move abroad. That it's a *good* thing – for the economy, for the nation's reputation, and for the people you love the most.

***

It seems less likely that people would be encouraged to leave wealthy nations, such as Britain. But as we mentioned before, many more people left the UK than arrived, in almost every year before 1984. Around half-a-million people still leave that country each year.

I feel that my ultimate emigration was the result of several factors, which were *nurtured* within me while I was growing up in Britain...

The first was the British culture of *vacationing*: Almost half the country goes abroad each year. We're a nation of international travellers. It can come as no surprise, therefore, that so many retirees move to the Algarve or the Costa del Sol. The chances are, they've already visited those places on holiday, and had a grand old time. They know what they're getting into.

The second factor was the British culture of the *"Gap year"*: Several British youths travel around the world, before heading to university. They follow in the footsteps of the Ancient Greeks, and those rich Europeans who went on "Grand tours". It's a rite of passage, and a part of their education.

I couldn't afford to do that myself, although I did go backpacking when I was older – an experience that opened my eyes to the world.

The third factor was *family*: I just mentioned that one of my cousins moved to Prague. Another cousin whizzed across Europe and the Middle East, while working in IT. So I had nomadic role models, when I was at a young and impressionable age.

The fourth factor was my internal migration for *work*: In my mid-twenties, I moved to Liverpool to complete my master's degree. After that, I moved to Burnley, Bristol and Northampton – to take up various positions, while pursuing a career in sports management. So I was already uprooted – living away from my hometown, friends and family. Moving abroad didn't seem like such a massive leap.

And the fifth factor was *economic*: The prohibitive cost of living encouraged me to move abroad – to find somewhere I could survive, whilst establishing myself as an author – and to find a place where I could afford to buy a home. I don't think I was alone: A good chunk of the British retirees in Southern Europe have moved there because of the cheaper housing. Millions of Americans travel abroad each year, to access affordable healthcare.

The British authorities might not encourage emigration *by design* – in the same way that the Canadians encourage immigration. But the country's *culture* does inspire people to leave. Brits have to move around for work, they choose to travel for leisure, they're inspired by the foreigners they meet in their daily lives, and they have an economic incentive to relocate. It's little wonder that so many of us make the move!

THE BENEFITS OF EMIGRATION

The money transfers my wife sent to her parents, are known as "Remittances". And these are classed as a kind of *export*.

That might sound a little strange. So please allow me to explain...

When we think of exports, it's easy to picture a product being sent overseas. But in purely economic terms, what makes something an export, is the money that flows in the opposite direction. When a firm exports a car, it *receives* a payment – the money which was paid by a foreign customer. That's what makes it an export.

Nothing physical has to leave the country: When the Premier League sells its broadcast rights around the world, it's *exporting* those rights, because money is leaving other countries and heading back to Britain.

Sometimes, the products can be consumed on home soil: If a French family goes for a holiday in London – spending money at restaurants and hotels – then economists would say that Britain "Exported" a holiday. Those restaurants and hotels weren't sent abroad. But the money they received had flowed out of France and into Britain.

Now think of remittances...

When Filipinos move abroad for work, they almost always take a chunk of their salary, and send it back to the Philippines. Money flows out of another country, and arrives in the land of their birth. In purely economic terms, we're witnessing an "Export".

The Philippines is exporting workers, and it's receiving a significant amount of money in return: In 2019, expats sent over $33b back to the Philippines. That's equivalent to almost a tenth of the nation's GDP, and over 30% of the nation's export earnings. (data.worldbank.org). (Yeung & Bacani, 2019).

That shouldn't be taken lightly: The Philippines imports some pretty basic stuff, including almost four-million tons of rice a year. It needs foreign currency to pay for these vital imports. And it needs remittances, to secure that foreign currency. (Phoonphongphiphat,

2023).

It's little wonder that Duterte hailed the "Invaluable contribution" made by people who'd already left the country. They were still supporting their nation.

***

The Philippines might be famous for its diaspora, but it's far from unique.

Across the globe, expat workers sent $31b home, back in 1990. But by 2021, that figure had risen twenty-five-fold – to $781b. The growth has been exponential. And these numbers don't include all the unofficial transfers, which go unrecorded.

In 2021, remittances produced half the GDP of Tonga, 38% of the GDP of Lebanon, and a third of the GDP of Samoa. (Ratha, 2022). (Emmer, 2011).

Remittances provide the *largest source of foreign income* for countries in the developing world. They deliver more money than foreign direct investment. And they account for more than double the amount that's received in foreign aid. (Goldin et al, 2012).

Remittances are also more *reliable*.

Foreign aid can go missing. It can be stolen by corrupt officials, and it can be squandered on vanity projects that fail to serve the people. But when an expat sends money to someone they love, they check that it's been received. If a peso or rupee has gone missing, they'll contact Western Union or Wise, and kick up a fuss until it reappears.

Foreign investment is volatile. Some firms might feel skittish at the thought of investing in a developing economy. Others might jump ship at the first sign of instability. But remittances can smooth the waters. They're *counter-cyclical*: When Mexico suffered a financial crisis, in 1995, and when Indonesia followed suit, in 1998 – both of those nations began to receive more remittances almost straight away. Relations sent money, to help ease their families' woes. And expat entrepreneurs invested more – taking advantage of the weakened currency, to buy up more land and expand their operations.

Indeed, a great deal of the money which is received from abroad is *invested*.

A survey of six-thousand small Mexican businesses, found that foreign remittances supplied around a fifth of their initial funding. Most of that money had been sent home by relations who were working in the States.

In Nigeria, people who received remittances spent very little on themselves – using just 10% to buy food, and spending just 5% on healthcare. By contrast, they used over a third of that money to purchase land and housing, and they invested over a fifth of their remittances in a business. (Ratha et al, 2011).

Of course, remittances are also used to fund consumption. Some are spent on luxuries. But a good chunk is spent on necessities. And this can help to *reduce poverty*.

It's been estimated that remittances have lifted 11% of impoverished Ugandans above the poverty line. Around half of the decrease in poverty we've witnessed in Nepal, is thought to have come about thanks to money which was sent home from abroad.

And this has a knock-on effect: When he studied the data from eighty-two countries, Christian Ebeke found that higher remittances led to a *reduction in child labour*. Another study, carried out in rural Pakistan, found that families who had a relative overseas, were 54% more likely to send their daughters to school. (Ratha et al, 2011). (Guest, 2011).

***

There's another way we might achieve these kinds of outcomes...

That's because nations don't only earn export earnings when their overseas workers send money home. They also receive money when their citizens return home in person.

When we first moved to Bulgaria, my wife and I rented a flat which was owned by a lovely (and rather handsome) man named Kostadin. Kostadin left Bulgaria almost every summer. He'd been to Britain, I think to work as a fruit picker. And he'd also worked in the States.

Kostadin saved most of his wages, and brought them back to Bulgaria in person. He used them to buy the apartment we rented.

(Kostadin lived with his family). And he used them to open a hire shop – supplying tourists with skis, snowboards and boots.

These things were good for Bulgaria: There was a surplus of unsold housing in Kostadin's town – people needed to buy it up. The country needs people like Kostadin, who open shops and create jobs for themselves. And the money they bring, flows into the country's economy, in much the same way as remittances. It also helps to improve their balance of trade.

***

This is all well and good. Families who have relations overseas, can benefit from the cash they send home in the form of remittances, and the money they bring home in person, after completing a contract abroad.

But what about their compatriots?

If a Filipina nurse moves to Canada, *her* family might be better off, but there'll be one less nurse left to care for everyone else. This is sometimes called a "Brain Drain".

In reality, people who complain of brain drains, are being a little myopic. They fail to consider the *ripple effects* that migration can inspire. They're essentially saying that the size of the pie is fixed – if we send a slice overseas, then there'll be less for everyone else. Whereas in reality, we can *grow* the pie. We can experience a "Brain Gain".

We already encountered this idea above. Nurses do leave the Philippines to work abroad. But some of them also *return*. When nurses come back, after working overseas, they arrive with more experience and a wider pool of contacts. They offer a better quality of care.

And there's an even more significant factor at play: Do you recall my wife's anecdote? She was *inspired* by her friends' parents – people who'd gone to work abroad. Well, that's a fairly common story over here: When nurses leave the Philippines, they inspire the next generation. Kids up and down the land think, "I want to be like them. I want to become a nurse, travel the world, and send money to *my* family". Some of them are so inspired, they enrol on a course, and train to become nurses themselves. *The pie gets even bigger.*

Of course, some of those newly trained nurses will eventually migrate – a large slice of the pie will end up abroad. But the majority *won't*. They might meet a partner who doesn't wish to emigrate, they might have to stay to care for a relative, they might have a change of heart, or they might procrastinate forever – saying, "We'll emigrate next year", without ever making the move. One of my school friends studied to be a doctor, because he wanted to travel the world with Médecins Sans Frontières. Seventeen years after graduating, he's still in Britain – raising two teenage girls, and paying off a mortgage! And I reckon that must be a pretty common story. There must be loads of other doctors and nurses who'd intended to work abroad, before life got in the way.

***

This isn't some kind of hypothetical mumbo-jumbo. The data back up the theory...

In 2001, around ninety-thousand Filipinos were training to become nurses. By 2008, that number had increased more than *fivefold* – to almost half-a-million. Hundreds-of-thousands of young people had been inspired to study. The pie was getting bigger.

The brain gain was real, although it came at a cost: It was *too much of a good thing*. There were so many nurses, the government was struggling to employ them all. Around 150,000 were out of work, in 2008, and nurses' pay began to stagnate. (Pring & Roco, 2012).

Some nurses were forced to move, because there weren't enough vacancies at home. Some emigrated because it'd been their dream all along. But around 65% of those nurses remained in the Philippines – caring for their compatriots.

These numbers add up.

According to figures from the World Bank, the Philippines had 5.4 nurses or midwives for every one-thousand residents, in 2018. That's not particularly exceptional – the USA had 15.7, and the UK had 8.9. The Philippines came in just below Israel (5.6) and just above South Africa (5.0). But that's still pretty impressive, when you consider that the Philippine's GDP-per-capita is one-fifteenth of Israel's, and a half of South Africa's.

The average country in the "East Asia & Pacific" region only had

3.9 nurses for every one-thousand residents. So the Philippines was doing considerably better than its neighbours. It wasn't losing out to a "Brain Drain". Its emigrants were inspiring their peers – fuelling a "Brain Gain", which was benefitting the nation. (data.worldbank.org).

***

Again, the Philippines is hardly unique...

According to a study of 127 nations, the adverse effects of the "Brain Drain" only outweigh the positive impact of the "Brain Gain", when more than a fifth of a nation's graduates decide to emigrate. And that's incredibly rare. It tends only to happen when there are extraordinary circumstances, such as a war or a famine. (Beine et al, 2008).

***

In some situations, migration can also result in *higher wages*.

When people move abroad, labour becomes scarce. Employers have to compete to lure those workers who remain, by offering them higher wages. Governments might also increase the salaries they pay to their staff, to discourage them from leaving the public sector.

A 2007 study found that wages were between six and nine percent higher in those Mexican states which sent a large number of emigrants to the USA, than in those states which only sent a few.

Another paper found that whenever the size of the Polish diaspora increases by 1%, wages in Poland increase by between 0.01% and 0.02%. That's a tiny figure – it amounts to under $5 per worker per year. But the numbers can add up: If we were to double the size of the Polish expat community, the average worker back in Poland would gain just under $500 a year. That's the kind of pay rise which can make a real difference.

And again, these examples aren't the exceptions. They're the norm: A range of studies have investigated what would happen were a country to experience a "10% *Emigrant Supply Shock*". It found that wages would increase by 2% in Honduras, by 3.2% in Moldova, and by up to 5.6% in Mexico. (Mishra, 2014).

***

It's little wonder that countries are trying to nurture a culture of emigration.

Emigrants send billions of dollars back home every year. They bring their savings, whenever they return. This money lifts people out of poverty. It leads to a reduction in child labour. And it's used to fund investments.

Emigration also creates a "Brain Gain" – both when people return with new skills, and when they inspire their peers to study. It can also help to boost wages for the average worker.

What's not to love?

A MATTER OF "NECESSITY"

"Imagine there was a single measure that could wipe out all poverty everywhere, raising everybody in Africa above our Western poverty line, and in the process put a few extra months' salary in our pockets too. Just imagine. Would we take that measure? No. Of course not. After all, this measure has been around for years. It's the best plan that never happened. I'm talking about open borders."

Rutger Bregman

We've already mentioned the Gallup poll, which estimated that almost a billion people would like to move abroad. But we didn't delve into the numbers.

There are massive variations, on a country-by-country basis.

Topping the charts, was Sierra Leone: Just over three-in-four Sierra Leonians wanted to relocate. But they didn't wish to flee from a military conflict. It's been more than twenty years since the civil war ended. Those people wished to flee from *poverty*. GDP-per-capita in Sierra Leone was just $480, in 2021. This means that the average person must survive on $1.59 a day. Most will have to survive on less. It's little wonder that so many wish to leave – to flee from their poverty, and increase their life expectancy.

Lebanon was next on the list: More than six-in-ten Lebanese people showed a desire to emigrate. Lebanon wasn't so poor. Its GDP-per-capita was $8,985, in 2019 – over eighteen times higher than in Sierra Leone. But the economy had just experienced a financial crash, which the World Bank said, "Is likely to rank in the top ten, possibly top three, most severe crises since the mid-nineteenth century". By 2021, GDP had fallen to less than half its previous level. People had experienced a taste of a better life. That life had been snatched from their grasp. They wanted to get it back.

And in third place was Honduras: 56% of Hondurans wanted to emigrate. That nation produced $2,771 of economic output per person, in 2021 – about $7 per person per day. That's far higher than in Sierra Leone, but it's still fairly low. What's more, *inequality* was also an issue. The 2018 figures show that over half of Hondurans had to survive on less than $5.50 a day. One-in-six had to get by with less than

$1.90. (Pugliese & Ray, 2023). (Data.WorldBank.org). (Al-Saeed & El Khalil, 2021).

ESCAPING ECONOMIC HARDSHIP

We're beginning to see the bigger picture...

People aren't only fleeing from *poverty*. They're fleeing from the *instability* brought about by an economic crash, and from extreme *inequality*.

If their nations had stable economies – and if they could expect to earn $20,000 a year – then most of these people *wouldn't* wish to leave. They're being *forced* to leave, because of circumstances which are beyond their control.

In the economic jargon, a person is said to be "Living in extreme poverty" if they have to survive on under $2.15 a day (at 2017 prices). As of 2022, just under 650 million people were suffering from this sort of poverty. (www.WorldBank.org)

I use the word "Suffering" quite deliberately.

Gandhi said that, "Poverty is the worst form of violence." Poverty leads to starvation: Over 850 million people were estimated to be undernourished, in 2009. And this can be deadly: Around 25,000 people die of hunger *every single day*. This number includes more than ten-thousand children. (Holmes, 2009).

Let's put that in context: Just over half-a-million people die each year as a result of armed violence. This means that for each person who dies in a warzone, around seventeen are killed by malnutrition. (Field & Bel, 2015)

And let's not forget that a lot of those people who die as a result of violence, also do so because of poverty – because poverty can lead to violence. (Anser et al, 2020). (Flemming, 2011). (Calnitsky & Gonalons-Pons, 2020).

People migrating out of poverty, are also likely to be escaping from crime-infested locales. They might be fleeing from diseases they cannot afford to cure. They might be escaping from working conditions that no-one would wish to endure. Or they might simply be searching for a better life: Over a billion people don't have electricity, over 600 million don't have access to clean water, and around half the population of the planet don't have adequate sanitation. It's little wonder that they wish to move. (Koulouris, 2019).

***

But do they?

You may have noticed an issue with the Gallop poll: It estimated that 900 million people would *like* to migrate. But most won't take the plunge.

Most people born in Mississippi don't move to New York State, even though they can, and even though wages are higher in the Big Apple.

People in Niger have the right to move to Nigeria, which is six-times richer. Romanians have the right to move to Sweden, where the average person is also six-times better off. But most Nigeriens and Romanians *don't* relocate. (Shah, 2020).

Most people don't possess that Wanderlust Gene. Some are change-averse. And many cannot afford to travel.

Do you really think that the average Sierra Leonian, surviving on $1.59 a day, is going to be able to save up enough money to pay for a journey to a distant country? What about their compatriots, who must survive on *less* than this amount?

The IMF has found a trend: The lower a country's per capita income, the more likely it is that a person living there will choose to leave. This stands to reason: The more poverty a person is forced to endure, the more likely they are to say "Enough is enough", and flee from that poverty.

But this trend goes into reverse, in countries which have a GDP-per-capita of less than $7,000. Below this threshold, the poorer a person's nation, the *less* likely they are to escape. They cannot *afford* to flee. They're trapped by their poverty. (Piazza et al, 2020).

***

Yet despite the difficulties and the reducing odds, a sizeable minority *do* leave the Third World. And the rewards are clear to see...

According to World Salaries, the average firefighter in Somalia is paid 1,765,300 shillings a year. That's just over $3,000. Meanwhile, the average American firefighter receives over $54,000. That's almost *eighteen times as much*! The average Somali bricklayer ($1,460 per year) could increase their salary by just *over* eighteen times – to $26,500 a year – simply by moving to the States.

The ratios are fairly constant for every other profession I tested: The average data entry clerk could expect to earn 17.43 times as much for the same work, simply by moving from Somalia to the USA. For the average accountant, the ratio stood at 17.67. For the average nanny, it was 17.13. And for the average farmer, it was 18.06. (WorldSalaries.com).

In the West, people get angry – and rightly so – when they hear that men get paid ten or twenty percent more than women. *But Americans get paid 1700% more than Somalis*! The difference is obscene.

It's little wonder that so many people wish to move. They can do the same work – utilizing the same skills, expending a similar amount of effort – and they'll be paid eighteen times as much! For most Somalis, that means escaping from the violence of poverty.

***

The numbers speak for themselves...

Back in Somalia, in 2021-22, only 1,595 people enjoyed an income of more than $30-a-day. That's less than 0.01% of the population. In the USA, 66,390 Somalians – over 63% of the total – received *more* than that amount. The contrast is stark. And yeah, there's going to be an element of selection bias: The Somalis who made it to the States, must've been richer to begin with. They could afford to pay for their flights. But this cannot explain the entire gap. Somalians were over *630-times* more likely to earn more than $30-a-day, after moving to the USA. (Bier, 2023).

***

It's not just Somalis who have so much to gain...

To earn enough money to buy a kilogram of flour, a construction

JOSS SHELDON | 147

worker in the USA would only have to render four minutes of labour. In Mexico, that same labourer would have to work for over an hour. And in India, they'd have to work for almost two hours. (Pritchett, 2006).

Nearly half of those Mexicans who've gone from earning less than $10-a-day, to earning more than that amount, have done so by crossing the American border. Four-fifths of those Haitians who've escaped from poverty, have done so by moving to the States. The lives of tens-of-thousands of infants are saved each year, because their parents left somewhere poor, and moved to a richer nation. (Clemens & Pritchett, 2008).

These people aren't driven by *greed*. They're driven by *need*. They have to move, to secure the incomes they need to buy things like food, water, clothing, accommodation and healthcare.

Without these things, they might suffer a premature death. In Somalia, a person's life expectancy is around seventeen years shy of the global average. But by emigrating, a Somalian can expect to enjoy the sort of full life that we all deserve to live.

OPENING OUR BORDERS WOULD ERADICATE POVERTY

Rutger Bregman opines that, "Borders are the single biggest cause of discrimination in all of world history." Borders lock in this crazy sort of geographical inequality – through which a person born in the USA, who goes on to earn the median wage, will be among the wealthiest 4% of people on the planet – not because their work is particularly special, but because they just happened to have been born in that place – all while a billion people, born in other regions, must survive on just 1% of global consumption. Even Americans who rely on food stamps, enjoy a lifestyle that marks them out as royalty when compared to people who were born in the world's poorest nations. (Bregman, 2017).

But if we were to open our borders, this wrong would be corrected.

John Kennan, an economist at the University of Wisconsin, has argued that open borders would enable wages to equalise across international boundaries – allowing a firefighter in Somalia to receive the same salary as a firefighter in the States. The price of labour would be almost the same in *any* place – in much the same way that the price of an iPhone is pretty much the same, no matter where it's sold. There are some differences – an iPhone might cost slightly more in one market, to cover the cost of delivery and local taxes. But those differences are small, because there's essentially only one market for iPhones – the global market – and it produces a single, global price. In the same way, if there was free movement for labour, then the differences in wages – the price of labour – would also be fairly small. There'd be a single market for each type of labour – the global market – and it'd produce a singular wage.

According to Kennan's analysis of forty poorer nations, the policy would lead to an average gain of $11,046 per worker (in 2012 prices). In some countries, the figure would be even higher: The average Brazilian would gain $12,296 per year, and the average Nigerian would gain $21,940.

This means that the policy wouldn't only make life better for those people who move, but also for the *countryfolk they leave behind*. It'd eradicate global poverty. And, rather ironically, it'd therefore reduce the need for further migration. (Kennan, 2012).

***

Even if we don't go the whole hog, we could still alleviate some poverty, by allowing *freer* movement, rather than full-on *free* movement.

The Global Trade Analysis Project wondered what would happen if developed countries were to welcome 3% more immigrants. It concluded that the biggest beneficiaries would be the immigrants themselves: Skilled workers would increase their incomes by $8,000-a-year, whilst unskilled workers would gain $6,500. But the nations they left behind, would also benefit from remittances they'd receive.

Even if these individuals only remained abroad for three to five years, they'd still send back enough money to increase the wealth of their homelands by about $320b-a-year (in 2023 prices). That's almost double the amount that developing nations receive in foreign aid! (Walmsley et al, 2005).

Think about that for a minute...

We send a load of money to poorer nations, because we acknowledge that poverty is an issue, and we'd like to do something to help. We participate in charity drives, make donations, and commit to standing orders. Our governments donate billions of dollars of taxpayers' money. But we could have double the effect, simply by opening our doors to a few more global citizens. And it wouldn't cost us a cent. We'd actually benefit – because those immigrants would help to improve our nations.

***

The differences between this and other policies can be stark...

In the late twentieth century, there was a craze for "Microcredit". This enabled aspiring entrepreneurs from poor backgrounds to borrow a small amount of start-up capital. They might have used it to purchase a mobile phone – renting it out to other villagers, each time they made a call. The income they received, might lift them out of poverty.

Microcredit was so lauded, that Mohammed Yunus – the man behind the Grameen Bank, in Bangladesh – was awarded the Nobel Peace Prize for his work.

But its effects are miniscule, when we compare it to migration.

A Bangladeshi would gain more by working in the States *for just eight weeks*, than they would by taking out a microfinance loan, setting up a business, and operating it for their entire lifetime in Dhaka or Chittagong. If three-thousand Bangladeshis were to move to the USA, they'd gain more than everyone who'd *ever* received a microfinance loan from the Grameen Bank! (Guest, 2011).

***

When it comes to policies to eradicate poverty, nothing else compares.

The reason a Haitian might suffer in poverty, isn't because they were *born* in Haiti. It's because they continue to *live* in Haiti. A low-skilled worker in Port-au-Prince might be paid around $1,000-a-year. Move to Miami, and they could expect to earn *twenty-five* times that amount. (Caplan, 2019).

Across the globe, the average Haitian lived off $2,234, in 2000. But the average person who was still living in Haiti, had to survive on just $1,619 – 27% less. The difference between the first figure (the "Income per natural") and the second figure (the "Income per resident") is the result of emigration. A small number of expats, pulled up the average Haitian income by a sizable amount. (Clemens & Pritchett, 2008).

But those expats didn't receive higher wages because they'd become harder workers, with more talent and skill. It's because they were able to put the same labour *to better use* in a more advanced economy. They worked for more efficient employers, with better funding, infrastructure and organisation. They served more affluent customers, who were willing to pay more for their services. And they had access to high-tech, labour-saving devices.

Migration meant their labour could be used more effectively – to create *more* wealth. A part of that extra wealth was paid to them, in the form of wages. A part benefitted their customers. And a portion went to their employers.

But borders reduce the extent to which this can happen. *They prevent wealth creation*.

There are billions of potential movers – each of whom would be a lot more productive if they were able to work in a more advanced economy. Open the borders, let them through, and they'd generate *hundreds-of-trillions* of dollars. (Caplan, 2019).

Most economists agree this would happen, although they disagree about the figures...

In 2005, Ana María Iregui calculated that open borders would increase global economic output by 67.0%. A year earlier, Jonathon Moses and Bjørn Letnes released their own research – putting that figure at 96.5%. Paul Klein and Gustavo Ventura were even more optimistic. In 2007, they calculated that open borders would increase global production by 122%. And the first estimate of its type – published by Bob Hamilton and John Whalley, way back in 1984 – put that figure at 147.3%! (Clemens, 2011).

Economists rarely agree on the minutiae. But this represents an overwhelming consensus. Only one economist, George Borjas, is a vocal critic of the theory – and his arguments are based on the idea that most people won't actually move, even if they can. It's a fair enough point, but we won't know unless we give it a go!

The prize would be substantial.

Even if we take the lower estimate of 67%, and apply it to the global GDP – which was $12,647 per person at the time of writing – then we're saying that we could all have an extra $8,473 each year.

I don't know about you, but that sort of pay rise would make a massive difference to me, my wife, and our pets!

It'd certainly make a massive difference to those people who are living in poverty. That's enough money to provide everyone on the planet with food, water, shelter, healthcare and clothing.

As Nelson Mandela once said: "Poverty is not an accident. Like slavery and apartheid, it's manmade and can be removed by the actions of human beings."

It can be removed by abolishing borders.

FLEEING WAR, VIOLENCE AND PERSECUTION

The image of two-year-old Alan Kurdi – in his red t-shirt and denim breeches – became iconic overnight. It was shared on social media, and printed on the front cover of the daily papers. Time Magazine called it "The Most Heartbreaking Photo of 2015".

It was almost impossible to look at Alan's body – limp and alone on a Turkish beach – and not feel an emotional response.

The tale behind that image is less well-known...

Alan had always been a bit of a sweetheart. Shopkeepers used to pop free sweets in the family's bags – gifts for the toddler, who they dubbed a "Little angel". And his family had been content with their lives – residing in a comfortable home, on a jasmine-scented street in Damascus. That was until Syria descended into chaos, and his parents were forced to flee.

At first, they moved to the Kurdish enclave of Kobani. But things only went from bad to worse: Whilst playing football, two of Alan's relations witnessed a suicide bombing. The street was showered with flesh, bone and blood. A little while later, *fifteen* of their relatives were slain, during the Ramadan attacks of 2015.

The family crossed into Turkey.

From there, their mission should've been straightforward: They had an aunt – Tima – who lived in Vancouver. The family wished to join her. But Tima had tried all the legal routes, she'd lobbied her MP, and she'd come up short. In an act of desperation, she sent her brother five-thousand Canadian dollars, so he could employ a people smuggler.

And so it came to pass that they set out on that fateful journey – crossing the Mediterranean in a dinghy.

The sea had seemed so calm, at first. Young Alan had even exclaimed: "We're going to have fun, Daddy".

Then the weather turned. Their vessel capsized and Alan drowned, alongside his mother and one of his brothers.

That image became symbolic. It seemed to represent *all* the children who'd died en route to a better life. And it caught a nerve: That body wasn't bloody or mangled, like the corpses you might find in a warzone. It was almost peaceful. It looked like any other child on Earth. It could've been *your* son, or nephew, or cousin.

Indeed, it *was* somebody's son. (Kurdi, 2018).

***

The whole story is such a mess.

The family quite clearly needed to move – to escape a conflict that had killed fifteen members of their family. They were willing to sacrifice everything, including a beautiful home. They'd paid thousands of dollars for one small leg of their journey.

Alan's father and surviving brother did reach Canada in the end. Their whole family could've made it together. Indeed, they *would've* completed their journey, in a world with open borders. There was no need for Alan to die.

***

According to World Vision, a hundred-million people have been *forced* to flee their homes. Four-in-five of them were fleeing from poverty – they came from areas that were characterised by malnutrition and acute shortages of food. But this figure also includes people who were escaping from adverse weather, violence and persecution. And it includes people like Alan Kurdi, who were fleeing from war.

Most such people remain *within* their country. Twenty-seven million refugees have crossed an international border. And approximately five-million asylum seekers are still applying for refugee status. (www.unhcr.org/refugee-statistics). (UNHCR, 2021).

***

At the time of writing, the upsurge in refugees was mainly due to the war in Ukraine. That had displaced eight-million people, and sent a further six-million into exile.

Almost seven-million people had fled from the Syrian civil war. Over four-million had escaped from the economic instability that was engulfing Venezuela. And almost three-million had left Afghanistan. (Reid, 2022).

These people are human beings, just like us. They have hopes and dreams. They have fears and insecurities. They bleed when they're shot. They cry when they see a loved one die.

They deserve to find a safe haven away from the falling bombs, and away from prejudiced regimes.

But I don't wish to dwell on the subject for too long. Refugees and asylum seekers already dominate the conversation. They only represent a tiny fraction of the total human population. And by focusing on their stories, which can be so horrific, we might lose sight of the fact that migration is usually a beautiful, positive, life-affirming thing.

I just want to raise a couple of points...

Firstly, it's interesting to note just *where* they go: Most refugees don't leave the country of their birth. Of those who do, 69% end up in neighbouring lands. Almost three-quarters of those countries are classed as low or middle income. (UNHCR.org/refugee-statistics).

Very few make it to Europe or North America.

According to the World Bank, Turkey hosted 3.7 million international refugees – more than any other nation on the planet. Jordan welcomed 3 million. 2.4 million were in the West Bank or Gaza, just over 1.5 million were in Uganda, and almost as many were in Pakistan.

The first wealthy nation to make the list – Germany – came in seventh place. The USA was down in a lowly eighteenth. That's below Cameroon – a country with 8.2% of America's population, and well under 1% of its economic output. The UK was twenty-ninth in the charts. It welcomes fewer refugees than Niger and Tanzania. (data.worldbank.org).

Wealthy nations aren't being "Flooded" or "Overwhelmed" by refugees – no matter what the likes of Trump would have you believe. That'd be places like Turkey.

***

The second point to note, is that there might be a silver lining. That's because when refugees leave a nation, they're "Voting with their feet". They're saying, "No, these circumstances aren't acceptable". They're withdrawing their labour, consumer spending, and taxes. And that, in turn, might apply political pressure to a country's elite. It might even cause regimes to fall.

We shouldn't go overboard. This is rare. But refugees can still play a role whilst they're *outside* their countries' borders.

A famous example of this comes from apartheid South Africa, where Nelson Mandela's political party – the African National Congress – was forced into exile. Its members became political refugees. But they maintained an army with around five-thousand members – in places such as Tanzania, Zambia and Angola. They operated schools, hospitals, farms and factories. They lobbied, campaigned, produced propaganda, and eventually won support from the international community. After many decades in exile, they achieved their goal – bringing apartheid to an end, and winning power in a democratic election. One of the exiles – Thabo Mbeki – even went on to become South Africa's *president*! (Bundy, 2018).

This kind of campaigning continues today.

I wrote my first two books while living in McLeod Ganj, in India. That village is home to the Dalai Lama, a large community of Tibetans, and "The Tibetan government in exile". Like the ANC, those refugees are also campaigning – doing whatever they can to reclaim Tibet's independence. You never know – their efforts might also achieve results.

***

Open borders, therefore, would improve life for refugees in a few different ways...

They'd allow *everyone* to flee from danger, no questions asked, wherever they happened to live. People would be able to flee from homophobic and transphobic regimes. Non-believers would be able to leave theocracies behind. Political refugees could escape from countries like North Korea. Entire communities would be able to wave "Goodbye" to war zones, famine-hit regions, and areas afflicted by natural disasters.

Open borders would also allow everyone to *return* to the places from which they'd fled. Six-million Palestinian refugees would be able to return to their homes. Arab Jews would be allowed to return to their nations.

And open borders would provide the impetus for regime change. They'd allow groups like the ANC, and leaders like Thabo Mbeki, to find a safe place from which to campaign – applying external pressure on despotic regimes, and helping to effectuate their demise.

THE CLIMATE REFUGEES

Migration is a historical constant. Everything has always been moving. But *peculiar* types of movement can give a portent of things to come...

In March 2009, all the toads went missing from the San Ruffino Lake. A few days later, a nearby town was destroyed by an earthquake. Those toads must have known it was on the way!

In 2004, elephants in Sri Lanka began to march inland. The humans who followed, did not regret their decision. It saved them from the tsunami which arrived soon after.

Dogs, birds, snakes, fish, bees and ants have also behaved in unusual ways, in advance of a natural disaster. (Maier, 2014).

These journeys were born of *necessity* – a need to flee from an imminent danger.

And other living beings have also been forced to move, albeit more slowly, in response to *climate change*...

Data from the United States Forest Service, taken between 1980 and 2015, shows that three-quarters of the tree species in the east of the USA were on the move – heading towards colder lands, at an average rate of one kilometre-per-year. Conifers were generally moving northwards, whilst oaks and birches were mainly moving westwards. The white spruce had been rampaging northwards at a rate of *ten* kilometres-a-year!

Trees are also moving *upwards* – ascending hills and mountains, in search of cooler air. Birch trees in Scandinavia have gained as much as five-hundred metres of altitude in just twenty years. Alder and willow now cover hills in Alaska which had been bare in the 1940s. (Bridle, 2022).

Scientists have conducted a series of studies – tracking insects, birds, animals, and fish. They've found that around *half* their subjects have relocated in recent times. Land-based animals were abandoning their traditional homes, as they became hotter – migrating towards the poles, at an average rate of 1.7 kilometres-per-year. (Chen et al, 2011).

Marine creatures were moving at an average of *seventy-five* kilometres-per-decade. (Poloczanska et al, 2013). (Parmesan, 2016).

And even some types of coral are on the move! Two species, native to the waters around Japan, have been moving northwards at a rate of 14 kilometres-per-year. (Yamano et al, 2011).

***

Humans have also been affected...

Let's consider the case of Khadijo – a farmer from Somalia – and her youngest daughter, Sabirin...

Things had been good for the pair:

"We were farmers and used to live a comfortable life in our house, because we planted maize, beans and other crops. And we used to have cows (for milk)."

That was before their town was hit by not one, but *three* consecutive droughts. Khadijo was helpless – forced to watch on, aghast, as her crops failed, her cows perished, and the water disappeared:

"We hoped for rain the next year, but it also became drought. It became three consecutive droughts. When it became three consecutive droughts, we boarded a car and left."

They went to Mogadishu – Somalia's capital. But getting there proved to be a challenge: The family had to travel for seven days, without a morsel of food to eat. Khadijo's children fell ill. Sabirin, who was just two-years-old, became severely malnourished, and had to receive emergency medical aid.

***

Khalid, an eighth-grader from Sudan, was forced to live in the open, after his entire village was flooded:

"We moved our belongings to the highway, where we lived for weeks. We could only access the village using a boat."

Around 140,000 Somali children missed out on a part of their schooling, as a result of those floods.

***

Sabirin and Khalid weren't alone: In the six years leading up to 2023, an average of twenty-thousand children were displaced *every single day* – because of storms, hurricanes, floods, droughts, earthquakes, wildfires or extreme temperatures.

Some children were displaced on multiple occasions. Most – like Khalid and Sabirin – returned to their homes. But many are still displaced. (Knaus & You, 2023).

And it's not just children who are affected: In the eleven years leading up to 2019, an average of over twenty-million people per year were displaced by climatic disasters. That's more than double the number of people who were forced to flee from wars and conflict.

In 2019 alone, thirteen-million people were displaced by storms, and another ten-million were displaced by floods. (UNHCR, 2021).

***

These tales offer a glimpse of things to come...

Throughout human history, the vast majority of people have resided in regions with similar climatic conditions – with a mean average temperature of between ten and fifteen Celsius. That's certainly been the case throughout the last six millennia – back through medieval times, antiquity, the mid-Holocene – and probably much longer than that. People do live in other places. The average temperature in my town is a smidgen over twenty-four Celsius! But that represents the exception, not the rule.

Temperature seems to be the most significant factor, which determines where humans live. We can acclimatise to places which have different levels of rainfall, and varying types of soil. But we tend to gravitate towards places with a milder climate. It's our "Environmental niche". Our crops, livestock, cultures and economies have evolved to function in these conditions.

With this in mind, we're going to be in for a mighty shock!

That band of territory where the average temperatures are between ten and fifteen Celsius, is set to shift by a greater distance in the next fifty years, than in the entire course of the last six-thousand years.

We can exist outside this niche, but only within certain limits.

As things stand, just 0.8% of the world's surface experiences an average temperature of more than twenty-nine Celsius. That zone is mainly in the Sahara – the sort of place where very few people choose to live. But if the projections prove to be correct, then *one third of the world's population* will be living in areas which experience this kind of heat by 2070.

The chances are that they'll need to relocate – to move to a place that enjoys a more hospitable climate.

Think about that for a minute...

There are around eight-billion people on our planet. If a third of them were forced to move, because their towns were as hot as the Sahara, then we'd see over 2.6 billion people on the march. That's before you factor in that many regions will be slightly cooler than the Sahara, but still incredibly hot. People in those places, might also wish to move. With this in mind, scientists have estimated that *3.5 billion* people could become climate refugees, within the next fifty years! (Xu et al, 2020)

***

But people won't only be fleeing from extreme temperatures...

As the ice caps melt, sea levels will rise, and low-laying homes will *flood*. As things stand, a tenth of the world's population lives within ten metres of sea level. Two-thirds of the world's largest cities – those with over five-million inhabitants – are positioned at this low altitude. And these are the sorts of places which are growing the fastest, as people move from rural to urban locales – a kind of internal migration that has been common in recent years.

They're not just located in one hub.

The list of countries which have the highest proportion of people living at under ten metres of altitude, includes: The Netherlands (Europe), Egypt (Africa), Vietnam and Bangladesh (Asia), and the Bahamas and Suriname (the Americas).

Around *half the world's population* lives in coastal areas, albeit at higher altitudes. (McGranahan et al, 2007).

An estimated 180 million people might be forced to move homes, as a result of rising seas, by the time that 2100 rolls around.

To that number, we need to add another 145 million people who are expected to leave their land because of *soil degradation*. This includes sixty-million people who might leave sub-Saharan Africa when the desert expands. (Nicholls et al, 2011). (United Nations Development Programme, 2022).

***

When we think of climate refugees, we tend to think of people in the Global South. And with good reason: Those people are being affected the most. But in reality, *no-one* will be safe.

Of all the coastal cities on Earth, New York and Miami top the charts when it comes to "Asset value at risk". In 2019, New York experienced power outages as a result of a heatwave. Its subways and streets are vulnerable to flooding. Parts of Miami have already been submerged.

According to BlackRock, most American properties west of the Mississippi are located in flood-prone locations. When the Missouri and Mississippi rivers burst their banks, the waters can destroy roads, bridges, homes and nuclear reactors.

America's breadbasket – states like Oklahoma, Dakota and Nebraska – might struggle to grow the food Americans require. They've already been affected by floods and droughts.

Boston is expected to suffer from thirty days of high-tide flooding, every single year. Logan Airport is expected to sink under the sea.

So this isn't a south-north issue. It's going to affect us all. *You* might become a climate refugee yourself. (Khanna, 2021).

MOST PEOPLE MOVE FOR
MULTIPLE REASONS

In this chapter, we've spoken about people who migrate out of *necessity* – to escape from poverty, violence, and natural disasters.

These things are often interconnected...

Climatic events, such as droughts and floods, can cause crops to fail. This leads to a shortage of food and water, which can lead to malnutrition – the telltale sign of *poverty*. This poverty might lead to an outbreak of *violence*, as individuals fight each other for food. It might even provoke a war.

Take Afghanistan as an example.

Climate change, overgrazing, and the excessive collection of firewood – have destroyed the plant-life, whose roots used to bind Afghanistan's earth. Now, when there are storms, the heavy rains cause rocks and earth to cascade down the hills. A deluge of muddy water sweeps over the land – turning villages to rubble, killing livestock, and destroying crops.

At other times, it doesn't rain enough. Droughts have affected almost every province in the land. (Mena et al, 2019).

The consequences are plain to see: By the beginning of 2019, an estimated 16.9 million Afghans – just under half the population – didn't have enough food. Over five-million were facing what the World Food Organisation called, "Critical levels of acute food insecurity". (World Food Program, 2021).

The latest figures, for 2021, show that the average Afghan must survive on just a dollar a day. Many get by with less.

This is fertile ground for violence: People with so little money, and such limited access to food, are bound to become desperate. They'll do whatever they must to survive. They'll even join an armed militia, if that group offers to feed and clothe them.

Afghanistan has been at war for years, and it's now fallen back into Taliban control. It's little wonder that so many people would like to leave. (UNHCR, 2021).

***

We see something similar in Syria...

The desertification of Syrian farmland, between 2006 and 2010, affected the entire economy: 85% of the livestock died. Food prices surged. Hundreds-of-thousands of people lost their jobs. And 1.5 million people were forced to abandon the countryside.

The villages they left behind became so impoverished, they were an easy target for Islamic State. Many villagers were recruited, and dispatched to fight in the war.

It's hard, therefore, to classify the almost seven-million people who've fled the nation. They're climate refugees, *and* economic refugees, *and* refugees of war – all rolled into one.

And this is the norm: Nineteen out of every twenty people who've been displaced by violent conflicts, come from regions which are vulnerable to climate change. The overlap is huge. (McAllister, 2023).

***

We can take several things from this discussion...

A lot of people *are* forced to migrate, due to circumstances beyond their control. This is hardly "Free" movement. But it is "Necessary".

If we were to open our borders, and grant these people the freedom they need to move, they'd be more likely to make it to safety. Open borders could save millions or even billions of lives.

But we don't have open borders. And most people *aren't* escaping.

Over 80% of those people who *do* move, aren't refugees. Most international citizens move because of *nature* or *nurture*, not because of *necessity*.

Although I can't help but think that these things might also be factors, even when it comes to those people who have been *forced* to move. People can be suffering from the effects of poverty, climate change and war – and still remain where they are.

What makes some people move, while others remain where they are?

Some individuals might not have the money required to migrate. Others might be turned away at the border.

But I expect the decision will also have a little to do with *nature*: Risk takers are more likely to take a gamble, leave their homes, and seek asylum – without knowing what challenges they might face along the way. Change-averse folk will stay in the places they've always lived, for as long as they possibly can.

And I think it might also have a bit to do with *nurture*: If you live in a society in which migration has become the norm, you'll probably be more willing to move. If you see hundreds-of-thousands of your countryfolk on the run, you might be inclined to join them.

You need three things to start a fire: Heat, fuel and oxygen. You can apply a spark to a flammable gas, but it won't ignite if there isn't any air.

In the same way, a person will require a little of each of these things – nature, nurture and necessity – before they decide to move abroad. Refugees are mainly motivated by necessity. Nomads are nurtured by their societies. Explorers are driven by their nature. But they're also influenced by these other factors – albeit to lesser degrees.

***

There's one last thing to note...

Those people who rail against the "Waves of immigrants flooding our shores", might sound a tad dramatic. The overwhelming majority of people still live in the country where they were born.

Even so, the naysayers might have a point. That's because of climate change – which could create 3.5 billion refugees.

It's hard to see how closed borders will stop their march. People who are fleeing for their lives, will find a way around any wall and across any sea. They'll break any law that stands in their way. If you want to stop these people, it'd be far better to combat the things which are forcing them to move – to focus on the *causes*, rather than the *symptoms*.

You don't want to face a "Deluge" of climate refugees?

Okay then! Invest in renewables, end fossil fuel subsidies, improve public transportation, plant more trees, have fewer children, eat less meat, insulate buildings, protect the oceans, and consume less plastic. Climate change will be reduced, and there'll be fewer refugees.

You don't want to provide a safe harbour for the victims of war?

Okey dokey! Stop waging wars.

If we didn't start wars in places like Libya and Iraq, there'd be far fewer refugees coming out of places like Libya and Iraq! If we abolished the arms industry, people wouldn't have to flee from the bombs we'd made.

And you have a problem with the so-called "Economic

migrants"?

Well, there's an answer to that as well: Abolish poverty! Wipe away third-world debt, pay reparations for the crimes of empire, abolish patents on medication, redistribute land and wealth, invest in health and education, and increase the social and physical infrastructure of the developing world. There'd be far less poverty, and far fewer migrants.

We could drastically reduce immigration, *without* closing our borders or impinging upon personal freedoms. But it'd require a whole lot of political will – reaching out to *help* our neighbours, rather than to *stop* them.

INTEGRATE? OR CONTRIBUTE?

"Britain has a German royal family, a Norman ruling elite, a Greek patron saint, a Roman/Middle Eastern religion, Indian food as its national cuisine, an Arabic/Indian numeral system, a Latin alphabet, and an identity predicated on a multi-ethnic, globe-spanning empire."
Akala

Bangu was a fairly nondescript place, back in the 1800s. Positioned a little to the west of Rio de Janeiro, it must have felt like a different world, when compared to that bustling metropolis. For most of the century, there'd only been a single road. Then a train track appeared, in 1890 – providing the catalyst for further development. Still, it was a hot, leafy old village – shadowed by the hills on either side, and cut into sections by a hotchpotch of meandering streams.

But the land was cheap. And that was a lure for investors.

Farms expanded. They began to grow cotton. And a mill soon appeared.

But a mill is of little use, without machinery or skilled labour. And so the mill's owners looked to Britain – importing machines, installers and instructors.

Among the first people to arrive, was a Scot named Tommy Donohoe. A burly lad, Tommy was one of seven children, all of whom had worked at their local dye works.

Donohoe seemed happy to move. But he wasn't so willing to change his ways. The lad knew what he liked, and he liked what he knew!

And so Tommy didn't look to the local community – participating in *their* leisure pursuits. He was steadfast in his conviction – to practice the one hobby that had come to define his life, even if it wasn't a part of the Brazilian culture.

When it became clear that he wasn't going to be able to find the equipment he needed, Tommy wrote to his wife, who was still in Scotland.

In August 1894, Eliza Donohoe sailed across the Atlantic, to meet up with her erstwhile spouse. She brought Tommy's boots. And she also brought the ball that Donohoe had requested. But it wasn't just any ball. It was a football. The *first ever football in Brazil.*

Tommy got down to business. He marked out a pitch, on a field beside his workplace. He improvised a pair of goals. And he rounded up as many expats as he could cajole. Together, they played a game of six-a-side – the first football match to be played on Brazilian soil.

News began to spread. And before too long, Tommy had inspired enough people – from different nations – to stage full games on a regular basis. (Campbell-Whittle, 2023).

***

It was another globetrotter who helped the game to flourish in the land of carnival and caipirinhas...

Charles Miller was born in Brazil. He was the son of a Scottish engineer, who'd been lured to São Paulo to help build the railways, alongside thirty-thousand other workers. But the Millers moved back to Britain, while Charles was still a child.

Encouraged by his headmaster, Charles developed into a serious talent – playing football for Saint Mary's Football Club (who were renamed "Southampton", and would go on to compete in the Premier League).

Miller returned to Brazil, aged twenty – also in 1894. But, unlike Donohoe, he came prepared – travelling with two leather footballs, and a copy of a rulebook.

He was a man on a mission.

Not content to play informal games, with other members of his community, Miller convinced the São Paulo Athletic Clube – a multisport establishment, founded by expats – to adopt the sport as its own. Within a year of Miller's arrival, he'd arranged what was thought to be the first *official* game in Brazil, between workers from *different* firms: The São Paulo Railway and the local gas company. And within six years, he'd launch Brazil's first ever football *league* – a five-team competition, called the "Liga Paulista de Foot-Ball".

Miller's team won the first three editions. (Keith, 2015).

***

One thing should be clear by now: These trendsetters didn't *assimilate* into the Brazilian culture. Donohoe didn't play "Peteca" – a badminton-like sport, which predates the arrival of the Portuguese. Miller didn't dedicate himself to "Capoeira" – that melange of martial arts and dance. They stuck to their ways – playing a foreign game, which had roots in an alien culture.

And just look at their impact...

A survey, conducted in 2020, found that 46% of Brazilians classed themselves as "Football fans". Another 32% said they "Followed" the sport. (López, 2021).

A second study found that 6.8% of Brazilian adults play the game themselves. It's more popular than any other sport in the land. (Guimarães Lima et al, 2019).

The Brazilians have created their own characteristic style – "Joga Bonito". They've invented their own variants of the sport: Beach Football and Futevôlei. Their men's national team is the most successful in the world – the only team to have won five men's FIFA World Cups. The country has exported talents such as Pele and Ronaldinho, who've won the affections of supporters across the globe. And their yellow shirts have become iconic – the symbol of a nation.

I doubt many people would remember Donohoe and Miller, if they'd merely *assimilated*. But these two men did something more remarkable: They *contributed*. They helped to create a *new* Brazilian culture.

***

So, should immigrants attempt to improve the prevailing culture, like Donohoe and Miller? Or should they respect their hosts' traditions?

It's a divisive subject.

There are certainly people who believe that immigrants should assimilate – differentiating between a kind of "Good Immigrant", who conforms to their host's culture – and those "Bad immigrants", who maintain their individual ways.

This sentiment was expressed by President Trump, in 2016:

"We also have to be honest about the fact that not everyone who seeks to join our country will be able to successfully assimilate... We've admitted 59 million immigrants to the United States, between 1965 and 2015. Many of these arrivals have greatly enriched our country. But we now have an obligation to them, and to their children, to control future immigration – as we have following previous immigration waves – to ensure assimilation, integration and upward mobility."

Trump was differentiating between those immigrants who'd already "Enriched" the country, and those new arrivals, who might not "Assimilate" – playing the old off against the new.

He was putting a positive spin on his agenda: He wasn't attacking *other* cultures. No way! He was defending the American way of life.

But earlier that year, Trump *had* gone on the offensive, while speaking to NBC.

"Belgium is no longer Belgium," he declared. "Belgium is a horror show right now. This all happened because, frankly, there's no assimilation. They are not assimilating for whatever reason. They don't want laws that we have, they want Sharia Law. And you say to yourself, at what point, how much of this do you take?" (Stump, 2016).

Whatever the angle, one thing was clear: For Trump, immigrants were only welcome if they changed their ways, conformed, and acted "American". They didn't have the right to be themselves.

Yet it would be wrong to single out Trump.

Tony Blair, who likes to portray himself as a far more moderate sort of chap, has also echoed this sentiment:

"There is a duty to integrate, to accept the rules, laws and norms of our society that all British people hold in common... Government cannot and should not be neutral on this question. It has to be a passionate advocate and, where necessary, an enforcer of the duty to integrate... Integration is not a choice. It's a necessity." (Savage, 2019).

***

This begs a question: What, exactly, would this "Integration" entail? What are these "Laws and norms... that all British people hold in common"?

To assimilate into a culture, one has to be able to *define* that culture. And this is easier said than done.

Culture and "Norms" can vary dramatically, across *class divides*. I may be British, but I have more in common with most Frenchmen, than with most members of the British aristocracy – with their fox-hunting, pretentious titles and stately homes.

Cultures can vary *within* a country: Many people from the north of England like to pour gravy over their chips. Many people from the south, think that they're insane!

Cultures can change over *time*: Very few people go wassailing or chimney-sweeping these days. Britain's pagan traditions have mostly been forgotten.

And cultures can be *contrary*: I'm writing this during King Charles's coronation. Monarchists are out on the streets, cheering him on. Republicans are also out on the streets, chanting "Not my king".

What's a poor immigrant to do? Both celebrate *and* oppose the monarchy? Cheer *and* boo the king? Who gets to decide which is the *correct* tradition? Surely, British monarchists and British republicans are both as British as each other.

The whole thing is a mess.

***

Fortunately, there's no need to go down this rabbit hole. We can do something better: Rather than demand that immigrants *integrate*, we can give them the opportunity to *contribute*. Rather than force them to *maintain* a country's culture, we can allow them to *improve* it.

Not everyone will agree with this idea. But it's not nearly as unpopular as Trump and Blair would have you believe.

A poll by the Sunday Times, found that 41% of Brits believed that immigrants, "Should leave behind their own cultural traditions and try to live like British people". But this means that almost six-in-ten Brits *did not* hold such a belief.

And a study by Ipsos MORI asked what Brits thought about "Multiculturalism". It found that 38% of the nation did believe it "Threatens the British way of life". But 30% disagreed, saying that "Multiculturalism makes Britain a better place". (Duffy & Frere-Smith, 2014).

IMMIGRANTS ENRICH THE SPORTING LANDSCAPE

Donohoe and Miller certainly made Brazil a "Better place". They improved the country's sporting culture. And I reckon most Brazilians are grateful for that.

But those men were far from alone.

Europeans had already introduced football to Argentina, *before* it arrived in Brazil. A Dutch schoolteacher introduced the game to Paraguay. A Chilean took it to Bolivia. Scottish players took "Soccer" to New Zealand. And an array of foreign sailors, soldiers, traders and missionaries – spread the sport across Africa. (Weil & Giulianotti, 2023).

***

Football is far from a singular case...

Basketball is the most-played sport in the USA. But it was invented by a Canadian! James Naismith was born in Almonte, Ontario. He didn't move to the States until he enrolled at the YMCA Training School, as a young adult.

It was while he was there, that Naismith saw a need to create a new indoor game, "That would be interesting, easy to learn, and easy to play in the winter" – when the fields were covered in snow.

Naismith was inspired by the sports he'd played in his youth – copying the jump ball used in English rugby, taking the passing technique from American rugby, and modelling his ball on the one used for soccer. He borrowed two peach baskets from the college's janitor, wrote the rules in the space of an hour, and taught the game to one of his classes. (Cooper, 2022).

Naismith's students – missionaries from the YMCA – loved it so much, that they began to spread the word. They took basketball to China and France, just two years after it'd been invented. From there, it spread to Portugal, Spain and Russia. Other travellers took the game to Latin America. American troops took it to the Philippines. (Anderson, 2023).

***

Volleyball has a similar history: That sport was also invented by a member of the YMCA, and spread by missionaries.

Volleyball evolved in the *Philippines*, where the process of setting and spiking the ball was introduced. It was revolutionised in *Hawaii* – the birthplace of beach volleyball. And it came under the international control of the Federation Internationale de Volleyball (FIVB), at a meeting which took place in *France*. (Olympics.com).

***

I've mentioned these sports because they're among the most popular in the world. But I reckon you'll find a similar story for any sport you research. The chances are, they'll have been spread by a mixture of travellers, immigrants, missionaries and sailors.

But the traffic is far from linear.

Participants migrate in every imaginable direction. Tennis players and golfers are almost nomadic – travelling the globe to entertain fans on every continent. Other professional athletes move to improve local *teams*. Four-in-eleven cricketers on any IPL team come from abroad, and two-in-three footballers in the English Premier League are foreign. These players and coaches deliver star quality. They improve standards – helping local players to improve. They bring new philosophies, playing styles, coaching techniques and diets. And they garner international interest – inspiring their compatriots to watch them on television.

To satisfy the demand, networks compete for the broadcasting rights – parting with massive amounts of money. And a lot of that money ends up in the pockets of *local* players: In 1982-83, when there were very few foreigners in the competition, the average NBA player was paid $246,000 a year. Skip forward to 2020, when 23% of players were foreign-born, and the average wage had skyrocketed to $7,700,000! Those foreign players had attracted foreign interest, which had generated foreign income – most of which was paid to *American* players! And this trend isn't limited to basketball. We see something similar in the MLB and the Premier League. (Anderson, 2020).

***

We should also consider the cases of those players who are naturalised, who immigrated *before* embarking on a career in sports, or who were born to immigrant parents – some of whom have represented their adopted country.

I expect my British readers are expecting me to say "Sir Mo Farah", right about now.

For those of you who don't know, Sir Mo was a long-distance runner. But his story begins many years before he shot to fame – when his father was killed, while taking care of the family's cattle. His mother was certain that Mo would also perish, if he remained in their village – in an area of Somaliland which was at the heart of a military conflict. And so she'd been willing to allow him to go to a safer place – Djibouti – while she took care of the family's home. Being separated from her child was heartbreaking. But she felt it was necessary, to protect her son.

When he was nine-years-old, Mo was trafficked by a woman, who said she was taking him to live with his relatives in London.

His real name was Hussein Kahin. But he was given the name of another child – Mohammad Farah – so he could use that child's papers to enter the country.

When they arrived in Britain, the trafficker destroyed the note which contained Mo's relatives' phone numbers, and forced him to work as a servant – showering her children, cooking their meals, and cleaning their room. Whenever Mo refused, his food was withheld. He was told, "If you ever want to see your family again, don't say anything (to anyone else)."

After a couple of years, Mo was allowed to attend school. But it was a struggle. He was unkempt, uncared for, unaccustomed to the culture, and unable to speak the language.

There was, however, a language that Mo *could* understand: Sport. He came alive during physical education. And, eventually, he opened up to his teacher, who helped him to find a home with a different family.

That was when things picked up.

Mo dedicated himself to athletics. He won race after race, in a style which appeared to be effortless. He collected the English Schools Championship, and was selected to represent his country at an international event.

But Mo couldn't travel, because he didn't have a passport. So his teachers campaigned on his behalf. They made two trips to the Home Office, wrote letters, and completed the necessary forms.

Farah was granted British citizenship, in 2000, even though a barrister would later tell him that it was technically "Obtained by fraud or misrepresentations", and that it could be rescinded at any time.

The rest is the stuff of legends.

Mo won the five-thousand *and* the ten-thousand metres at the London 2012 Olympics. Draped in a Union Jack, his face became the iconic image of the games – symbolising British success. Farah would go on to claim another two Olympic titles and six World Championship golds – making him the most successful male long-distance track runner of all time.

***

These days, Mo Farah certainly seems British. He's never far from a Union Jack. But it's impossible to say if he's fully "Assimilated". I have no idea what metric you're supposed to use, when measuring such a thing.

When he finally returned to the village of his birth, Farah welled-up, saying:

"It felt amazing: That's my mum. They are my real brothers... And I think, as a kid, that was just me, and that was my name, and that was my twin brother, and that was my mum, and this is the village. *This is where I'm from*... It is what it is. You are who you are."

Perhaps every immigrant feels this kind of attachment to the places they leave behind. Perhaps we all leave a little part of ourselves in the homes where we used to live.

Whatever the case, however much you judge Farah to have *assimilated*, one thing cannot be denied: He's *contributed*. He created a seminal moment, which brought joy into millions of households, up and down his adopted land. (Burley, 2022).

***

We find similar tales when we consider *team sports*...

France won their first ever FIFA World Cup, in 1998, when their squad contained nine players who were either immigrants or the children of immigrants. Its star, Zinedine Zidane, had two Algerian parents.

They would go on to win a second championship, in 2018. That time, their squad contained *seventeen* players who were either first or second-generation immigrants. Its shining light, Kylian Mbappé, is the son of a Cameroonian.

***

The French team stands out because of their success. But they're far from unique.

When we consider *all* the men's FIFA World Cups, we see that around one-in-ten players were born outside the country they represented. Around one-in-eight players were foreign-born at the third World Cup, in 1938, so it's hardly a recent phenomenon.

As of 2018, the United States had taken *forty-eight* foreign-born players to various World Cups – more than any other nation. Sixteen of Ireland's players at the 1994 World Cup, had been born in the UK. Morocco selected seventeen foreign-born players, for the 2018 edition. (Van Campenhout et al, 2018). (Oonk, 2022).

***

Let's surmise...

Some sports were invented by immigrants. Most sports spread because of migration. Players move between nations, to play in different leagues – attracting foreign investment, and thereby helping to increase the incomes of local players. And immigrants go on to represent their adopted nations – winning them trophies, Olympic medals, and international acclaim.

Immigrants *contribute*.

But they don't just contribute on the sports field. They contribute to pretty much *every* aspect of society...

IMMIGRANTS ENHANCE THE ARTS

The American lifestyle is famous around the world, thanks to the films it exports – most of which were made in Hollywood. But who do you think created Hollywood itself?

I'll give you some clues...

Metro-Goldwyn-Mayer, or "MGM", was formed after a merger between Goldwyn Pictures (which was founded by Samuel Goldwyn, a Jew born in Poland), and Louis B. Mayer Pictures (which was founded by a Russian-born Jew). Universal Pictures had several founders, including Carl Laemmle (a Jew born in Germany), David Horsley (an immigrant from England), and Charles Baumann (a Jew whose family had moved from Poland). One of Paramount's three founders, Adolph Zukor – "The father of feature-length films" – was a Jew who'd moved from Austria-Hungary. Another Austrian Jew, William Fox, founded the Fox Film Corporation, which merged to form Twentieth Century Fox. Warner Brothers was established by four Jewish brothers, who'd immigrated from Poland. Columbia Pictures was created by two Jews, whose parents had moved from Russia and Germany (along with a third Jew, whose parents were born in the States).

Are you beginning to see a theme?

These people came to America with almost nothing to their name – no money, very few qualifications, and only a limited amount of professional experience. Most of them would've failed the sorts of immigration tests which are coming into vogue today. But they arrived with something else – something that's impossible to measure. They came with a *dream*: To go from the "Outsiders" of Eastern Europe, to the "Insiders" at the heart of America.

They weren't alone: They made the journey alongside 2.5 million other Jews – four-fifths of whom had headed to the States.

But they weren't exactly met with the warmest of receptions.

They were excluded from the financial services industry, and most "Honourable" businesses. The best schools, such as Harvard, had a quota system which denied entry to most of their children. And they weren't allowed to live in the swankiest parts of town.

They could work for slave wages, and live in tenement slums. But they hadn't left their homes, and travelled halfway across the planet, to settle for such lousy conditions! If they'd been willing to be second-class citizens, they'd have stayed in Eastern Europe.

There was only one solution: They had to create a space for themselves within a *new* industry, which wasn't fully formed, and so wasn't such a closed shop.

But first, they had to accrue some capital.

Louis Mayer's father founded a scrap metal firm. But most of Hollywood's moguls started life as salespeople. Carl Laemmle was a bookkeeper-turned-promoter for the Continental Clothing Company. William Fox sold candy as a child, and clothing as a young adult.

And so when the first movies began to garner mass appeal, they saw an opportunity: This was something they could *sell*!

They established their own picture houses – mom-and-pop stores, the size of regular shops. And they sold, sold, sold – until every seat was taken, for every single screening. Then they upsized – opening regular theatres, and expanding to form chains – mainly in Boston, Chicago and New York.

It wasn't enough. They wanted to *make* the movies they were showing. But there was a problem: Thomas Edison had created a cartel – imposing a monopoly on cameras and film, charging a tax on their use, and forcing his competitors out of business. Those budding entrepreneurs couldn't get going, until Carl Laemmle challenged Edison's monopoly, under the Sherman Act, in 1912.

Three years later, Laemmle headed west – where there was less prejudice. It was there, in a valley north of Hollywood, that he established "Universal City" – a gargantuan place – the first ever "Movie-making city". It even had its own postal code, mayor, and police force.

That facility churned out hundreds of movies a year. But, more significant than the *quantity*, was the *content*.

Edison's films had tended to feature short skits, mired in class and racial prejudice. But Universal's output offered a vision of unity and hope – celebrating African American culture, glorifying the working class, and extolling middle-class values. Their films rarely mentioned Jews in any explicit sense. But they *Americanised* Jewish concerns about persecution and exclusion. They took their own stories, as Jewish immigrants on the run from Tsarist oppression – as outsiders who'd dreamt of a better life, persevered, and turned their dreams into a reality – and they rebranded it as the *American* story. Or, if you prefer, the *American Dream*.

"My Fair Lady" is a film about a working-class woman's effort to find a place in upper-class society. In "King Kong", the audience sympathises with the outsider – an oversized ape. In "The Jazz Singer", the immigrant father is rejected, for clinging onto the old world, while the son is celebrated for embracing American culture.

The typical Hollywood romance included two lovers from different classes, races, religions or nations – outsiders to each other, who allowed love to bridge the divide.

Hollywood created a fantasy America: The scenery in those early films was replete with picket fences, gleaming streets, and sparkling houses. The characters were wholesome citizens. There was an almost spiritual sense of family. The stories were imbued with optimism. They usually concluded with a happy ending.

When America joined World War Two, Hollywood was asked to produce propaganda movies to unite the nation. It obliged – depicting integrated army units, replete with white folk, black folk and Jews.

It was all a lie: America wasn't all pristine housing and picket fences – there were plenty of slums. The American army wasn't integrated during that war.

The world that Hollywood depicted wasn't a reality. It was portraying a dream. The *American Dream*: A dream invented by a group of immigrants, who'd moved from Eastern Europe.

***

Those foreigners didn't assimilate, at least not at first. They refused to accept the America they encountered. They weren't prepared to be second-class citizens, living in squalor, and working for poverty pay. They *challenged* Edison's monopoly.

But they did integrate a little, once they'd established a niche for themselves: They anglicised their names, hosted Easter egg hunts, celebrated Christmas, married non-Jews, and raised their children in a secular or Christian environment. When they were excluded from country clubs, they built their own versions in the American style. They wore tailor-made suits, and lived in the same kind of mansions which were owned by the American upper classes.

They were a genuine success story – people who'd left the old world without a penny to their name, and accrued riches which exceeded their wildest imagination. At one point, Louis Mayer – who celebrated his birthday on the fourth of July – received a higher salary than anyone else in the world.

But these immigrants didn't only integrate. They did something way more significant: They *contributed*. They had a massive influence on American society. They invented the "American Dream". They established the biggest, most iconic movie industry in the world. They invented the Oscars. And they produced movies which promoted America in cinemas across the globe. (Gabler, 1989). (Jacobovici & Samuels, 1998).

***

At the same time as the likes of Louis Mayer were establishing the film industry, other immigrants were becoming its stars...

Al Jolson, who was born in modern-day Lithuania, became the highest-paid entertainer in the nation. He was no saint – he had an overinflated ego, and he's been criticised for his use of blackface. But he left an indelible mark – transforming the American arts.

Jolson created a whole new style. His performances were more physical and emotional than anything that had hit Broadway before. He brought sound to the cinema – playing the lead in the original feature-length "Talky". And he inspired a generation of stars. (Gioia, 1998). (Hirschman, 2013).

Another pair of Jews had a similar effect on the American *music* scene...

Benny Goodman (whose parents had moved from Kaunas and Warsaw) and Artie Shaw (the son of an Austrian and a Russian), both integrated their bands, in a time of segregation – showing that black and white folk could produce beautiful things together. Shaw hired Billie Holiday. And he was original – combining European classical music with American Jazz, to create a whole new genre fusion. (Firestone, 1994). (Shaw, 1992).

The godfather of American *ballet* – George Balanchine – was born in Russia. He moved to the USA after being inspired by images of Ginger Rogers and Fred Astaire. Balanchine established the New York City Ballet – showcasing a new art form, which combined European classical dance with the razzmatazz of the new world. He opened a ballet school – investing in the youth of his adopted land. And he choreographed eighteen Broadway hits. (Horowitz, 2009).

Second-generation Russian immigrants also contributed to the theatre stage: Michael Kidd ("Guys and Dolls"), Jerome Robbins ("West Side Story"), and Helen Tamiris ("Touch and Go") – won a third of all the Tony Awards for choreography, between 1947 and 1973. (Hirschman, 2013).

And the majority of American *directors* who've won two or more Academy Awards, were either immigrants or the children of immigrants. We're talking of people like Frank Capra ("It's a Wonderful Life"), who was born in Italy – William Wyler ("Ben Hur"), who was born in Germany – and Billy Wilder ("Some Like It Hot"), who was born in Austria. (Hirschman, 2005).

***

Back across the Atlantic, another group of immigrants were influencing *British* culture...

The "Windrush Generation" got their name from the "Empire Windrush" – the boat which brought the first batch of arrivals across from the Caribbean. Between 1948 and 1971, 123,000 people followed in their wake. (Shaw-Roberts, 2022).

The Windrush Generation were enticed to Britain by the promise of good jobs and a better life for their families. But, just like the Jews who'd arrived in America, they were in for a rude awakening.

Despite their talents and qualifications, those people were often put to work in the worst available jobs. Several landlords refused to rent their properties to black people.

But this prejudice came with a silver lining: Those people had little choice but to cluster together in the few parts of town where they *were* welcome. They formed new communities – places which were characterised by the smells of rum, drum chicken and marijuana – by the colourful fashions of the West Indies – and by the musical genres which those immigrants imported: Reggae, ska, blues, calypso, gospel and jazz. (Hebidge, 1997).

Sound systems – walls of speakers, pumping out loud bassy music, sometimes accompanied by an MC – became an emblematic feature of these communities. They reminded the immigrants of the islands they'd left behind. And they inspired a kind of nostalgia, which helped the new arrivals to cope with the struggles of daily life. (Ward, 2017).

***

The Windrush Generation also inspired the *white youth* of the late 1970s, especially the Mods, who were roused by the resilience of underground reggae – a genre which persisted in a carefree culture, even though it was snubbed by the mainstream media. The young, white working class of that time felt that they were also being marginalised and overlooked. They felt that they had a lot in common with their Caribbean peers.

Thus, 2Tone music was born...

It began in Coventry – an industrial town in the East Midlands, which was famous for manufacturing cars. People came from around the world, to work in Coventry's factories. They brought reggae to the area, formed bands with the locals, and created a mashup sound – a sort of reggae punk, with moments of up-tempo ska, and an angsty lyrical style that could've only been made in Britain.

2Tone bands tended to feature both black *and* white members – hence the name. Even the artwork, featured on album covers by bands like The Specials and The Beat, was produced in those two simple shades.

It was political: They were saying that black and white people – Brits *and* immigrants – could get along just fine. They even wrote songs with political messages: Tunes like "Stand Down Margaret" and "Free Nelson Mandela". (Finch, 2020).

***

Sound systems would also inspire another British culture in the early 1990s: Rave culture...

Those stacks of sonic-boom-inducing speakers, were taken from the streets and placed in fields and forests – where they blasted out music, all the way through the night. (Henriques, 2011).

Some of the genres of music, which were played at those raves, were invented by the children of the Windrush generation. Those second-generation immigrants would go on to invent jungle, drum and bass, garage, dubstep and grime. (Finch, 2020).

It's almost exhausting! Just over a hundred-thousand people arrived in Britain as part of the Windrush project. Between them and their children, they introduced variants of at least six different types of music. They helped to create at least another five genres, while living on British soil. And they established the Notting Hill Carnival – Europe's largest street party.

Those immigrants didn't just assimilate into the British music scene. They revolutionised British music – contributing way more than anyone could've ever predicted. They acted as ambassadors for their adopted nation, whenever they toured the globe. And they endeared Britain to music lovers in hundreds of other nations.

***

Immigrants from the Caribbean weren't the only people to bring new musical styles to the UK. The families who arrived from South Asia, introduced genres like bhangra. And their children created a brand-new British sound of their own – The Asian Underground – which was made famous by bands such as Cornershop and Asian Dub Foundation.

It wasn't all one-way traffic...

The Beatles were so inspired by their trip to India, that George Harrison began to write songs in the Indian style. John Lennon picked up a sitar, and used it while performing "Norwegian Wood".

Fela Kuti invented afrobeat, after embracing jazz while studying in London. When he returned to Nigeria, he fused English jazz with African beats and chants – creating a whole new Nigerian genre.

When musicians travel, they're exposed to new cultures, sounds and styles. They take inspiration from the music they encounter, experiment with it, and invent *new* genres – creating music that brings joy to the world.

Opening our borders, allowing *every* musician to find inspiration in *any* location, would give birth to an unlimited number of new styles. Who knows what sort of mashups we might produce? A genre born out of Seattle grunge and Inuit throat singing? French chanson spliced with klezmer?

We'll never know, unless we open our borders and give it a go.

IMMIGRANTS CREATE NATIONAL DISHES

If there's one thing that defines a national culture – perhaps even more than its sports, music and arts – that thing is probably *food*.

Food is ubiquitous – we see it wherever we go. It's essential – we all have to eat. And it's central to a region's identity: If you see some hummus and falafel, you'll probably think of the Middle East. If you hear the word "Tapas", the chances are your mind will be drawn to Spain. If someone says, "Let's throw some shrimps on the barbie", you might guess they were Australian, even if their accent hadn't already given the game away.

The same can be said of so many famous dishes:

If I said "Fajitas", what country would come to mind?

What if I said "Bratwurst"?

"Chow Mein"?

"Jerk chicken"?

"Tom Yum"?

"Sushi"?

Am I making you hungry?

And would it surprise you if I told you that many so-called

"National dishes" actually had *international* roots? That they were taken around the world by immigrants who refused to assimilate?

***

Let's begin by considering one of the most quintessentially British meals of them all: Fish and chips.

Over ten-thousand "Chippies" specialise in this traditional fare – deep-frying fish fillets in batter – serving them up on top of a bed of chunky fries. We Brits buy 360 million portions of the oily treat, from fish and chip shops, every single year.

But is it actually British?

Well, err, not really!

The tale begins sometime after 1497...

When the Portuguese king married a Spanish princess, he buckled to her father's demands: The Spanish were pursuing their "Inquisition" – forcing Jews to emigrate or convert. The Spanish king refused to give his daughter's hand in marriage, until the Portuguese promised to do the same.

Some Jews did convert to Catholicism – either of their own free will, or as a result of physical coercion. But they were still persecuted by the state.

A great number were forced to flee. Some of them moved to Britain.

It's hard to know if they "Assimilated" – eating the sorts of foods that were popular at the time: "Pottage" and "Frumenty" (soupy stews containing meat, vegetables, cereals or bran), "Garbage" (a stew made from chickens' heads, feet and gizzards), and "'Umble Pie" (stuffed with deer entrails). It's unlikely that they ate the types of meat which the aristocracy was known to consume: Roasted swans, peacocks, beavers and hedgehogs. They probably didn't eat any cats – following the old British tradition: Burying the cat's headless body in the ground, digging it up, roasting it, and serving it in a garlicky broth. But they might have tried sheep's penis, following another traditional recipe: Stuffing it with egg yolk, saffron and fat – blanching it, roasting it, and polishing it off with a cinnamon glaze. (Martisiute, 2018).

We do know one thing for sure: These immigrants ate an alien dish, the likes of which had never been seen in a British kitchen: Fried, battered fish.

They had a good reason to indulge.

Jewish people aren't allowed to do housework during the Sabbath. So some Jews in Southern Europe had struck upon a nifty custom: Just before the holy day began, they filleted some white fish – usually cod or haddock – dipped it in flour or matzo meal, and fried it in oil. The batter helped to preserve the fish – ensuring it retained some of its flavour and moisture, when it was eaten the following day.

Those immigrants didn't hide their foreign dish away. They weren't ashamed of their differences. They were so proud of their outsider-food, that they took to the streets of London's East End – displaying it on trays, and selling portions to anyone who was willing to give it a try.

Fried, battered fish came to be synonymous with Jews.

The American president, Thomas Jefferson, wrote about his dalliance with "Fried fish in the Jewish fashion", after completing a visit to Britain. A British cookbook, from 1781, refers to "The Jews" way of serving fish.

It just needed a side dish.

So, what of the trusty old chip? Was that a British invention?

Well, err, not really.

Chips are made from potatoes. And potatoes come from the Andes, in South America. They're hardly an indigenous ingredient! They weren't even brought to Europe until the sixteenth century. The first European account we have of the staple, comes from the memoir of Pedro Cieza de Leon – a teenage conquistador – who wrote of "A kind of earth nut which, after it's boiled, is as tender as cooked chestnuts".

Potatoes were popular from the get-go. But they were tiny – not much bigger than a cherry. It took time for them to evolve, and become the size we're familiar with today – big enough to peel and chop into batons. (Ovchinnikova, 2011).

No-one really knows where the humble chip was first invented.

Potatoes may have been fried soon after they arrived in Spain.

The first *pomme frites* were cooked in lard or butter, and sold by street vendors on Paris's Pont Neuf, in 1789. But the consensus seems to suggest that chips were created in Belgium: Villagers living on the banks of the River Meuse, were accustomed to eating fried fish for most of the year. When the river froze, they had to make do with potatoes. And so they cut them into fish-shaped pieces, and fried them in oil – pretending they were fish.

The Americans call chips "French fries", because the recipe was brought back across the Atlantic by Thomas Jefferson, who'd encountered them on a visit to France. Perhaps they were brought to Britain by another traveller. Or perhaps they were brought by an immigrant. We may never know. (Rupp, 2015).

What we do know, is that the two dishes were eventually paired, and the first chippies appeared soon after. But this didn't happen until 1860 – around forty-thousand years after the first people stepped foot on British soil. And the first fish and chip shop wasn't opened by some kind of "Indigenous" Brit. It was opened by another Jewish immigrant – a man named Joseph Malin. (Rayner, 2003).

***

Fish and chips are made from a universal ingredient (fish), a South American ingredient (the potato), a Belgian invention (the chip), and a recipe for fish which was imported by Portuguese refugees. The first chippy was probably opened by a Jew from Eastern Europe. And yet we're supposed to believe that it's as British as roasted cat, frumenty, and sheep's penis!

It *is* British in the sense that it evolved in Britain. It came to define British culture. And it certainly has mass appeal: According to a survey by Statista, fish and chips was the joint most popular meal in Britain. (Wunsch, 2022)

Brits embraced the combo, in much the same way that Brazilians embraced football. They said to those Jews who refused to assimilate: "Actually, you might be onto something". And they absorbed that foreign dish into *their own culture*.

***

What about the other dishes that define British culture?

The one dish that Brits enjoyed just as much as fish and chips, according to that Statista poll, was roasted chicken.

Once again, we'll have to concede that the chicken isn't native to Britain. It evolved from wild jungle fowl in Southeast Asia. Chickens spread across the world as a result of conquest, trade and migration – only arriving in Britain around three-thousand years ago.

But Brits didn't eat their chickens back then.

This is what Julius Caesar had to say on the subject:

"The Britons consider it contrary to divine law to eat the hare, the chicken, or the goose. They raise these, however, for their own amusement and pleasure."

The original British tradition, was to *worship* the chicken. It took the arrival of a group of foreigners – the Romans – for chicken to make its way to the dinner table. And it was probably the *French* who first roasted the bird, sometime in the Middle Ages. (Fox, 2020).

***

Let's just consider one more British delicacy.

According to the Encyclopaedia Britannica, it's *chicken tikka masala* that's "Widely considered the country's national dish". The curry is made from "Marinated boneless chicken pieces, that are traditionally cooked in a tandoor, and served in a subtly spiced tomato-cream sauce."

There's a folkloric tale behind the meal...

According to legend, a diner at an Indian restaurant once complained that his chicken was too dry. The chef, Ali Aslam, took the plate back to his kitchen and added some creamed tomato soup, which he'd been using to treat a stomach ulcer. The customer was so happy with the resulting concoction, he returned with some friends, and encouraged *them* to give it a try. The rest, as they say, is history.

This story may or may not be true. Some claim that the dish was imported by people who'd moved from Punjab. Others say it was Bangladeshi or Pakistani chefs who developed the dish – adjusting the recipe for shahi chicken masala, which they'd found in a cookbook by Balbir Singh.

Whatever the case, one thing is clear: Curries came from the

Indian subcontinent. They were brought to the UK by travellers. They evolved to suit British tastes. And they became part of the British culture.

Curries were being served in London cafes, as far back as 1733. But they didn't become ubiquitous until after the Second World War, when immigrants began to buy up cafes which had been bombed in the Blitz – using them to sell curries alongside fish, pies and chips. Those establishments stayed open into the early hours – enticing punters as they poured out of the pubs. The midnight curry became a British tradition. Those restaurants stopped selling pies, and dedicated themselves to South Asian cuisine.

These days, there are apparently more "Indian" restaurants in Greater London than in Mumbai. Around two-thirds are run by Bangladeshi immigrants. Together, they contribute more than £5b to the British economy – employing more people than the British shipping industry. And they've become a part of British culture – serving traditional British dishes, such as chicken tikka masala. (Mukherjee, 2017).

***

Britain's three most iconic dishes, all have foreign roots.

But what about Britain's national *drink*?

Tea was first brought to Britain from China, by Dutch traders, in the early 1600s. It was a novelty, and didn't come to define British society until Catherine of Braganza arrived from Portugal, to marry King Charles the Second – travelling with a chest of tea among her possessions. Catherine would go on to popularise the drink among members of the upper classes.

When India began to mass produce tea, in the 1800s, prices began to fall – meaning that regular folk could afford to drink the beverage. At some unknown point, people began to add milk. The tea bag was invented in 1908.

The British had taken the drink and made it their own – but only after they'd received a dollop of help from the Chinese, Indians, Dutch and Portuguese. (Kowaleski-Wallace, 1994).

***

That's just Britain. But I expect you'll find a similar story wherever you look.

Take the USA, for example...

Something might be as "American as apple pie", but that's not particularly American. Pies were invented in England. And a great deal of the apples in America, descend from the trees which were planted by Puritan settlers, soon after they'd moved from Europe.

The hamburger was brought to America by people from *Hamburg*. The name gives the game away. Although burgers weren't a German invention. They were created by the Tartars, in the time of Genghis Khan.

Hot dogs, also known as frankfurters, came from... Can you guess where?... Yeah, they came from Frankfurt. The American version was created by combining several recipes, which had been brought to America by different travellers, from various parts of Europe.

The tradition of frying chicken, has roots which can be traced back to Scotland and West Africa. French fries, as we have mentioned, either came from France or Belgium. They were brought to the States by Thomas Jefferson's chef, who also introduced macaroni and cheese (an Italian dish). Pizza was brought to the States by Italian immigrants, sometime in the 1800s. Polish Jews introduced the beigel to New York. And doughnuts were brought to Manhattan by the Dutch. (Hodge, 2020).

***

Take any national dish, look up its origins, and I reckon you'll find a foreign influence. Here in the Philippines, the national dish – adobo – is heavy on soy sauce. But that condiment was introduced by the *Chinese*. The name, "Adobo", is a *Spanish* word. It means "Marinade".

I've laboured the point quite hard, but with good reason: Food is central to a nation's identity. It defines the rhythm of our lives.

It also happens to be pretty darned international!

Most "National" dishes have *international* roots. They were introduced by immigrants who refused to assimilate, but who chose to contribute instead.

<u>IMMIGRANTS IMPROVE OUR LANGUAGE</u>

An immigrant might eat national dishes, play popular sports, and listen to local bands. And yet that probably won't be enough for those people who champion "Assimilation". They also like to demand that their foreign guests speak a country's *language*.

It's a theme you hear over and over again.

Take this quote, from Barack Obama:

"If you're going to be here, then you should learn the language... Because we need to have some sort of common language in which all of us can work, and learn, and understand each other."

He almost has a point: Communication leads to understanding, which leads to social cohesion. That's a fabulous thing.

But it does seem a little coercive, to demand that we all speak in a certain way. If an individual has an incentive to learn a language – if it's going to enable them to get a job, study on a course, or set up a business – and if they have the means and the ability to learn it – then the chances are that they'll pick it up of their own accord. They won't need to be cajoled by one of the most powerful men on the planet – someone who used to control the biggest army in human history.

Other politicians have gone even further.

This is a quote from Donald Trump:

"I think that when you get right down to it, we're a nation that speaks English. I think that, while we're in this nation, we should (all) be speaking English... Whether people like it or not, that's how we assimilate."

***

This view is problematic from the start...

What if someone is nomadic – they wish to stay in a country for six months, and then go to live elsewhere? Should we expect them to learn a language each time they move, even if it means studying ten or twenty different languages? They'd never have the time to do anything else!

What if someone is reclusive? If they wish to live in a forest? They wouldn't ever speak to anyone else. So why would they need to learn the local language?

How much of a language should we ask people to speak, before we're willing to accept them? How long do we give them to learn? Are they supposed to pay for their own materials, even if they're struggling to find money for food? Or should the taxpayer foot the bill? Are these new arrivals allowed to choose the dialect they use? Or does that have to be mandated by a Trump-like figure? If we witness a person speaking a second language, are we supposed to confront them and ask them to stop? Are we supposed to snoop on our neighbours, and snitch on them if they say "Gracias" rather than "Thank-you"?

The "Learn the language" trope seems even more ridiculous when you consider that English isn't even American. It was brought to the USA by *immigrants*. Languages such as Navajo, Cherokee and Ojibwe – have a much longer history in that land. French was spoken across a vast swathe of the USA, before the Louisiana Purchase. Spanish remained common in Texas, even after it joined the union.

English isn't even the only language in the United Kingdom. Plenty of people speak Welsh. And different words are used in different regions. The Scots say "Ken" instead of "Know", "Bairn" instead of "Baby", and "Aye" instead of "Yes".

It feels strange to hear Brits demand that other people speak English, when only one-in-three Brits speak a second language themselves. Plenty of Brits who move abroad, struggle to pick up the local dialect. Some don't integrate at all. There are expats in Spain who only eat at British restaurants and drink in British pubs – barely speaking a word of Spanish. Learning a language is hard. People might try, but they need time. And even then, they might ultimately fail.

***

There can be beauty in that failure...

Sometimes, when a person cannot find the right word in a foreign language, they borrow one from their mother tongue. They *contribute* a new word, and make the language better for everyone else.

Examples of foreign words which have been absorbed into the

English language include: banana (Wolof), lemon (Arabic), ketchup (Chinese), karaoke (Japanese), ballet (French), wanderlust (German), paparazzi (Italian), penguin (Welsh), victim (Latin), and guru (Sanskrit). (Mark, 2020).

Trump might rally against those Mexicans who speak Spanish while living in the States. But Trump speaks Spanish every time he refers to the states of "Montana" (the Spanish word for "Mountain"), "Nevada" (the Spanish word for "Snowfall"), and "Florida" (the Spanish word for "Flowery"). Plenty of American towns have Spanish names – such as San Francisco, Los Angeles and El Paso. Americans regularly use words with Spanish roots: Words like "Macho", "Cargo" and "Mojito". And they use words which have been adapted from the Mexican language of Nahuatl: Words like "Avocado" (from the Nahuatl word "Ahuacatl"), and "Chocolate" (from the Nahuatl word "Xocolatl"). (Jordan, 2021).

Shakespeare is considered to be quintessentially English. But he used blank verse in his plays – a style of writing which was introduced into Britain when Henry Howard translated the Æneid – an epic poem which was written by a *Roman* poet. Shakespeare was also famous for his sonnets. And yet sonnets were invented by Giacomo da Lentini, and popularised by Francesco Petrarca – both of whom were *Italian*. (Winder, 2010).

In fact, pretty much *all* the words in the English dictionary arrived in England from abroad. The language has been influenced by the Vikings, Anglo-Saxons, Romans and Normans. Around two-thirds of its vocabulary can trace its roots back to Latin or Greek. Over a quarter is Germanic. We use the Latin alphabet whenever we write, and Hindu-Arabic numerals whenever we perform a calculation. (Ullman, 1922).

***

What was once considered the local language, is barely recognisable today...

This is a line from Ælfric's "Homily on Saint Gregory the Great", written a little over a thousand years ago:

"Eft he axode, hu ðære ðeode nama wære þe hi of comon."

Can you make sense of that?

The word "He" hasn't changed. Perhaps you guessed that "Nama" means "Name", and that "Comon" means "Came". But could you decipher the overall meaning – "Again, he asked what might be the name of the people from which they came"?

Some words, such as "Axode" – "Asked" – have evolved. Others, such as "Eft" – "Again" – have disappeared from the lexicon. The word order is inverted: It says "From which they came", not "Where they came from". Ælfric's text includes gendered nouns and adjectives. He uses two imperative and four subjunctive forms – none of which exist today. And he used Old English letters, such as "Thorn", "Eth" and "Ash" – "þ", "ð" and "æ" – which have fallen out of use. (Merriam-Webster.com/help/FAQ-History).

***

Languages evolve...

Words are added, letters are abandoned, and the grammar is simplified.

What's more, it's usually *immigrants* who improve our vernacular. They offer an outsider's perspective – picking up on the anomalies that others can miss. It happened in the past, when the Romans and the Normans arrived in Britain. And it's happening in the world today.

A young generation of Arabic and Turkish Germans are creating a new variant of the German language. They're not saying, "Morgen gehe ich ins Kino" – "Tomorrow go I to the movies". They're saying, "Morgen ich geh Kino" – "Tomorrow I go movies". It's a little shorter, which is convenient. And it corrects a clunky quirk of the language – replacing the rather jerky, "Tomorrow go I", with the smoother, "Tomorrow I go".

This variant, known as "Kiezdeutsch", is being spoken among *all* the children of immigrants – regardless of whether their parents arrived from Kurdistan, Somalia, or anywhere else.

Other German residents have begun to communicate in English – an international language, spoken by peoples from different places. Some have even created their own variant – "Denglisch" – using *English* words and phrases, while speaking in *Deutsch*.

Similar linguistic adaptations are popping up in Sweden,

Denmark, Norway, and the Netherlands. In Senegal, people who've learnt Wolof after moving to the cities, have created a simplified version – using a single gender, rather than the eight (or more) genders which are usually found in that language. And in the Congo, the children of migrant workers have created a simplified version of Swahili – "Shaba Swahili" – which is spoken by *millions* of people. (McWhorter, 2015).

You never know, perhaps one day Kiezdeutsch will be spoken by millions of people in Germany. Perhaps it'll supplant contemporary German, just as modern English replaced the version which was spoken by Ælfric.

That'd simplify the language, making it easier for new arrivals to learn. And that, after all, is what the likes of Obama and Trump seem to want.

IMMIGRANTS CONTRIBUTE IN COUNTLESS OTHER WAYS

Immigrants don't only help to enhance our sports, arts, cuisine and language. They improve almost every aspect of society.

They're a boon for *science*: Albert Einstein, one of the most famous physicists in history, was a refugee who'd escaped from the Nazis. Enrico Fermo created the world's first nuclear reactor, after moving to the USA. Andrew Grove invented the processors found in most personal computers, after fleeing from Budapest.

Our foreign-born peers save lives, thanks to their *medical research*: David Ho – whose work has helped millions of people to survive with HIV – moved to the USA from Taiwan. Mani Menon made a similar journey from India, before pioneering robotic surgery for cancer. Julio Palmaz developed intravascular stents – used to open blocked or narrowed arteries – after leaving Argentina behind. Elias Zerhouni improved MRI technology, after emigrating from Algeria.

International scientists have also contributed to *aviation*: The high-wing monoplane was invented by an Italian American – Giuseppe Bellanca. The U-2 Superwing was invented by a Scottish American – Don Mitchell.

When you put all these things together, the numbers tell a story: Between 1990 and 2004, *over a third* of all the American scientists who won Nobel Prizes, were born *outside* the USA. These people overachieve! (Wulf, 2006). (Skorton, 2018).

***

Globetrotters get involved in *politics*...

Who could forget Arnold Schwarzenegger's time as governor of California? Or Madeleine Albright – America's first female Secretary of State? Well, Schwarzenegger immigrated from Austria, whilst Albright moved from Czechoslovakia.

King George the First was a member of the *House of Hannover*. Every monarch who's sat on the throne since he passed away, in 1727, descends from that immigrant king. The current monarch, King Charles, is the son of a Greek refugee – Prince Philip – a man who was smuggled out of his country as a child, hidden inside a crate which was supposed to hold oranges!

Guyana, Ireland, Portugal and Britain have all had heads of state who are of Indian descent. And two British prime ministers were born overseas: Boris Johnson in New York, and Bonar Law in Canada.

***

People born abroad also advance *fashion*...

Oscar de la Renta, who moved to the States from the Dominican Republic, has dressed everyone from Jackie Kennedy to Taylor Swift. Levi Strauss, the man behind blue denim jeans, was a German immigrant. And Diane von Fürstenberg, who invented the "Wrap Dress", was born in Brussels. (Gouveia, 2020).

***

Immigrants contribute to *literature*...

Joseph Pulitzer, the man behind the Pulitzer Prize, moved to America from Hungary. Khaled Hosseini ("The Kite Runner") arrived there after emigrating from Afghanistan. Chimamanda Ngozi Adichie ("Half of a Yellow Sun") travelled from Nigeria.

Britain has welcomed Kazuo Ishiguro ("Remains of The Day"), who moved from Japan – Joseph Conrad ("Heart of Darkness"), who moved from Ukraine – Harold Pinter ("The Birthday Party"), who was of Eastern European descent – and Salman Rushdie ("Midnight's Children"), who was born in India. Doris Lessing moved to the UK from Iran, V. S. Naipaul migrated from Trinidad and Tobago, and T. S. Eliot came from the States.

Even some of our beloved *characters* came from abroad: Sir Lancelot is French, and Hamlet is Danish.

One of Britain's most famous historians – Simon Schama – was born to parents who'd immigrated from Kaunas and İzmir. One of its foremost architectural historians – Nikolaus Pevsner – was born in Leipzig. And one of its most influential feminists – Germaine Greer – was born in Melbourne. (Winder, 2010).

IMMIGRANTS CONTRIBUTE WITHOUT COERCION

Let's wrap things up...

This chapter has been a mishmash. We've spoken about sports, cinema, music, food, language, science, politics and literature. We've chucked in some anecdotal tales, some lists, and some statistics. I hope you've managed to cope!

There was a reason to take this approach: Immigrants contribute in such a vast array of ways. It's important to give an overview – to appreciate the sheer breadth of their contributions. And it's important to remember that they're individual human beings, with their own unique stories to tell.

Not every immigrant will have as large an impact as the Brits who introduced football to Brazil, the Eastern Europeans who founded Hollywood, or the Bangladeshis who championed the chicken tikka masala. But they'll help things along in their own little way. They might contribute through their work. They might create jobs for others. Or they might donate their time: A 2013 study found that around 15% of American immigrants were volunteers. (Frausto, 2016).

One thing seems certain: It's crazy to force people to integrate.

How would you measure the extent of their integration? What would you do if they didn't assimilate enough? If you're going to test immigrants, are you also going to judge the locals by the same criteria? What if *they* came up short? And what if a new arrival only fails the test, because they don't perform well in exam conditions?

None of this is necessary.

If you just sit back and relax, things will usually turn out for the best – often in ways you'd have never predicted. Immigrants might not speak the language as well as a local, or play the most popular sport. But they might introduce new words, popularise a foreign sport, or establish an entire industry.

***

Having said all this, it should be noted that people *do* assimilate on their own.

Money plays a part.

When we were living in Bulgaria, my wife and I ate the local delicacies: Meatballs and white cheese. We hadn't made a conscious decision to assimilate. But this food was cheap and accessible – available at almost every grocery store, market and restaurant. I still preferred cheddar, but I settled for a more affordable alternative.

Time plays an even more significant role.

When people first arrive in a prosperous nation, there's a high probability they'll be poorer than their peers – they'll work in junior positions and receive lower pay. But studies in the States have shown that these differences evaporate within the space of a single generation. The children of immigrants tend to get the same kinds of jobs as their neighbours. There's a good chance they'll end up in a professional or managerial role. They receive the same rates of pay – accounting for race, age and gender. They experience the same rates of poverty, have the same number of babies, and suffer from similar diseases. (Waters & Gerstein-Pineau, 2015).

Nowhere is this phenomenon more relevant, than when it

comes to *speech*.

It used to be the case that people with foreign roots took several generations to adopt the local language: The Huguenots continued to speak French for centuries, after moving to England in the 1500s. The Portuguese followed suit. Newspapers printed in the Yiddish language, were a fixture in New York for several decades. And the first Germans to settle in the States, continued to speak their mother tongue. This led Benjamin Franklin to ask: "Why should the Palatine Boors be suffered to swarm into our settlements... (They) will never adopt our language or customs." (Winder, 2004). (Caplan, 2019). (Guest, 2011).

But their children *did* "Adopt" the lingo.

Today, around fifty-million Americans have German ancestry. They've intermarried and intermingled to such an extent, that it's impossible to tell them apart. Almost all of them speak English. Most *don't* speak any German.

What's more, Americans have embraced the *German* culture: These days, millions of Americans watch sport on the weekend, whilst drinking clear beer and chomping on frankfurters. They might tell you this is an American pastime. But it came from Germany.

German medicine, engineering and philosophy – have also been incorporated into American culture. (Guest, 2011).

***

Learning a language is tough. Many first-generation immigrants struggle with the task. But unlike in the time of the Huguenots, it doesn't take hundreds of years for their families to catch up. The German Americans only took a few generations. These days, families are taking even *less* time than that.

In the USA, only 37% of Hispanic immigrants can speak English proficiently. But *91%* of their children are fluent. And that figure is on the rise. It'll probably be even higher in the near future. (Funk & Lopez, 2022).

The numbers are even more promising, when we consider people from other regions. In all, half the foreign-born population in the States say they speak English "Well" or "Very well". Their descendants usually drop their mother tongue, and become monolingual, within the space of three generations. (Waters & Gerstein-Pineau, 2015).

***

There's another problem with the logic of assimilation: It assumes that the native culture *has to be maintained.*

But what if it's flawed?

The incarceration rate for new arrivals in America is around a third *lower* than the norm. But the children of immigrants commit just as many crimes as their peers. Their behaviour converges to the norm – they assimilate – and we end up with *more* crime.

New arrivals tend to have better health. They're also more likely to live in two-parent households. A generation later, this is no longer the case. Their children assimilate, by having *worse* health and *more* broken homes. (Waters & Gerstein-Pineau, 2015).

I certainly see undesirable cultures, here in the Philippines: People drive without licences. They don't give way to oncoming traffic, when exiting minor roads. They sing karaoke at full volume, in residential zones. They have a fetish for single-use plastic. They drop litter. They keep their dogs in tiny cages.

I *could* assimilate. I *could* drive in a manner that endangers people's lives. I *could* blast music through people's windows. I *could* abuse my dogs.

But my moral compass won't allow me to assimilate in these particular ways – doing things which might cause pain to others, or damage the natural environment.

***

It can be hard for people to see the flaws in their own society. Lots of Filipinos won't see a problem with the way their compatriots drive, because they've never known anything different. Some Filipinos *do* despise loud music. Our neighbours once complained about a karaoke shop, and got the authorities to shut it down! But if you mention "Noise pollution", most Pinoys won't know what you mean. They have no concept of a peaceful existence.

This is one of the reasons that immigrants are so great: They see their adopted lands with a fresh perspective. They can spot issues. And they can offer solutions.

This is why Eastern Europeans were able to transform the American movie industry: They saw the shortcomings of contemporary American films, and took action to make them better. And it's why immigrants are improving Germany's language today: They're spotting issues with the grammar, and correcting it themselves.

***

I'm certainly not suggesting that immigrants should *force* these changes. I'm not supporting a kind of imperialism, in which *nations* occupy other nations. My last novel, "Other Worlds Were Possible", rallies against this very thing.

Open borders would allow *individuals* to arrive as guests. They might introduce some foreign food, sport, music and fashion. But the locals would remain in charge: They might choose to embrace these things. Then again, they might not.

Immigrants like Charles Miller didn't only introduce football to the São Paulo Athletic Clube. They also introduced cricket. The Brazilians didn't fall in love with that sport. But still, no harm was done. A few Brazilians were able to give cricket a go, and I expect they were grateful for that.

Indian cuisine took off in Britain for two reasons: There were plenty of Indians who wished to cook curries, naan bread and samosas. And there were lots of Brits who enjoyed that spicy food. At the same time, people from the Caribbean were also opening restaurants – serving jerk chicken, saltfish and ackee. But those dishes haven't come to define British cuisine. And who cares? They still add variety. They're still available, for anyone who wishes to indulge.

The fact is, we cannot be sure what impact a new arrival is going to make until *after* we've opened our doors, welcomed them, and given them a chance to do their thing. Some will invent new products, objects, genres, sports and industries – the likes of which we couldn't have ever imagined. But we won't find out *how*, until several decades have passed.

This is why "Points-based systems" are prone to failure: They don't judge people according to their humanity, or on what they *might* contribute, but according to a rigid mathematical formula.

Take the UK's new system as an example: To gain entry, a worker must have a job offer, an "Appropriate skill level", and the ability to speak English at the "Required level". They must be set to earn a reasonably high wage, or fill a vacancy in a specific industry, or hold a relevant PhD. (www.gov.uk).

Such a system would've excluded the Jews who brought fish and chips to Britain. It might've denied entry to several members of the Windrush Generation – people whose children would go on to invent jungle, grime and dubstep.

The criterion does allow entrepreneurs to live in the country, but only if they arrive with £50,000 in cash. That'd have excluded people like Louis Mayer and Carl Laemmle – the founders of MGM and Universal Pictures – who emigrated without a penny to their names. It would've blocked several of the entrepreneurs who we'll encounter in the following chapter.

The next time someone turns up at the border, with or without papers – perhaps without a profession, any qualifications or capital – we should ask ourselves what that person *might* contribute, given time. We should ask what their *children* might invent, thirty-odd years down the line. We should ask what they might contribute to society, *outside the workplace*.

These things cannot be measured by a fixed criterion. No form can predict the kind of impact a person's unborn child is going to have. A "Points-based system" doesn't give points for intangibles such as culture. It reduces humans to numbers – ignoring the things which make us all unique.

And that's the thing with immigration: It's predictably unpredictable. You know it'll produce some beautiful things. But it's impossible to say how, what, when or where. You just have to open your borders, mix yourself a mojito, sit back, and watch the magic unfurl.

THEY CREATE OUR JOBS!

"I owe everything to this country. I want others to dream big, come here to start their businesses, and create American jobs."
Max Levchin

In February 1986, Soviet Life Magazine published an interview with Vitalii Skliarov – Ukraine's Minister of Power and Electrification. In that article, Skliarov boasted of a power plant which was producing a gargantuan amount of energy. When asked about the dangers, the politician remained defiant, claiming: "The odds of a meltdown are one in ten-thousand years."

Two months later, a reactor at that facility – Chernobyl – experienced the very kind of "Meltdown" that Skliarov had deemed so improbable. The building's roof was torn asunder. The skies shimmered with radioactive waste. And a ten-year-old boy, named Max Levchin – who'd been asleep, ninety kilometres away – had to be evacuated from his home.

At the train station, the passengers were tested for radioactivity. Max's family embarked without an issue. His brother stepped on board. But when the Geiger counter scanned Max's foot, it went ballistic: *Beep, beepy beep-beep, beepy beep.*

Max was in hysterics. His foot was radioactive! It'd have to be amputated. He'd struggle to walk. People would turn their heads, whenever they passed him by.

Max was a handsome boy, but he was hardly butch. As an infant, he'd suffered from a life-threatening respiratory disease. He'd learned to play the clarinet, to improve his lung capacity, and he'd survived against the odds. But now he was going to lose a foot!

His grandmother spoke up:

"Check the boot," she demanded.

And with that, the crisis was averted.

The culprit had been a radioactive thorn, embedded in Max's shoe. That thorn was removed, and Max stepped onto the train.

***

Max's world would never be the same again...

His mother – a scientist at the Institute for Food Science – saw her workload increase, in the wake of the Chernobyl disaster.

The Soviet government sent her a couple of ungainly computers, to help shoulder the load.

Max wasn't particularly impressed, at first. But his opinions changed, when he discovered an early version of Tetris, and the "Pascal Compiler" – a program which allowed users to code.

He was hooked. He found the instruction manual – a pirated book – took it home, and treated it like a holy scripture.

It was as though he was looking into the future. He could tell a machine to do something, and it'd do that very thing! This contraption was going to change the world. *He, Max Levchin*, might use it to change the world.

Up until that point, Max had always wanted to be a teacher. But not anymore! *Now* he just wanted to code.

***

Max was only allowed to use the "Robotron" computer after his mother had finished her work. So he went to the park, filled his notebooks with code, waited, waited some more, and inputted that text just as soon as his mother was done.

The Robotron was a fairly rudimentary piece of kit. If Max made a single mistake, his entire program would go kaput. And so he had to ensure that his code was perfect.

This left him with exacting standards – standards that would enable him to get ahead, once his family had moved abroad...

***

The Levchins became *refugees*. They were fleeing from antisemitism. (A star of David had been graffitied on their door). And they were also *economic migrants*. They were fleeing from the fall of communism – searching for a better life, in a more prosperous land.

They kept their emigration a secret, whilst they waited for an agency to process their sponsorship. Then they were off – clasping hold of their life savings – wearing winter coats, even though it was a midsummer day, so they wouldn't have to declare them at customs.

It was a good job too: By the time they landed in the States, the rouble had collapsed. Their savings, which they thought would be worth thousands of dollars, were only worth seven-hundred. They had to sell those coats, to get the money they needed to survive.

***

Max was determined to get ahead...

He found a broken television in the trash, took it home, repaired it, and began to watch American shows – learning to speak English, by studying the sitcom "Diff'rent Strokes".

Within a couple of years, he'd earned himself a place on a computer science program at the University of Illinois.

***

One Friday night, while Max was in the computer lab, two students approached him from behind – lurking in the shadows, before confronting the young Ukrainian.

The first student, Luke Nosek, was also an immigrant. He'd moved from Poland in the 1970s. The second, Scott Bannister, was a native of Kansas City.

Nosek began the inquisition:

"What are you working on?"

"I'm making an explosion simulator."

Bannister, a little confused, pushed for an explanation:

"But... what does it do? What purpose does it serve?"

"What do you mean? It's beautiful. It's in real time, and it recomputes a random explosion."

Nosek repeated his friend's question:

"Okay, but *why*?"

"I don't know. It's cool."

Bannister took over:

"It's Friday night. Don't you have somewhere else to be?"

"No... I love this. Don't *you* have somewhere to be?"

And that was when Nosek made the statement that would change Max's world:

"We're going to go start a company. You should come with us."

***

It wasn't all plain sailing, as Max would tell a reporter from his old university:

"The very first company I started, failed with a great bang. The second one failed a little bit less, but still failed. The third one, you know, proper failed, but it was kind of okay. I recovered quickly. Number four almost didn't fail. It still didn't really feel great, but it did okay. *Number five was PayPal.*"

***

Max hadn't gone it alone.

PayPal was born from a merger between *Confinity* and *X.com*. Confinity was a security firm, which enabled clients to store encrypted data. It was established by Max (a Ukrainian), Nosek (a Pole), and a German-born financier named Peter Thiel. X.com was an online bank, which had been set up by Harris Fricker and Christopher Payne (Canadians), Elon Musk (a South African) and Ed Ho.

Between them, they established a company which has gone on to create over *25,000* jobs – mostly in the States.

IMMIGRANTS PLATFORM OTHER FIRMS

It'd be wrong to stop here.

After PayPal, Max invested in Yelp, which had over four-thousand employees at the time of writing. Musk formed SpaceX – keeping the "X" from X.com. That employed almost ten-thousand workers. And Thiel was the first outside investor in Facebook – a company with over seventy-thousand members of staff. Facebook was co-founded by another immigrant – a Brazilian named Eduardo Saverin.

***

PayPal also inspired several of its *employees*, who went on to invest in a second batch of firms...

David Sacks – a South African, and PayPal's Chief Operating Officer – became an angel investor in Facebook, Airbnb (which has over six-thousand employees), and Uber (which has over thirty-thousand employees, and five-million drivers). In fact, the three people who established Airbnb, are *all* of foreign descent – one has a Polish father, whilst the others have Italian ancestry. One of Uber's founders is a Canadian.

Reid Hoffman – an American – was one of PayPal's original directors. When PayPal was sold to eBay, in 2002, he co-founded LinkedIn with Eric Ly – a refugee whose family had fled from Vietnam. At the time of writing, LinkedIn employed just under twenty-thousand people.

Roelof Botha – another South African, and PayPal's Director of Corporate Development – became known for his work in investment funds. He finances start-ups, which have created jobs for another tranche of American workers.

And Premal Shah – a product manager, who was born in India – went on to form Kiva. That non-profit has issued loans to two-million entrepreneurs, in eighty countries. Who knows how many jobs *they've* gone on to create?

***

When PayPal first launched, Max Levchin returned to his old university, to recruit some of their students:

"We selected people like us... We said, 'We want kids that have nothing to lose, that are going to go big or go home every time, that basically all think this is their final training ground. Their next company is going to be their own."

Some of them did "Go big".

Russell Simmons, PayPal's "Lead Software Architect", went on to create Yelp, along with another PayPal employee and Illinois student – Jeremy Stoppelman. (Soni, 2022). (Hayden, 2018).

And three of Max's other recruits, went on to launch *YouTube*...

***

The story begins with a mass assassination.

Sheikh Mujib, the "Father of Bangladesh", had just been slaughtered in a bloody coup. And a young man named Naimul Karim was responding in an unpredictable fashion – making the spontaneous decision to move to East Germany. He told his family, didn't give them a chance to protest, and hopped on a flight to Berlin – with only $50 to tide him over.

Naimul was taken to Leipzig, where he studied German. His course was led by a woman who began by writing two sentences on the board: "Ich bin Frau Lehmann. Ich bin ihre Lehrerin." ("I am Misses Lehman. I am your teacher"). She repeated these words, until everyone understood that she was Misses Lehman, and that she was their teacher. No English was ever spoken in Lehman's classroom, but the lessons were effective. Naimul picked up the language in next to no time.

He said it was like gaining his sight:

"Each day, as I walked around the city, I deciphered another signpost. As I looked out while riding a tram, I understood another nugget from a billboard... With every improvement in my comprehension, I could catch more bits and pieces of conversations... The experience was like moving gradually from deafness to hearing, from incomprehension to comprehension, and ultimately from darkness to light. I do not know anyone who was cured of blindness. But that is the closest analogy I can come up with."

Naimul moved to Merseburg, where he began his degree, married a local, and had a son.

But the couple – a Bangladeshi and a German – stood out from the crowd. And that made them a target for the local racists.

Naimul moved his family to the other side of the Iron Curtain, to escape the abuse. But the prejudice followed them west, and so they decided to leave.

In 1992, the Karims arrived in Minnesota, where Naimul found work as a corporate scientist – putting aside enough time to pursue his hobbies: Line dancing, hiking, tennis, and the "Intellectual deconstruction of The Matrix". (Naimul.net).

His son, Jawed, was thirteen-years-old at the time. It'd take a decade for Jawed to finish his schooling, complete a degree in Illinois, move to California, and begin life at PayPal – two years after the company was formed.

It was whilst working for that firm, that Jawed met an American named Chad Hurley, and another Illinois alumni – Steve Chen – who'd immigrated from Taiwan.

Together, the three programmers went on to create YouTube.

Jawed would even star in the first ever YouTube video – a nineteen-second skit, entitled "Me at the Zoo", in which he tells viewers that elephants have "Really, really long trunks. And that's cool". The video has received millions of views, and Jawed has millions of subscribers – even though he's only ever posted this solitary clip.

***

We could focus on the basic message: That two immigrants and one American, launched a website – YouTube – which created 2,800 jobs. But this would barely scratch the surface.

That's because YouTube doesn't only employ people itself. It provides a *platform*, on which users can invent new jobs *for themselves*.

Some of those jobs are obvious: A few "YouTubers" are so successful, their videos attract enough views to earn them a full-time income. These content creators benefit from free access to the video publishing industry, and they're able to reach a global audience – things which would've been impossible, before a Bangladeshi-German and a Taiwanese immigrant got to work.

These content providers might make their money from adverts, sponsorships, affiliate links, donations or monthly subscriptions.

Other YouTubers make a living by using their channels to *promote goods and services* which they or their firms produce – making their money indirectly, from the sale of those items. A band might post a music video – hoping it'll attract new fans, who'll pay to see them in concert. A hardware firm might upload tutorials, showing people how to use their tools – in the hope that some viewers might go out and purchase those gizmos.

Together, these people create jobs: Over a third of American YouTubers employ *staff* to work on their channels. Some employ a full-time team.

The *advertisements* shown on YouTube, also create employment: It takes a lot of people to write a script, audition the stars, build a set, film and produce those videos. Other people must be employed to manage these adverts – posting them online, choosing which demographics to target, managing bids, and monitoring their expenditures.

Next, we must account for the goods and services which these adverts help to sell. The firms that produce *these* products, must also employ people – to satisfy the demand which was just generated by their adverts on YouTube. They'll have to employ more customer service agents, to deal with their new customers – and more bookkeepers, to oversee their accounts.

Another set of firms ply their trade by selling audio-visual equipment to the YouTubers themselves – things like video cameras, microphones, and editing software. People have to be employed to produce these things as well.

All of these items have to be sent in the mail. That creates work for delivery drivers. It creates jobs at the firms which produce packing paper, cardboard boxes, bubble wrap and adhesive.

And YouTube also platforms educational videos. Viewers can study these shows, learn a new craft, and turn that into a job. Workers can watch training videos *after* they've been employed, to help them upskill and retain their positions.

***

It should be clear, by now, that Jawed and his colleagues didn't only create 2,800 jobs at YouTube.

According to reports by Oxford Economics – who surveyed thousands of YouTubers, viewers and businesses – the website supported the equivalent of *390,000* full-time jobs in the United States, the equivalent of another forty-thousand full-time jobs in the UK, and many more jobs elsewhere. The platform was worth $35b a year to the American economy, in 2022 alone. (Galloway & Gambarin, 2023). (Goodwin & Serra, 2022).

It's hard to envision how any of these jobs would exist today, if it weren't for a German-born man with a Bangladeshi father, and a second man who was born in Taiwan – both of whom moved to the States, where they teamed up to create the site.

If Jawed Karim's father had raised his family in Bangladesh, do you really think that Jawed would've invented a multibillion-dollar business, which created hundred-of-thousands of jobs? In Bangladesh, he wouldn't have had access to the sort of education he received in Illinois, or the sorts of servers which are common in the States. He wouldn't have benefitted from the techy environment he found in Silicon Valley. He wouldn't have been able to recruit the programmers who got YouTube off the ground. And he wouldn't have been nurtured by a firm like PayPal.

If Max Levchin had been left on his own – working on a Robotron computer, somewhere near Chernobyl – do you think he'd have created PayPal? Do you think he'd have recruited Jawed Karim, Steve Chen and Chad Hurley? Do you think he'd have mentored them – giving them the tools they needed to launch YouTube?

It seems unlikely.

Immigration created these jobs. A larger amount of immigration, would create a larger number of jobs. Open borders, would create the *largest* number of jobs.

THEY'RE THE STARS OF SILICON VALLEY

YouTube is far from a freak example.

PayPal also creates jobs in the wider economy. It helps other businesses, such as eBay, to process payments – enabling them to do business – something which requires *them* to employ staff.

eBay was established by a chap named Pierre Omidyar, in 1995. Pierre moved from France to the USA, back when he was a child. (Viegas, 2006).

At the time of writing, the company employed over eleven-thousand people. But again, this underestimates its impact: The website provides an online marketplace, which allows *others* to trade. According to the site's Chief Communication Officer, eBay had six-million sellers in the United States, in 2017. Between them, they were shifting $90b of merchandise a year. eBay estimates that, "Commercial sellers and full-time entrepreneurs on the eBay platform are responsible for creating more than 690,000 jobs." Most work for small and medium firms. Over a third come from small towns and rural areas. (Tarman, 2018).

***

Let's turn our attention to an even more famous website: Google.

Would it surprise you if I told you that one of Google's two founders was also an immigrant? Sergey Brin was born in Moscow. He left the USSR with his family, moved to the USA, and enrolled at Stanford, where he met Larry Page. The two youngsters began to code – creating a new kind of search engine, which would become "Google".

How many jobs has the Russian programmer helped to create?

Google's parent company, Alphabet, employed 190,000 people in 2022 – including 115,000 in the States. That number was rising every year.

But again, this is a massive underestimation.

Can you even begin to imagine how many items are sold, after someone uses Google to search for "Dishwasher for under $300", "The best brand of bread-maker" or "Flamenco gigs near Barcelona"? Now think of all the people who have to be employed to promote, produce, and deliver *those* items.

We don't know quite how many jobs these searches have created, *indirectly*, but it has to be huge.

The firm's corporate website does claim:

"The Android app economy, including Google Play, helped create two-million American jobs – from software engineers and developers of mobile applications, to the marketing and human resources teams that support them." (EconomicImpact.Google)

***

Before we move on, let's consider one more immigrant: A political refugee named Miguel.

Miguel left Cuba when he was sixteen. He made the journey to the States alone – his parents were even forbidden from entering Havana's airport. And he only spoke Spanish at the time.

Miguel learned to speak English, began a thirty-two year career at Exxon Mobil, married a woman called Jackie, and adopted her son – a boy named Jeff.

Jeff would speak fondly of his father:

"He had those tough experiences. I think in every immigrant, you'll find a deep optimism and a deep resilience too... My Dad is an intense hard worker. My Dad is warm and he teaches an easy smile." (Wenger, 2022).

It seems like Miguel was an inspiration for Jeff.

In 1994, Miguel's son created the largest online retailer in the world: Amazon.

Amazon employed over 1.5 million people, in 2022, according to Statista. But, yet again, this underestimates the total number of jobs that the website creates.

You probably wouldn't be reading this book if it wasn't for Amazon. Most of my titles are bought on that site. Amazon's subsidiary – Kindle Direct Publishing – prints a good proportion of my paperback and hardcover editions. As loathe as I am to admit it – I owe a great deal of my success to the site (and to an immigrant named Miguel).

I'm not alone: Kindle Direct Publishing has published books by a million independent authors, in forty languages.

Like eBay, Amazon also allows third parties to sell on its platform. Small and medium firms, selling on Amazon's dot-com site, employ an estimated 1.1 million members of staff. Across all of Amazon's domains, these businesses have created over 2.2 million roles.

Amazon also has a business-to-business channel, which provides a platform for another 150,000 sellers. And they partner with 2,200 delivery firms, who employ over 95,000 drivers.

That's not bad for a business which was established by the son of a man who arrived in the States with nothing – not even a word of English! (Quaker, 2022).

***

So, contrary to popular belief, immigrants don't come to *take* our jobs. They come to *make* our jobs. They make jobs for you, your family, and your friends. They create some businesses which are so nurturing, they inspire their employees to create *other* businesses. And they create platforms which provide a leg up for millions of firms and creatives.

According to the 2017 Internet Trends report, fifteen out of the twenty-five most valuable tech firms in the USA were established by first or second-generation immigrants.

That list includes some fairly big hitters...

Apple was created by Steve Jobs, whose biological father had immigrated from Syria. He would've been denied entry into the country, if he'd arrived while the "Muslim ban" was in place.

Apple had 116,000 employees at the time that report was released.

Oracle was co-founded by Bob Miner, whose parents were from Iran – another nation affected by Trump's ban.

Oracle employed 136,000 people.

Cognizant Technology was created by Francisco D'Souza (who immigrated from India), and Kumar Mahadeva (who was born in Sri Lanka).

Cognizant had 261,000 employees.

And one of IBM's founding fathers – Herman Hollerith – was the son of German parents.

IBM had 380,000 members of staff.

***

A different study reached a similar conclusion: It found that over half the engineering and technology firms in Silicon Valley, had at least one founder who was an immigrant.

That report also showed that the majority of those entrepreneurs had moved to the States to *study*. People tend not to head for California, with the sole intention of setting up a business. They live in the States for an average of thirteen years, before creating a firm of their own. (Wadhwa et al, 2007).

Yet this doesn't mean that they don't create jobs in the meantime. They do! Because foreign *employees* can also create jobs, at least if we're to believe Bill Gates.

Gates has claimed that each time Microsoft employs someone on an H-1B visa – the visas which are issued to highly-educated people with "Speciality occupations" – the firm creates another "Four or five jobs... (to *support*) those engineers." They employ more foreigners, and that creates *more* American jobs. (Norris, 2008).

The reverse can also be true.

When Donald Trump suspended the H-1B visa program – to prevent Indian software engineers from moving to the States – firms in Silicon Valley responded by outsourcing work to places such as Hyderabad and Hanoi. Immigration was reduced, and Californians *lost* their jobs as a result. (Khanna, 2021).

FOREIGNERS CREATE ALL SORTS OF JOBS

It'd be wrong, however, to only focus on the digital domain.

Immigrants create jobs in *almost every sector...*

In the previous chapter, we spoke about the immigrants who established Hollywood. Well, according to the local government, "During 2016, the Los Angeles County Film and Digital Media Industry generated 640,500 jobs." That number included 265,000 people who were employed within the industry, and another 375,000 people who supplied filmmakers with services such as catering and cleaning. None of those people would be in work, if it hadn't been for immigrants such as Louis Mayer and Carl Laemmle. (LACounty.gov).

A study by the National Foundation for American Policy, found that immigrants had helped to establish over half the nation's start-ups which were valued at more than a billion dollars. Between them, these new businesses were worth $168b – almost as much as the entire stock market in a country like Russia or Mexico. (Anderson, 2016).

And research from the Center for American Entrepreneurship, published in 2017, found that 43% of the firms in the Fortune 500 had at least one co-founder who was either a first or second-generation immigrant. This number went up to 52%, when they focused on the largest twenty-five firms.

Just let that sink in: *Over half of the largest businesses in the States were established by foreigners or the children of foreign nationals!*

We're talking about some pretty traditional corporations: The likes of Costco, Verizon, Ford, J.P. Morgan, AmerisourceBergen, Walgreens, Kroger, General Electric, Boeing, AT&T, and Home Depot – as well as Apple and Amazon. Between them, these companies have created millions of jobs. They've employed people for several decades, across the length and breadth of the nation. (Dumitriu & Stewart, 2019).

***

But new arrivals don't only create big businesses. They're also more likely to create *small and medium firms*, when compared to sedentary people...

Between 2005 and 2010, 0.83% of working-age immigrants started a new business in the States, compared to just 0.46% of people who'd been born inside its borders. In total, just over 7% of foreign-born residents had opened a business – compared to just 4% of the sitting population. This means that immigrants are opening businesses at almost *double the rate* of their peers. (Azoulay et al, 2020).

Immigrants are a small minority – they only constitute one-seventh of the US population. But they're more likely to be employed – they do one-sixth of all the work. And they're more likely to be entrepreneurs. Around a *quarter* of new American businesses are launched by non-nationals. (Beyer, 2021).

Indeed, the New American Economy has calculated that there are 3.2 million active, first-generation immigrant entrepreneurs in the States. Between them, they've directly created almost eight-million jobs. (Feinblatt, 2019).

IT'S THE SAME ON BOTH SIDES OF THE ATLANTIC

We see something similar in Britain...

Statista has ranked the "Largest companies based in the United Kingdom". Tesco – a chain of supermarkets – came in second place. It employed 293,000 people, worldwide, in 2020. And it was founded by a chap called Jack Cohen, who was the son of two Polish parents.

In third place, HSBC Holdings was created by a nomadic Scot, while he was working in Hong Kong. HSBC employed 235,000 people.

And in fourth place, Unilever was formed by a merger between an English firm, and a firm which was established by Dutch entrepreneurs. Unilever had 149,000 members of staff.

Other famous British brands founded by immigrants include...

Marks and Spencer's, a high-street retailer founded by a Belarussian (Michael Marks) and a Brit (Thomas Spencer). It employed 65,000 people at the time of writing.

EasyJet, a budget airline, was founded by a Greek (Stelios Haji-Ioannou). It had 12,000 employees.

Burroughs Wellcome, a pharmaceutical firm, was established by two Americans (Silas Burroughs and Henry Wellcome). It merged to form GlaxoSmithKline, which employs 69,000 people.

And Associated British Foods – the firm behind Twinings (tea), Silver Spoon (sugar), Kingsmill (bread), and Primark (clothing) – was founded by Willard Weston, who was Canadian. It had 132,000 members of staff.

In fact, one-in-five of the businesses which are listed in the FTSE 100, have a founder who was a first-generation immigrant.

Smaller British firms which were established by immigrants, include: Burtons menswear (founded by a Lithuanian), Chicken Cottage (created by a Pakistani), Cobra beer and Patak's spices (established by Indians), Caffè Nero and Selfridges (created by Americans), and Rimmel cosmetics (founded by a Frenchman). (Mitchell, 2017).

These are established, household names. But things come into even starker contrast when we consider those businesses which are still bursting onto the scene. That's because, whilst just 14% of British residents were born overseas, 49% of the country's fastest-growing start-ups have at least one foreign founder. And they're a pretty eclectic bunch: Those entrepreneurs migrated from twenty-nine different nations.

Syndicate Room has classed fourteen British start-ups as "Unicorns" – businesses worth more than a billion dollars. Of these, nine had at least one co-founder who'd moved to the UK from overseas. That means that almost two-thirds of Britain's most successful new start-ups, were established by non-nationals. We're talking about businesses like Revolut (created by a Russian and a Ukrainian), Wise (created by two Estonians), and Deliveroo (created by two Americans). Deliveroo is already a bit of a behemoth. It coordinates work for 180,000 drivers. (Dumitriu & Stewart, 2019).

***

Once again, we've started by focusing on the big guns. And with good reason: These businesses have created millions of jobs. But it'd be wrong to exclude those individuals who run smaller enterprises. They might only employ a handful of people, but there are so many of them, that the numbers can still stack up.

My family fits into this category: When my great-grandparents moved to Britain, they didn't take jobs from other people. *They created jobs for themselves.*

One of my mum's grandfathers was a self-employed tailor. He worked on the family's dining table, whilst a budgerigar perched upon his spectacles. Two of my great-grandfathers were furniture makers.

Their *children* were an entrepreneurial bunch.

My mother's uncle opened a factory in London's East End – making eiderdowns and bedding. After his section of the family was evacuated to Oxford, on the eve of the Second World War, they opened a shoe emporium, a ladieswear shop, an estate agent, and a grocery store – all on the very same street.

My father's parents were also in on the game: They opened two babywear shops, which evolved into haberdasheries over time.

***

In most English towns, you only have to walk down your local high street to find a store that's owned and run by a person who was born overseas...

When I was growing up, there was a stereotype of the Pakistani immigrant who opened a convenience store on a street corner, and the Indian immigrant who ran a restaurant. These days, you're just as likely to see a "Polski Sklep", run by a Polish-born entrepreneur. In London,

South Asians seem to have cornered the market on laptop repair.

Such stereotypes aren't always well-intentioned. And they aren't always accurate: A lot of "Indian" restaurants were opened by Bangladeshis. But they contain a nugget of truth: Foreigners are almost 70% more likely to open a business in the UK than the average Brit: Over one-sixth of immigrants start a company. But only a little over one-tenth of all the locals ever take the plunge.

Nearly half-a-million people have launched a business after moving to Britain. These individuals come from 155 different countries – around three-quarters of the nations on Earth.

The average foreign-born entrepreneur is around eight years younger than their British counterpart – so they give themselves more time to grow their empire. They're more likely to be female. And they're most likely to go into construction or real estate. They're quite literally building the homes and infrastructure that the country desperately needs. (Johnson & Kimmelman, 2014).

FOREIGN CONSUMERS CREATE JOBS

Now let's look at things from the opposite perspective...

So far, we've focused on the *businesses*, founded by immigrants, which employ millions of people. But a foreigner doesn't have to be an entrepreneur, to create jobs in their local community. We all create jobs, each time we spend our money. That's because workers have to be employed, to supply us with the things we buy.

Some of these professionals are employed *directly*: Immigrants create work for the immigration lawyers who process their papers. If they cannot speak the language, they might have to employ a local translator. And there's a good chance that they'll go on to study the language – employing teachers along the way.

But most of these jobs are created *indirectly*...

Imagine a scenario in which ten-thousand foreign people suddenly turn up to work. Puff! They materialise out of thin air, and take jobs as fruit-pickers, construction workers, and brain surgeons.

At the end of every month, they receive their paycheque.

What do you think they're going to do with their money?

They may send a little home – helping to lift their loved ones out of poverty. They might save a little for a rainy day. But they're going to have to spend a fair chunk on the things they need to survive – things such as housing, electricity and water. They might buy a few of life's little luxuries, or pay for some leisure activities.

It's not unreasonable to suppose they might visit the local supermarket – to buy food, toiletries and cleaning materials.

All of a sudden, that supermarket will be awash with new customers. Ten-thousand people will be parading along the aisles, picking up cans of baked beans, throwing satsumas into their trollies, and marching upon the tills.

Don't you think that the supermarket will have to employ some more staff, to cope with this surge in demand?

Of course, they will!

They'll have to employ more people to restock the shelves. They'll have to employ more checkout staff, to scan the products. They'll have to employ more administrators, to manage their inventory. And they'll have to employ more drivers, to deliver new produce.

But it's not just the supermarket which will have to employ more people. It's also their *suppliers*.

If these new customers buy a decent amount of spaghetti, then the firms who make pasta will also have to up production. They'll have to hire more staff to work in their factories, and more drivers to deliver their products. They'll also have to buy some more flour. And so wheat farmers will also have to employ more staff, to produce even more wheat than before.

We could say the same for every product those immigrants buy: Bakers will have to bake more bread for them to eat. Clothes-makers will have to produce more clothes for them to wear. Toothpaste producers will have to produce the toothpaste they're going to use.

But we shouldn't stop here. That's because there's a second iteration to this tale.

Now we have several *local* people with new jobs at supermarkets, food production facilities, wheat farms, toothpaste factories, and delivery companies. *These people* will have more money than before – when they were unemployed, or in jobs with lower wages. The chances are that *they'll* begin to buy more things.

Along with the ten-thousand new arrivals, this second group of workers might visit restaurants, bars, golf courses, cinemas and cafes.

These organisations will have to recruit a *third tranche of employees*, to cope with the surge in demand. And their suppliers will have to employ a *fourth* set of workers, to produce the inputs which these companies will need.

These workers will also begin to spend more money – creating even more demand. And another set of firms will have to employ a *fifth set of workers* in order to cope.

We could go on forever.

In reality, the effects will diminish with each new iteration. That's because workers don't spend *all* their wages at once. They might buy some imports – sending their money abroad. And firms don't use all their income to pay workers and suppliers. They also pay taxes. They repay debts, and issue dividends.

But the knock-on effects do add up. It's what economists call "The Multiplier Effect": If you have a surge in demand – such as the one which occurs when new workers begin to spend their wages – then the effects will ripple through the economy, creating a benefit which is *multiple* times greater than it might've first appeared.

***

We know that immigrants create new jobs, each time they spend their money. But *how many* jobs do they create?

To answer this, we need to begin by looking at the total amount of money that immigrants spend: Research from the New American Economy, shows that they spent $1.3t in the United States, in 2019 alone. (Beyer, 2021).

Next, we need to convert these revenues into jobs, which we'll do in three successive steps...

First, we'll look at the *direct jobs* which this spending creates. In the previous example, this'd be the jobs which were created at the supermarket, where the new arrivals bought their food.

We then need to consider *supplier jobs*. In the previous example, these would include the jobs which were created at the firms that produced spaghetti and toothpaste. It would also include several jobs which were created at *service providers* – at the accountancy firms who audited the supermarket's books, and at the banks who processed their payments.

Finally, we need to consider *induced jobs*. These are the jobs which are created when money is *re-spent*. This includes the jobs which are created at the businesses that supply the suppliers – the jobs which are created when the second and third groups of employees begin to spend their wages – and the jobs which are created *in the public sector*, using the tax revenues which are generated along the way.

The Economic Policy Institute has looked at all three types of jobs – "Direct Jobs", "Supplier Jobs" *and* "Induced Jobs" – in every industry in the United States.

According to their figures, the vast majority of industries generated between ten and fifteen jobs, each time they received a million dollars. The median industry provided 12.75 jobs. The mean average was a little over thirteen.

Let's take this last figure, and apply it to the $1.3t of consumer spending which is generated by immigrants in the USA each year.

The impact is significant: Simply by spending their money in the States, foreign residents create around *seventeen-million jobs*. That's 10.9% of all the jobs in the nation!

Now, let's put these things together: Immigrants create jobs by establishing new businesses, such as PayPal. They invent platforms, which enable other people to create jobs for themselves. They create industries, such as Hollywood, which employ hundreds-of-thousands of people. And they create jobs, each time they spend their money.

Our international guests create millions of new jobs.

If you're unemployed, you'd better pray for even *more* foreigners to arrive on your shores, because they might just create the work you so desperately need! (Bivens, 2019).

Indeed, according to one piece of research – published by the National Bureau of Economic Research – each time ten new people arrive in an area, they help to create *twelve* new jobs. The majority of those positions are filled by people who've always lived in the vicinity. And over three-in-five of these jobs are "Non-tradable". They supply things such as haircuts and restaurant meals, which cannot be sent in the post, but which have to be supplied by locals. (Hong & McLaren, 2015).

***

What we have here is a *relationship*: When immigration goes up, unemployment goes down.

To see an example of this in practice, consider the USA in the late 1990s: Immigration was high and rising. It peaked around the year 2000. At the same time, unemployment rates were dipping below 4%, and real wages were *increasing* for almost everyone – rich and poor alike. (Griswold, 2002).

This follows a historical precedent.

In 1899, immigration was pretty low. Only three immigrants arrived in the country, for every thousand people who were already there. Unemployment was fairly high at the time – it stood at 12%.

Eight years later, in 1907, the country was experiencing five-times as much immigration. *Fifteen* people were arriving for every one-thousand American residents. But unemployment had plummeted. It was just 3% – a historic low.

Immigration had gone up, and unemployment had gone down.

And this trend continued throughout the century...

Looking at the period from 1890 through to 2014, we see that in those years which had *higher*-than-average rates of immigration, an average of 5.7% of people were unemployed. In the years which had *lower*-than-average immigration, the rate of unemployment went up to 7.2%. Unemployment was 1.5% *lower*, whenever immigration was *higher* than the norm. (Bier, 2016).

This relationship also holds when we compare *states*...

Between 1960 and 1990, the ten states with the highest proportion of foreigners, had an average unemployment rate of 5.9%.

In the ten states which had the lowest proportion of non-nationals, the average unemployment rate was 6.6% – 0.7% *higher*! (Vedder, 1994).

Although we should offer a word of caution: Correlation does not imply causation. Just because higher immigration and lower unemployment go hand-in-hand, we cannot say that one is responsible for the other. It could be that immigrants are creating new jobs. But it could be the other way around: When fewer people are unemployed, businesses struggle to find staff. They might have to *entice* people from elsewhere, to fill their vacant positions. (Bier, 2016).

THE REAL JOB THIEVES

We've spent a lot of time on this subject, and with good reason: To counter the narrative, pushed by the anti-freedom brigade, which states that foreigners *steal* jobs from nationals.

This is a quote from Donald Trump:

"We are going to have an immigration system that works, but one that works for the *American* people... Decades of record immigration have produced lower wages and higher unemployment for our citizens."

Trump was playing a game of "Divide and rule" – pitting foreigners against Americans – suggesting that immigrants were responsible for mass unemployment.

I think we've debunked that nasty myth!

It's not the case that there's a fixed number of jobs – that if some go to foreigners, then there'll be fewer for everyone else. Foreigners enlarge the pie. They create at least as many jobs as they take, and therefore help to *reduce* unemployment. (Bier, 2016).

Yet despite this reality, many people still fall for the lie.

In 2008, 63% of Brits believed that a reduction in immigration would be a good thing, because it'd mean "More jobs for British-born workers". A YouGov poll, from 2013, found that six-in-ten Brits believed that, "Immigrants are taking the jobs and driving down (the) wage rates of British-born workers". And a 2011 poll, by IPSOS Mori, found that a similar proportion believed that immigrants made it *more* difficult for people to get jobs. Only 20% of respondents saw this for the falsehood it was.

Just over half the people in Hungary, Spain and Italy were also labouring under the delusion that immigrants take jobs which would've otherwise gone to a local. So it's a widespread misconception. But it's certainly not universal: That same study found that just 23% of Swedes believed that immigrants steal jobs. 45% *disagreed* with this statement. And that's cause for hope. It shows that perceptions can vary. People might change their minds, if we present them with the facts. We just need to spread the word! (Duffy & Frere-Smith, 2014).

***

So, are foreigners taking *any* of our jobs?

Well, yeah, sort of.

Whenever a company shuts down a factory in your country, and moves it to the so-called "Third World" – and whenever a business relocates one of its departments overseas – then jobs really are being lost at home. Someone on the other side of the globe is taking a position which had previously been filled by one of your neighbours.

According to Zippia, two-thirds of American businesses outsource at least one department. Around 300,000 American jobs are sent abroad, *every single year.*

And according to a Princeton study, thirty-million American positions – almost a fifth of the jobs in the country – are vulnerable to outsourcing in the near future.

Between 1979 and 2009, eight-million American manufacturing jobs were sent overseas. These days, it's jobs in accounting and IT which are the most vulnerable. Jobs in marketing and call centres are also under threat. (Boskamp, 2023).

But these jobs aren't being *taken*. They're being *given away* by chief executives, who are looking to cut costs, so their firms can make more profit. And they're not going to people who've moved to your country. They're going to sedentary people who've stayed where they were before – many thousands of kilometres away.

There's very little upside.

Those people won't spend their wages in your local area, they won't pay taxes to your government, and they won't establish businesses in your vicinity. It'd be much better if they *had* migrated. At least that way, they'd be creating new jobs near you.

***

Immigration into your country might even help to *reduce* the outsourcing of jobs...

If businesses can employ affordable foreign labour to do the less glamorous tasks – working at night, or cleaning the toilets – then their costs will be reduced, and they'll be *less* likely to move production overseas. The immigrants who perform these essential roles, help to keep workplaces up and running – thereby helping to keep the locals employed.

***

So, let's focus on the real villains: It's not the *foreigners*, "Coming for your jobs". It's the greedy *bosses*, who are sending your jobs overseas. And it's the duplicitous *politicians*, who scapegoat immigrants for "Stealing jobs", when they're doing nothing of the kind.

***

This might all prove to be a moot point.

Automation is set to reduce the need for the vast majority of jobs which exist today. Robots could end up picking our food, making our devices, and loading our shopping onto drones. A great deal of our art and literature might be produced by AI. Entire buildings might be built using 3D printers. Most healthcare could be made redundant, thanks to gene editing. Surgery might be performed by lasers which are far more precise than a shaky human hand.

The Bank of England conducted a study in 2015, which predicted that fifteen-million jobs would be lost to automation, within the space of a few decades. That's around two-fifths of British jobs.

Karl Frei and Michael Osborn, of the University of Oxford, have estimated that 47% of all American jobs face a high risk of being automated, and that a further 19% face a medium risk. (Bastani, 2019).

This doesn't have to be a bad thing. So long as we have access to the things we want, it could be pretty nice to be freed from the obligation to work. But it does make you think: If something *were* to come for our jobs, it probably wouldn't be a foreigner – a Guatemalan or a Romanian. It'll probably be something which contains a microchip, a motor and a camera.

IT'S WIN, WIN, WIN

"Imagine there's no countries. It isn't hard to do.
Nothing to kill or die for, and no religion too.
Imagine all the people, living life in peace.
You may say I'm a dreamer, but I'm not the only one.
I hope someday you'll join us, and the world will be as one."
John Lennon

When the USA joined World War Two, it posted so many men abroad, that it needed to find a new set of workers to fill the positions they'd left behind. And so its government came to an arrangement with the Mexican authorities.

The "Bracero" scheme benefitted both nations: American firms received the workers they needed to sustain the railroad, mining, construction and agricultural sectors. In return, the Mexican economy benefitted from the remittances those labourers sent home. Their workers gained valuable experience. And some of them invested their earnings, after they'd returned to Mexico – helping to develop their homeland.

The Bracero program continued to recruit Mexican workers, on short-term contracts, even *after* the war had ended. But the focus had shifted: Now, the Braceros were only put to work as farmers. The vast majority went to either California or Texas. (Kosack, 2021).

Evaristo Sierra was one of around four-million Braceros who took advantage of the scheme.

He'd been a farmhand since he was nine – herding animals, gathering firewood, and tapping sap from agave. His father and uncles were also farmers. You could say farming was in his blood. So it was an easy decision to make: Evaristo was going to do the same work as before. Only now, he'd receive a much higher wage, in a slightly different location. And he'd be helping the people he loved:

"I became a Bracero *to help my parents* buy a house. I wanted to help *them*."

The bureaucracy was a chore.

After being persuaded to apply by an agent, the twenty-two-year-old had to make the arduous journey to his nearest recruitment centre. He had to wait in line for several hours, pass a series of exams, and provide evidence to show that his labour wouldn't be missed at home.

He was ready to head north.

Evaristo was stopped at the border, where he was sprayed with a lice-killing chemical. He passed a medical examination, and continued on to McAllen, Texas, where he worked for forty-five days – thinning weeds and picking tomatoes – before returning to his Mexican village.

He wouldn't have to wait long for a second assignment.

This time, he was sent to Los Angeles, where he spent a year – weeding, harvesting, and caring for the animals. And from there, he was headhunted by Takahashi Farms.

Evaristo formed a bond with the Japanese-American owner of that establishment. And he made friends with the other Mexican workers. They chatted in the fields, listened to the radio together, played cards, and visited the local town:

"There were about seven or eight of us that got together and went to the cinema. We watched a lot of films." (Alonso, 2020).

It'd be wrong to view Bracero life through sepia-tinted lenses. Whilst Evaristo spoke fondly of his time in the States, other Mexican workers were abused by the locals. Some were underpaid. A few had to travel in dangerous vehicles. Others were made to sleep in chicken coops, tents or barns. (Rosas, 2014). (Mize & Swords, 2010).

But Evaristo achieved everything he'd set out to accomplish. He met the woman of his dreams, returned to his village, got married, built a home, and raised a family. (Alonso, 2020).

***

Evaristo's story ticks so many boxes: He helped to fill a labour shortage. He produced something vital – the food which fed his host nation. He did well for his employer. And he earned the income he needed to settle down.

But the next generation of Mexicans wasn't to be granted the same opportunity as Evaristo.

In 1959, a commission was formed to analyse the Bracero

program. It was hardly neutral: The only member with any research training, Rufus von Kleinsmid, was a eugenicist who believed that Mexicans belonged to a genetically inferior race. Yet despite its obvious flaws, the panel's findings proved to be influential.

President Kennedy cited the commission's report, when he said this, in October 1961:

"Studies of the operation of the Mexican labour program have clearly established that it's adversely affecting the wages, working conditions, and employment opportunities of our own agricultural workers."

The following year, Kennedy's administration attempted to disincentive farmers from recruiting Mexican staff, by boosting their minimum wage. And in 1964, his successor – Lyndon Johnson – terminated the program.

Just under half-a-million Braceros were sent south. Most returned to Mexico almost immediately. The others were gone within the space of a couple of years.

But did the policy have the desired effect? Were more jobs made available for local workers? And did their wages improve at a faster rate than before?

***

When the program was cancelled, more Braceros were employed to pick tomatoes than any other crop. Harvesting machines had existed since the 1950s, but very few were used. There was no need to buy that expensive equipment, whilst Mexican labour remained so cheap and abundant.

That all changed with Johnson's legislation.

In 1965, around sixty-thousand Bracero were picking tomatoes in California. By 1967, there weren't any. To fill the gap, farmers invested in the newish technology. And, by 1968, the transition was complete: Tomato harvesting had been mechanised across the entire state.

We see a similar story when it comes to cotton.

Automated cotton picking had been feasible since the 1920s. It took another couple of decades for complementary technologies to catch up – for more uniform strains of cotton to be developed, and for better herbicides to come onto the market. Yet the uptake remained low. In 1950, only 8% of cotton was harvested using heavy machinery. Then the Bracero program was brought to an end, and everything changed: Within a few years, *78%* of cotton harvesting had been mechanised.

The same thing happened when it came to the farming of sugar beets: Mexican labour was replaced by high-tech equipment.

But not *every* harvest could be mechanized. There weren't any machines which could pick things like asparagus, strawberries, lettuce, citrus and cucumbers.

Farmers couldn't switch from Mexican labour to newfangled machinery. But they didn't recruit American workers, to fill the gap. They simply reduced production.

This affected consumers: Many Americans had to go without the ingredients they loved. Others were forced to pay inflated prices, to import their food from abroad.

But it barely affected workers: There was a tiny bump in employment for domestic farmhands, in 1964 and 1965. But this affected those states which hadn't had any Braceros, as much as those that had. In the years which followed, employment levels actually *went down* for American farm workers. There were *fewer* opportunities than before – even in those states which had lost the largest number of Mexican workers.

The Department of Agriculture admitted as much, two years after the Braceros had been excluded:

"Neither the growers nor the State Employment Service were able to recruit a labour force which would take over the jobs formerly performed by the Braceros."

And this was despite the fact that the government had launched a charm offensive, in a vain attempt to recruit more American workers.

The effect on wages was equally muted.

Salaries did increase after the Braceros departed, although this was hardly surprising – they'd been rising for years, even while the Braceros were employed. But earnings didn't shoot up at an unprecedented rate – they stuck to the long-term trend. And farmhands in those states which had welcomed the greatest number of Mexicans – Texas and California – didn't benefit any more than the farmhands in other states. Their wages increased at a *slower rate* than in other parts of the country.

IMMIGRATION BOOSTS WAGES

The Bracero program is interesting, because it gives us a real-world example of what happens when you remove a huge number of people in one fell swoop.

Just under half-a-million Braceros were dismissed from the workforce, in the space of a couple of years. These Mexicans all worked in a single industry: Agriculture. Most of them worked in a couple of states: California and Texas.

If the rhetoric was correct – if immigrants did take jobs from the locals, and drive down their rates of pay – then we'd expect to see the reverse occur when those people departed. We'd expect there to be more jobs and higher wages for the Americans they left behind.

Indeed, this was why the program was scrapped: Kennedy wanted to exclude the Mexicans, "(Who) were adversely affecting the wages (of Americans)."

But Kennedy was clearly wrong: The Mexicans weren't taking jobs from Americans. Americans didn't fill the positions those Braceros had vacated. And the Mexicans weren't driving down wages: Pay didn't surge when they headed south.

Some work was automated. The production of other crops went into terminal decline. And that was the end of that. (Clemens at al, 2018).

***

Contemporary policy-makers would do well to take note.

When accepting his party's nomination, Donald Trump claimed that: "Decades of record immigration have produced lower wages and higher unemployment for our citizens."

Immigration might have been relatively high, and wages might have been decreasing. But this doesn't mean that the two things are linked.

The previous example shows that expelling immigrants *doesn't* benefit the people they leave behind: Americans were *worse* off after the Braceros left: They didn't have more jobs. They didn't have better pay. And they were left with a *smaller* selection of homegrown food.

We've seen something similar in Britain: When the UK left the European Economic Area, in February 2020, citizens of the other EEA nations lost their automatic right to live and work in the country. The Institute for Fiscal Studies noted that there *was* an increase in job availability, but that this *didn't* lead to an increase in wages: The hospitality sector lost a quarter of its European-born workforce. But wages grew at a *lower* rate in this sector, than in most other industries.

The Chartered Institute of Personnel and Development surveyed employers in the summer of 2021. It found that over three-quarters of businesses who were experiencing staff shortages, had no plans to increase the salaries they were offering.

Firms looked to alternative sources of labour: A few attempted to employ prisoners on temporary release. Others attempted to recruit asylum seekers. Some worked with the government to cajole the long-term unemployed into work. Some firms paid a one-time bonus, to entice recruits. Others increased wages at a steady rate, in line with inflation. But there was little evidence of a bump. Indeed, the withdrawal of immigrant labour coincided with a "Cost of Living Crisis", in which many Brits were left *worse off* than before. (Sumption et al, 2022).

***

The Bracero and Brexit examples deliver a similar message: Drastically reducing the number of immigrant workers, *does not* increase in wages for the people they leave behind.

But what if we could go further? What if we were to suggest that more immigration, might make people *better off*? That higher immigration might lead to *higher* wages?

Several researchers have come to this conclusion...

A British study found that immigration did apply some downward pressure on wages, *but only for the lowest earners*. Each time a batch of immigrants arrived, equivalent in size to 1% of the native population, wages fell by 0.5% – but only for one-in-ten workers – and only for those people who were already earning less than their peers.

At the same time, wages *increased* for 85% of the workforce! Around half the workers saw their wages grow by *over* 0.5%. A worker on the median wage, saw their income increase by 0.6%.

Now, let's consider that during this period – between 1997 and 2005 – a number of immigrants equivalent to 3% of the native population arrived in the UK. This means that the average worker saw their income increase by around 1.8% – purely because of the effects of this immigration. (Dustmann et al, 2013).

This isn't to downplay the fact that a tenth of workers were left worse off than before. But the net effect was positive. A small minority of people lost out by a small amount, while the majority benefitted by a much larger amount.

And we could always compensate those lower earners – by increasing the minimum wage, reducing the lowest rate of income tax, or passing laws to empower their unions. Policies such as these, would be way more effective at increasing wages, than controls on immigration.

***

That British study was far from unique...

An Australian study focused on the years between 2005 and 2015. Looking at the effects of a visa program, which had encouraged skilled workers to move to the country, the report concluded that: "International workers *increase the wages of natives*... We find no evidence of negative effects of the visa programme on the wages of high-skilled or low-skilled native workers." (Crown et al, 2020).

We see something remarkably similar in the USA...

A study in the States looked at the long-term effects of all the immigration which took place between 1990 and 2004. Like in the UK, it found that a small section of the workforce did lose out: People who didn't have a high school diploma, "Lost 1.1% of their real wage". But this loss was outweighed by a much larger gain, experienced by 90% of the population: "In the long run, the average wage of US-born workers experienced a significant increase (+1.8%) as a consequence of immigration." Without that immigration, the average American worker would've been worse off. With open borders and *more* immigration, they'd have probably been much *better* off. (Ottaviano & Peri, 2008).

And we come to the same conclusion when we turn our attention to Europe...

A report from researchers at the World Bank and the University of California, concluded that: "Immigration has had a *positive average wage effect* on native workers". That report argued that Europeans should be more concerned with *emigration*. Losing workers to other countries *did* push wages down. But welcoming people from abroad, had an almost equal and opposite effect – forcing wages up. (Docquier et al, 2011).

***

These are just a handful of papers, from a small selection of academics. A cheerleader for freedom might quote from these studies. But a person with an anti-freedom agenda, might refer to the work of Borjas and von Kleinsmid – people who've reached very different conclusions. Although, it should be noted that their findings have been discredited by their fellow academics. (Borjas, 2003). (Card & Perry, 2016). (Clemens & Hunt, 2019).

So, what's the truth?

We'll have to concede that there remains an element of doubt. But it's not as though the experts are split down the middle.

In 2013, the Chicago Booth University surveyed forty-six leading economists. And we're talking about the crème de la crème: Academics from the likes of Harvard, MIT, Yale, Berkeley, Stanford, Princeton and Chicago.

Those experts were asked to respond to a statement: "The average US citizen would be better off if a larger number of low-skilled foreign workers were legally allowed to enter the US." Only four of the forty-six respondents disagreed with this claim. Half agreed. The rest were either unsure or failed to respond.

The results were even starker when those experts were asked about *high-skilled* immigration. This time, 89% of the experts agreed that, "The average US citizen would be better off if a larger number of highly educated foreign workers were legally allowed to immigrate to the US." There wasn't a single economist who disagreed with this remark. (KentClarkCenter.org/Surveys/high-skilled-immigrants).

***

It makes sense...

Immigrants are outsiders. They feel a need to prove themselves – to show they're worthy of a place in their new society. And so they work that little bit harder. They might even inspire their colleagues to follow their lead. Together, they'll create more wealth. And a little of that wealth should return to the workers, in the form of higher wages. (Bregman, 2017).

Of course, this isn't the only reason that immigrants help to boost wages. As we saw in the previous chapter, immigrants are more likely to open a business. But there's more to this tale. That's because those businesses are also more likely to pay higher salaries: Workers in firms which have a foreign founder, are paid 0.7% more for the same work, when compared to their counterparts at firms which were established by homegrown entrepreneurs. (Azoulay et al, 2020).

This can have a knock-on effect: Their competitors might feel a need to increase *their* wages – for fear that their employees might jump ship, and go to work for those immigrant-run firms.

Some non-nationals will end up doing the sorts of domestic work – as cleaners or nannies – which can liberate the locals from housework. This allows *them* to leave their homes, spend more time in the workplace, and return with a fatter paycheque than before.

Immigrants are also responsible for a lot of consumer spending, as we saw in the previous chapter. When they move to an area, they create demand for things such as haircuts and restaurant meals, which have to be supplied by local workers. This extra demand for labour applies an upward pressure on wages. (Hong & McLaren, 2015).

And there's another reason that immigration can help to boost wages: As we saw with the Bracero example, they're often willing to perform temporary seasonal work, in a variety of locations – whilst most locals prefer to secure long-term employment, near the people and places they love. Mobile and sedentary people do *different types of work,* and they work in *different regions*. That was why American farmers couldn't just replace the Braceros with local workers. The locals had no interest in picking fruit. Americans in other states weren't prepared to move to Texas.

Immigrants do work which *compliments* the work which is done by the locals. They help to create a more vibrant, more varied economy – doing jobs which their neighbours are *unwilling or unable* to do...

FOREIGNERS DO THE JOBS WE'RE UNWILLING OR UNABLE TO DO

Marta Escoto felt that she didn't have a choice. She *had* to leave home. One of her children was ill, and Marta was struggling to pay for their care. So Marta gathered her belongings, and travelled to the States, to earn the money she needed to save her child's life.

Marta didn't pass through the official channels. And so she was forced to do whatever work she could find, no matter the conditions.

In time, she'd find a job as a seamstress, producing uniforms for American soldiers. But her first port of call was a fish-processing plant in Massachusetts.

Skinning, filleting and deboning fish is a gruesome endeavour: Workplaces are malodorous, gungy, grimy and frigid. The work is monotonous, exacting and intense. Employees have been known to develop carpal tunnel syndrome. And accidents are common: Staff have lost fingers in the machines used for removing fish heads. Others have picked up infections from the blood-infused water which is used to clean the fish.

It's little wonder that so few Americans wish to do this kind of work. But it's essential stuff. A nation has to eat! (Felbab-Brown, 2017).

That's where immigrants like Marta come into their own. They fill a gap – doing the kinds of work which the locals tend to avoid.

***

In early 2020, the American government began to shut down parts of the country, in an attempt to curtail the spread of Covid Nineteen. They did, however, make an exception: Some workers were dubbed so "Essential", they were asked to continue their work.

These "Essential" workers – the very people who ensured that America functioned – were often foreign-born: 69% of foreign nationals did jobs that were classed as "Essential". 74% of undocumented people – such as Marta Escoto – did work which fell into this category. (Kerwin et al, 2020).

Foreigners only make up 18% of the American workforce. Yet at the time when Covid hit, 38% of home health aides were non-nationals. These were the people on the front line, waging war on the Coronavirus. They were going out into the community, risking their own lives, in order to save their American peers. (Batalova, 2020).

Like Marta, a great number of America's international residents were helping to keep the nation fed: Of all those people who did the most physically demanding work in this sector – as labourers, graders, sorters, crop producers, meat processors, and commercial bakers – three-in-ten were foreign-born.

In California, 69% of agricultural workers were born abroad. In Alaska, seven-in-ten seafood processors were immigrants. And in Nebraska, two-thirds of meat processors had moved from another country. (Ruggles et al, 2020).

America *needs* to attract these people.

Back in 1960, around half the men who'd been born in the USA were high school dropouts – the kind of people you might expect to do the most taxing kinds of work. These days, only one-in-ten Americans leave school before completing their education. That's great news for a large chunk of the population, who are likely to find less precarious work. But it leaves a gap. America *needs a different intake of people* to do the jobs which these Americans might've done in the past

– working in sanitation, home healthcare, and food preparation – as nannies, cotton pickers, and night watchmen. Fortunately, there *is* a group of workers who are up to the task: Nomadic souls like Marta Escoto. (Rawlins, 2011).

***

It's not just that foreigners are more willing to complete this essential work. They're also more likely to *move around a country*, to find themselves a job...

We saw this with the Braceros: Hundreds-of-thousands of Mexicans moved from place to place, each time they secured a new contract. During the 1970s and 1980s, another group of immigrants migrated to Texas in record numbers, to help the nation capitalise on its oil boom. And in the 1990s, a third group of new arrivals headed to Silicon Valley. (Orrenius, 2016).

This also happens in the UK: While we were living in Bulgaria, we met a couple who spent their summers picking fruit in Britain. They'd worked in Kent, Wrexham, Wisbech, and so many other places that I struggled to keep up! That couple tended to work in two or three different locations each summer. And why not? Nothing was tying them to one particular spot. And they liked to experience life in different villages and towns.

***

Foreigners are more likely to get their hands dirty, doing the sorts of hard graft that many sedentary people would rather not do themselves. They're over-represented in the hospitality industry, domestic service, construction, and light manufacturing. (Griswold, 2002).

And overseas workers are also more likely to work at the opposite end of the spectrum: More than four-in-ten of the medical scientists and software developers in the USA are foreign-born. International workers are over-represented when we look at university professors, engineers, mathematicians, nurses, doctors and dentists.

They're needed.

American firms are crying out for more people with STEM degrees. The number of positions in these sectors, rose by 34% in the

2010s. But universities aren't churning out American science graduates at anywhere near the required rate. The United States *needs* to attract foreigners, to fill the gap.

Fortunately, people are answering the call: When we look at all the PhD candidates and fellows at American universities, we see that almost two-thirds of those who work in computing came from overseas. 56% of physicists, and 55% of mathematicians, were also international. (Wildavsky, 2010).

***

Those foreigners are returning the favour...

A report for the New American Economy, found that of all those patents which were filed by the top American universities, three-quarters had been submitted by projects which included at least one foreign inventor. These people came from eighty-eight different nations. Between them, they contributed to 1,500 patent applications in a single year. (Bloomberg, 2012).

We find something similar when we focus on the most innovative organisations in the *private sector*: 72% of the patents filed at Qualcomm were submitted by immigrants. At Cisco, that number stood at 60%. At General Electric, it was 64%. And at Merck, it was 65%. (Goldin et al, 2012).

These numbers add up.

Foreigners in America hold *a quarter of all the patents*, even though they only represent around 14% of the population. (Azoulay et al, 2020).

And their creativity is contagious.

Whenever America welcomes 1% more people on H-1B visas, the number of patents which are issued goes up by *15%*. Those mobile people inspire their American peers, who file more patents themselves. (Goldin, 2011). (Kerr & Lincoln, 2010).

IMMIGRATION FUELS ECONOMIC GROWTH

Immigrants do *complementary* work – filling night shifts, cleaning the offices where we work, and picking our food. They fill empty positions in growth industries. They help firms to develop better products. They establish firms, and launch entire industries.

You put these things together, and the outcome should be obvious: These people *enrich* our nations.

Indeed, the data is pretty unequivocal: *Immigration leads to a more than proportional increase in GDP*.

The International Monetary Fund looked at those instances in which there'd been an "Immigration shock" in an advanced economy – where a large influx of people had arrived, in a manner which was out of kilter with the long-term trend. They found that when the immigration-to-employment ratio increased by a single percentage point, *total* economic output went up by almost 1%. That's not because there were a lot more workers. Total employment only increased by around 0.35%, and a large part of that was attributed to a 0.2% improvement in employment for *domestic* workers. The boon was brought about thanks to a boost in *productivity*. Those immigrants performed new tasks – employing a skill set that *complimented* the locals' work – enabling everyone to achieve more. (Piazza et al, 2020).

***

Different studies have reached similar conclusions...

Another IMF investigation, looked at eighteen advanced economies, over thirty-years – from 1980 through to 2010. It found that whenever the proportion of immigrants went up by 1%, relative to the total population of a country – total GDP went up by 2%. The benefits were felt by the entire population – rich and poor alike. (Jaumotte, 2016).

Economists based on four continents, came together to present a paper at Purdue University. They found that if developed countries were to welcome more workers from developing countries, by an amount equivalent to 3% of their current workforce, then the average *local* would gain $382, thanks to the boost in productivity which would ensue – without doing any extra work themselves. The larger part of this amount – $227 – would be generated thanks to low-skilled immigration. (Walmsley et al, 2005).

Focusing solely on the USA, the George W. Bush Institute also found that immigration helped to increase the amount of GDP which was received by the *sedentary* population. Their slice of the pie increased by between $36b and $72b each year, because of immigration. This means that the average American pockets an *additional* $150 to $300, *every single year*, because some *other* people managed to enter the country. (Orrenius, 2016).

And FWD – a lobby group established by Mark Zuckerberg – has calculated that welcoming in another two-million immigrants, would provide a dividend worth $2,500 per American per year, by the time that 2050 rolls around.

Their research finds that reducing immigration would make Americans *worse off*. (Connor, 2021).

***

The effect is greatest in those states which welcome more new residents...

States which have the lowest number of foreign citizens – such as West Virginia and Mississippi – also have the highest rates of poverty, and the lowest levels of GDP per capita. States with the highest number of foreign residents – such as New York and Massachusetts – are among the wealthiest in the land. (Yglesias, 2019).

This relationship holds when we consider the countries in the OECD: Places like Bulgaria and Romania, have a low proportion of non-nationals, and a low GDP per capita. Places such as Switzerland and Australia, have a high proportion of international residents, and a large economic output. (Hanson & McIntosh, 2016).

Once again, we should note that correlation does not imply causation: It could be that people are drawn to those nations which are already rich.

And so Giovanni Peri, an economist at the University of California, has crunched the numbers – investigating what happens when new immigrants move to individual states, to see the *direct* effect of their arrivals.

Peri concluded that those states which welcome the most foreign workers, experience the fastest rates of *growth*: When immigration swells a state's workforce by 1%, output-per-worker increases by 0.5%. *Everyone produces more* (on average) – even when they're performing the same tasks as before. (Peri, 2012).

And this effect is writ large across the globe: Only 3.6% of people have moved abroad. But they're responsible for 10% of global output. The average migratory worker produces almost three-times as much output as their sedentary peers! (Khanna, 2021).

***

None of this is particularly surprising. Immigrants are entrepreneurial, they work hard, and they innovate at an unprecedented rate. You throw these things together, and you'd expect to see more growth.

What isn't so obvious, is the fact that immigrants don't only enrich their host nations. They *enrich the entire planet.*

We touched on this in the "Nurture" section, where we showed that emigration was a boon for poorer nations. Emigrants send massive amounts of money back to their loved ones. They inspire the people they leave behind. Sometimes, they return home – arriving with new skills and expertise – opening new businesses and producing new things.

And we touched on this again, when we spoke about those people who move out of "Necessity" – to escape from their poverty. We mentioned that open borders would increase *global* GDP by a massive amount: Seven separate studies have found that "Gross Worldwide Product" would increase by between 67% and 172%, if we were to open our borders and allow labour to flow to those places where it could be utilized more efficiently. (Pritchett, 2010). (Kennan, 2012).

If just half the people in the world's poorest regions were to move to developed nations, and receive an additional $7,500 a year as a result, then they'd gain *$23t* between them. That'd represent a 38%

increase in global GDP!

Imagine if *more* than half the people moved. Imagine if they each gained more than $7,500 a year. The effects would be even larger! (Clemens, 2011).

According to the Harvard economist, Lant Pritchett, open borders could be worth as much as *$65t* a year. (Bregman, 2017).

Can you think of any other policy, which would be worth anywhere near as much?

DEFUSING THE DEMOGRAPHIC TIMEBOMB

We've already shown that some nations, such as Japan and Canada, are encouraging inward migration – to fill the gaps in their workforces...

As nations become richer, their birthrates tend to decline. We're already seeing a birthrate below the "Replacement rate" in several developed nations. At the same time, people are living longer than ever before. In Europe, the median age is forty-three. That's ten years higher than the global average.

When you put these things together, you end up with a demographic time bomb – with more pensioners, and fewer workers to support them.

The key statistic here is called the "Dependency Rate". This is the ratio of working-aged people (aged twenty to sixty-four) to retirees (aged sixty-five and over).

By 2050, the dependency ratio will be seventy-eight in Spain. This means that a hundred workers will have to produce everything they need for themselves, their children, and seventy-eight retirees. That's quite a tall order – especially when you consider that the ratio was only thirty-two, back in 2019!

Things will be even more extreme elsewhere: The dependency ratio will be seventy-nine in South Korea, and eighty-one in Japan. (UN Department of Economic and Social Affairs, 2019).

A Japanese person born today, has a life expectancy of *107*! But the population of that country is actually shrinking – at a rate of half-a-million people a year – because Japanese women are only giving birth to a small number of children. This means that there'll be a shrinking number of Japanese workers, in the years to come, but they'll have to support even *more* pensioners than they do today.

These countries aren't alone.

According to the United Nations, *one-in-six* people will be aged sixty-five or older, worldwide, by the time 2050 rolls around. Back in 1990, less than *one-in-sixteen* people fell into this category.

The old-age dependency ratio is expected to more than double in most parts of Asia, Latin America, the Caribbean, and Northern Africa. (UN Department of Economic and Social Affairs, 2019).

By 2030, a quarter of China's 1.5 billion residents will be sixty-five or older. China is already spending more on pension payments, than it receives in social security. And that gap will widen, once China's population begins to decline.

In the States, back in 1950, around sixteen workers were paying into social security programs, for every elderly person who was withdrawing their pension. But by 2035, there'll only be two workers to fund each retiree. (Wu, 2022).

Will those workers be able to shoulder the burden? Will they be able to produce all the food, electricity and healthcare that these people are going to need?

Automation will certainly help: "Care Robots" are already assisting the elderly in Japan. Panasonic is manufacturing hospital beds which can transform into wheelchairs.

But this might not be enough.

Immigration could help to plug the gap, in richer nations at least.

In the United States, it already is...

Without immigration, the American workforce would begin to contract within the space of two decades. But if people continue to arrive at the current rate, the American workforce would actually *increase* by thirty-million, during the next fifty years. (Griswold, 2002). (Felbab-Brown, 2017).

That will be crucial for the country's economy, if it's to retain a competitive advantage...

In 2010, the World Economic Forum predicted that the USA would have to entice 26 million people, during the following two decades, just to maintain the rates of economic growth it'd experienced during the previous twenty years. (Bennet, 2010).

This is because *most immigrants are of working age.*

According to the US Census Bureau, 78.7% of its foreign-born population were aged between sixteen and sixty-four, in 2019. Only 7.2% were under nineteen, and only 6.4% were over seventy-five. (Wu, 2022).

Countries need these people – aged sixty-five and under – to go to work, produce goods, supply services, provide care, and fund our pensions. These immigrants *keep the rest of us alive.*

IMMIGRANTS PAY TAX

When nations reemerged from lockdown, in the aftermath of the Covid pandemic, economic output began to rebound: It increased by 10.5%, across the OECD nations. And that resulted in an even *larger* increase in tax receipts. Government revenues surged by 12.8%, in those same countries, between 2021 and 2022. (Perez-Navarro, 2022).

It stands to reason: People who are underemployed, receive lower incomes, and therefore pay lower rates of tax. Get them back to work, put them on a full-time wage, and they'll move up the tax bands. They'll pay a higher *proportion* of their income in tax.

The same applies for business: After the pandemic, firms began to turn a profit once again. They paid tax on those profits. They also paid taxes on some of their sales.

Now put everything together: Immigration leads to a more-than-proportionate increase in GDP. And an increase in GDP, leads to a more-than-proportionate increase in tax receipts.

The conclusion should be obvious: A little immigration, will generate a large amount of taxation, which can be used to fund essential services.

***

But the effect isn't only indirect. That's because immigrants also *pay more tax...*

We already noted that immigrants are more likely to be of working-age. In the USA, more than three-quarters of foreign nationals are aged between twenty and sixty-four.

But we should also note that working-aged immigrants are more likely to actually work: According to America's Bureau for Labour Statistics, 65% of foreign-born residents over the age of twenty-five, participated in the labour force (in 2021). For locals, the rate was 3.7% lower.

Most immigrants are working-aged, and most are actually in work. This means that a much higher proportion of immigrants are earning a wage, and paying tax on their earnings.

The numbers add up.

In 2019, immigrants in the USA paid $492b out of the $1.6t the government received from workers. This means that immigrants paid just over 30% of all personal taxes. (Wang, 2022).

What's even more surprising, is that *undocumented* workers were also paying tax: In 2010, 1.8 million people were using *fake* social security cards, to help them get a job. Between them, they were contributing around $13b a year in social security. Since they weren't using real accounts, they might not benefit from those contributions, which does seem rather unfair. But it goes to show that they're paying their way – contributing more in taxes, than they can expect to receive in return. (Felbab-Brown, 2017).

And in addition to this kind of taxation – taken from employees' paycheques – anywhere up to three-quarters of undocumented workers also file their own tax returns! Once again, they have little choice but to invent a Tax Identification Number. And once again, this means that they might not receive anything back themselves. (Wang, 2022).

***

According to research from the OECD, the average immigrant pays more in taxation than the average local, in countries such as Austria, Ireland, Spain and England.

They also pay more than they receive.

When the OECD totted up the figures from twenty-five of their member states, they discovered that immigrants paid $2.5t in taxation. But they only consumed $2t in public services. This means that the countries which took them in, were rewarded with a kind of profit, worth *half-a-trillion dollars* a year! (Scarpetta, 2022).

The Office for Budget Responsibility, in the United Kingdom, has calculated that if the nation were to welcome another eighty-thousand international residents each year, its public debt would fall by 30% in the space of fifty years – because of these contributions. But if immigration were to proceed at its current, lower rate – then the nation's debt would *increase* by 39%. (Chote et al, 2018).

And the National Academies, over in the USA, has concluded that the average immigrant family paid $80,000 more in tax than they received, over the course of their lifetimes (in research from 1997). That figure jumped up to a staggering $198,000, when the researchers focused on families which had university degrees. Between them, immigrants in the USA were paying $11.5b *more* in tax, than they were receiving in return, *every single year*. (Smith & Edmonston, 1997).

In 2019, the average foreigner in the States paid $165.52 more to the state than they received in return. Americans, on the other hand, received $51.46 more than they paid. Foreigners' taxes were paying for services which were being used by their hosts! (Ranker et al, 2021).

These effects add up.

According to another study, immigrants paid almost $500m more in Social Security than they took out of the system, between 1998 and 2022. Their net contribution is expected to top the $2t mark by 2072. (Wu, 2022).

A more recent report by the Cato Institute supported these findings. It found that immigrants in the States were less likely to claim welfare: Between 97% and 98% didn't receive any cash assistance whatsoever. They also used less Medicaid: The average American received $984 worth of Medicaid, but the average immigrant only received $572. (Ku & Bruen, 2013).

We see something similar in the UK: Only 27% of foreigners bothered to claim benefits in Britain when they were unemployed. (Fernández-Reino & Rienzo, 2022).

Between 2001 and 2011, immigrants paid around £25b *more* into the system, than they took out. People from EEA nations, contributed 34% more than they received in return! Just like in the States, they were subsidising the local population, who received more than they paid. (Dustmann & Frattini, 2013).

Overseas students also pay *tuition fees* to the state: Their annual contribution was worth more than €45b in the USA, around €25b in Australia, just over €15b in the UK, and around €10b in Canada.

And immigrants' general taxation, can also help us to *spread the load*.

Governments have "Fixed public expenditures", which don't increase when a population grows. When a new batch of foreigners arrives on our shores, we might have to spend a little more on healthcare, because a few of them will get ill. But we won't have to fund any more national parks, galleries or museums. We probably won't open any extra military bases, or hold more parades. The taxes we'll receive from our guests can still be used to pay for these things – meaning that the rest of us won't have to pay quite so much ourselves.

BORDER CONTROL IS COSTING YOU A FORTUNE

Donald Trump was getting ready to address an audience, not far from the Mexican border. A couple of months had passed since he'd lost the 2020 election, but nothing seemed to have changed: Trump was still wearing a generic suit, with a white shirt and red tie. His face was still bronzed, his hair was still yellow, and his lectern was still emblazoned with a seal, marked "President of the United States".

The billionaire was in a celebratory mood, because his "Big, beautiful wall" had reached a landmark. It had gotten a little bigger. Now, it was over *seven-hundred* kilometres long.

As Trump strode into position, a song by Lee Greenwood blared out from the speakers. Its lyrics proclaimed: "I'm proud to be an American, where at least I know I'm free". And yet the irony seemed to be lost on the audience, who were celebrating a wall which was *reducing* their freedom to move.

Trump began:

"We've worked long and hard to get this done. They said it couldn't be done, and we got it done. One of the largest infrastructure projects in the history of our country... It's steel. It's concrete inside the steel. And then it's rebar. A lot of heavy rebar inside the concrete. And it's as strong as you're going to get and strong as you can have. But we gave you a hundred percent of what you wanted."

But what, exactly, did his audience *want*?

The border between Mexico and the USA is a little over three-thousand kilometres long. So the wall covered less than a quarter of its length. It was strong and imposing. But it only covered forty miles of new ground. Most of it was merely an upgrade – a more permanent version of a fence which had been constructed under the leaderships of Bush and Obama. And Trump hadn't managed to make the Mexican government pay, as he'd promised during his campaign. It had cost American taxpayers *$15b*!

That's such a large amount of money, it's hard to comprehend. But let's give it a go...

To build a new hospital in the USA, you'll need somewhere between $60m and $190m. So, for the same price as Trump's wall, the country could've built anywhere between 79 and 250 hospitals.

Let that sink in for a moment: For the price of an incomplete wall, which covered less than a quarter of the border, Americans could've had up to *250* sparkling new hospitals! Just think of the lives that could've been saved.

***

It'd be wrong to single out Trump...

His successor, Joe Biden, did promise a change of tack, stating: "(There) will not be another foot of wall". (Rodriguez, 2021).

And yet Biden is still committed to spending an exorbitant amount of money in America's war on mobility.

An official White House briefing, released in March 2023, stated that:

"The Biden-Harris Administration has secured more resources for border security than any of the presidents who preceded him, (and) deployed the most agents ever – more than 23,000 – to address the situation at the border... (The Biden-Harris) budget includes nearly $25b for US Customs and Border Protection, and Immigration and Customs Enforcement (ICE)... A new $4.7b contingency fund to aid the Department of Homeland Security... (And) more than $1.5b (for) the Executive Office for Immigration Review." (WhiteHouse.Gov).

These are staggering sums.

Back in 1990, the US government only allocated $263m to its "Border Patrol Budget". By 2021, that figure had skyrocketed to $4.9b. That represented a 1851% increase, in the space of just thirty-one years.

We see something similar when we look at the "CBP & ICE Annual Budgets". These rose from $9.2b in 2003, to $26b in 2021 – an increase of 183% in eighteen years. (Cruz, 2021).

We're not talking about the $15b cost of the border wall – a *one-off expense*. We're talking about spending $26b *every single year*.

Once again, it might help to break this number down...

On average, it costs $150,000 to treat an American who has cancer. For $26b you could treat 173,000 cancer patients *every single year*. You could treat two-million patients, in a little over a decade.

This is where the lunacy really begins to dawn: In order to stop people from entering the country – enriching its culture, opening businesses, creating jobs, pushing up wages, fuelling growth, and paying a disproportionate amount of tax – the American authorities are paying an unfathomable amount of money, which could've been used to build hundreds of hospitals, and save millions of people from cancer!

And border control doesn't even work!

Between 1980 and 2007, the American government spent increasing amounts of money to "Secure" the Mexican border. And at the very same time, the number of undocumented Mexicans in the USA *grew seven-fold*.

It wasn't only a colossal waste of cash. It was also counterproductive. (Massey, 2007).

***

So, what's the alternative?

If you can't stop people from crossing the border, you could always attempt to deport them *after* they've settled.

But that'd also cost a fortune – around $10,070 per person. Given that there are over eleven-million undocumented humans in the USA, the bill would come to somewhere in the region of $114b. That's around $440 for every American adult. (Wolgin, 2015).

There'd also be an *indirect* price to pay...

Removing undocumented people, would reduce the median income of the households they leave behind – from $41,000 to $21,000. That'd plunge several families into poverty. If one-third of US-born children were to remain in the States, after their parents had been dumped overseas, it'd cost another $118b to help care for them until they came of age. The nation's housing market would be thrown into disarray, because undocumented people have taken out more than a million mortgages. And economic output would take a blow: $4.7t would be lost in the space of a decade. (Warren & Kerwin, 2017).

***

So far, we've focused on the United States. But that nation is far from unique. Other nations are also squandering billions – doing an awful job of "Controlling their borders".

A 2021 report by the Transnational Institute, found that Canada was throwing away $1.5b a year, militarising its frontier. That sum was fifteen-times greater than the amount they'd committed to combating the climate emergency!

The United Kingdom and Australia each wasted $2.7b a year, in their war on free movement. Germany, Japan and France – were squandering $6.6b between them. (Miller et al, 2021).

***

It's insane.

If we were to open our borders, the immigrants who'd arrived would send so much money home – in the form of remittances – that we'd be able to scrap foreign aid, and their nations would still be better off than before.

Scrapping foreign aid would've saved UK taxpayers £12.8b, in 2022. It'd have saved American taxpayers $50b, in 2021.

***

We misuse billions of dollars of taxpayers' money each year – building walls, policing borders, processing applications, housing asylum seekers, imprisoning so-called "Illegals", staging elaborate court cases, and deporting human beings who share most of our DNA.

Just think of what we could achieve, if we used that money to do good – to eradicate poverty, heal the sick, or end homelessness.

Our leaders are psychopathic. They're wasting our money, whilst ignoring our real needs.

BUT WHY? (OH WHY, OH WHY?)

"In the early 1970s, an Indian lawmaker cheekily asked Indira Gandhi: 'Can the prime minister explain why Indians seem to thrive under every government in the world except hers?' She had no good answer."

Robert Guest

We've seen how immigrants contribute to their host nations. But we should also take a moment to ask why: *Why* do these new arrivals achieve so much?

It's not because they're inherently different. In the chapter on "Nature", we showed how people born abroad are almost identical to ourselves. Some might possess the Wanderlust Gene – they might have a penchant for taking risks, which could inspire them to open a business and create new jobs. But many people who move, *don't* possess this gene. Many sedentary people *do*. Pick any person, in any place, and at least 99.4% of your DNA will be the same. On average, 99.9% of your DNA will be a perfect match.

If it's not "Nature", it has to be something else.

"Circumstances" can play a role. International citizens aren't representative of the wider population. They're a self-selecting bunch.

Impoverished people cannot afford to travel abroad. People who own assets and land in a specific place, might feel inclined to stay put. And people who hold titles – such as "Lord" or "King" – might prefer to remain in those places where those titles are respected.

When people first arrive in America, they usually have a little stash of money. But they tend not to have much in the way of fixed assets. Many have skills and qualifications – the sorts of "Social capital" that can be moved from place to place. They tend to be young, but of a working age. Many are already doing well, before they embark on their journey. And most are fairly healthy: International people have lower rates of mortality, chronic disease and obesity – and they're less likely to smoke – when compared to members of their host societies. That remains the case, even if they hail from a poorer nation, and even when they're members of a lower socioeconomic group. (Lindstrom &

López-Ramírez, 2010). (Domnich et al, 2012).

Of course, not every international citizen is a cash-rich, super-healthy graduate. Refugees might arrive with nothing to their name. Globetrotters don't only achieve things because of their circumstances. They succeed because of the *experiences* they accrue along the way.

In the words of Felix Marquardt, "It's not so much that (migrants) left because they were exceptional, but rather that they *became* exceptional as a result of leaving."

Immigrants are forced to adapt, to survive in a foreign land. They have to use their initiative, find a niche for themselves, take risks, be a little bit curious, battle against the odds, form new alliances, and show a great deal of *ingenuity*...

CROSS-BORDER LIVING
FOSTERS CREATIVITY

The "Duncker Candle Test" is a bit of a classic...

Invented by Karl Duncker, back in the 1940s, the experiment involves a box of drawing pins, some matches, a corkboard, and a candle. Participants are asked to attach the candle to the board, and light it in a safe manner – without spilling any wax.

Can you deduce how this might be done?

There is a solution, but it requires some creative thinking.

You begin by removing the pins from their box. You then attach that box to the corkboard, using a few of those pins, such that it forms a kind of shelf. Then you place the candle inside that shelf – pinning it in place from below. Now, it should be safe to light.

It's hardly rocket science. But it's a nifty trick.

Lots of people pass Duncker's test at the first time of asking. But several come up short. Some try to attach the candle to the board using a pin. Others try to glue it in place using a dollop of melted wax.

The experiment is seen as a test of creativity, because it requires subjects to use an object – the pin box – in a new and original way.

Participants must move beyond a preconceived notion – that the pin box should be used for storing pins – and repurpose that object into something new: A shelf for a candle. (Duncker, 1945).

***

A younger generation of academics, at the Kellogg School of Management, revisited Duncker's experiment in 2007. They tested 205 MBA students, around two-thirds of whom had lived in another country.

The results were revealing: Those who had lived abroad, were approximately 50% *more* likely to solve the puzzle at the first time of asking.

What was more, the academics found a strong and significant correlation: The *longer* people had spent outside of the country of their birth, the more likely they were to discover the solution. (Maddux & Galinsky, 2009).

And this experiment was by no means unique.

In a separate study, participants were asked to write down all the things they could imagine doing with a bin bag. Those people who'd lived abroad, came up with significantly longer lists. (Leung et al, 2008).

The two studies reached the same conclusion: *People who'd lived abroad, were more creative.*

This might have a little to do with their genetics: The Wanderlust Gene isn't only associated with a willingness to travel – it's also associated with "Bursts of focused creativity". (Shah, 2020).

But this creativity is enhanced by their lived *experiences*.

When you move abroad, you get a taste of different cultures, and end up with *multiple frames of reference*. The chances are you'll be able to see more options, possibilities, interpretations and nuance. You'll be better placed to come up with creative solutions in life, society, business and the arts. You might combine reggae with electronica, to create jungle music. You might invent a business such as PayPal, or a platform such as YouTube.

You might not have much of a choice. You might have to improvise, just to get by.

Here in the Philippines, it's hard to get nice crusty bread. If you want some, you'll have to learn to make your own. Alternatively, you could adapt to the local diet – eating rice for breakfast, lunch and dinner.

I've had to start doing several things I was too privileged to do before: Slicing the corn off the cob by hand, instead of buying sweetcorn in tins. Removing the scales and organs from fresh fish. Arranging for drinking water to be delivered. Cooking my dogs' food, using whatever cheap cuts of meat I can find. And familiarising myself with different types of bananas – some of which have green peel, but are ready to eat. (You need to squeeze them, to see if they're ripe).

These things are normal for the locals, but they're new for me. I'm being forced to innovate and adapt.

I expect that every new arrival must face similar challenges, while they're settling down. They'll also have to learn to improvise. And that'll stand them in good stead, should they ever decide to open a business, become a musician, or embark on a new career.

THE SECOND-GENERATION ADVANTAGE

Even if you don't use that creativity dividend to get ahead yourself, there's still a chance that you'll push your offspring onto glory – reminding them of the sacrifices you made on their behalf, and inspiring *them* to go the extra mile. You might encourage, cajole, or even shame your children – persuading them to study more, practice for longer, and exert far more effort than their peers.

Parental pressure isn't always beneficial. Taken to extremes, it might cause depression, or result in low self-esteem. But exerted in moderation, it can help to provide those youths with a *second-generation advantage.*

Let's not forget that the children of immigrants won't have to endure the same struggles as their parents. They're born into the local culture. They'll speak the local language. But, at the same time, they're still going to have the same multicultural reference points, and the same steely determination which benefitted their parents.

Over the course of the previous few chapters, we've met a raft of people who were the sons and daughters of immigrants: Grime, 2Tone and dubstep were invented by the *children* of the Windrush Generation. Jeff Bezos was adopted by a Cuban father. The co-founder of Airbnb has a Polish father. Henry Ford's father emigrated from Ireland. IBM was created by an entrepreneur who had two German parents.

These things didn't come about by chance.

Studies have shown that the children of immigrants in the USA, are less likely to break the rules, less likely to drop out of high school, and more likely to go to university. On average, they achieve higher grades than their classmates. (Hao & Bonstead-Bruns, 1998). (Kao & Tienda, 1995). (Perreira et al, 2006). (Bankston & Zhou, 2002).

Asian Americans are a particular success story: Compared to their peers, the average second-generation Asian American ends up with a higher level of academic achievement, a higher wage, *and* a higher level of wealth. (Harris et al, 2008).

In general, first-generation immigrants in the USA have lower incomes than their neighbours. A 2013 report by Pew Research, found that the median household income for a first-generation immigrant family was $45,800. The median American family takes home $12,400 more than that. But this gap disappears within a single generation: Second-generation immigrant households have a median income which is pretty much the same as their peers.

Whereas only 29% of first-generation immigrants in the USA held a bachelor's degree, 36% of second-generation immigrants went on to graduate from university. That's five percentage points higher than the national average.

The poverty rate for first-generation immigrants was 18%. But for second-generation immigrants, it was only 11% – two percentage points *lower* than the national average.

The same study also found that second-generation immigrants were more likely to value hard work and career success, when compared to the general population. And they integrated more than their parents' generation: Their English tended to be better, they had more friends from other racial groups, and they were more likely to consider themselves "Typical Americans".

They also integrated *with each other*: Only 18% of Americans marry people from other races. But 15% of second-generation immigrants intermarry. For Asian Americans, that figure jumps up to 23%. And for Hispanics, it stands at 26%. (Taylor et al, 2013).

INTERNATIONAL CITIZENS TRADE ACROSS INTERNATIONAL BORDERS

Immigrants also have a natural advantage, when it comes to *international trade*...

Imagine that you spent your youth in one place, you moved to a different nation, and now you're looking to establish a business. Don't you think you'd use every resource at your disposal – sourcing supplies from one country, and selling your wares in the other? You're familiar with both economies. Why not put your contacts and knowledge to use?

***

This was certainly the case with a Chinese woman named Mei Xu...

When China opened up to the outside world, its government established some schools which specialised in foreign languages. It wished to train the next generation of trade envoys and diplomats.

Mei wanted a slice of the action! She sat a load of exams, held her breath, waited, and eventually made the grade. She was in! But this was just the start. Mei studied hard, went to university, and interned at the United Nations – putting her language skills to the test – arranging funding for various schemes, installing water pumps, and making friends along the way.

Then the "Bad thing" happened: In 1989, Chinese students protested against the government in Tiananmen Square. The authorities became suspicious of students. Several were packed off to "Re-education Camps", and Mei was sent to work in a warehouse.

It was a grind. Mei grew frustrated, applied for a place on a journalism degree, and moved to the USA.

When she graduated, she found herself in another tedious job – helping a firm to export merchandise to China. But this time, there was a silver lining: That position came with accommodation – an apartment near Bloomingdales. With a penchant for "Pretty things", Mei was enticed. But she noticed that something was amiss: That swanky department store had a fantastic array of clothing, games and gadgets. And yet its homeware section came up a little short.

So Mei and her husband did something that no local would've been positioned to do: *They got in touch with their contacts in China*, who sent over a selection of household items. Mei took those products to a trade show. She totted up her sales, realised that her candles were more popular than any other item, returned home, and began to experiment in her basement – making her own candles, using soup cans as moulds – combining an array of scents and colours.

Mei used her knowledge of the Chinese market again: This time she ordered in bulk – getting Chinese factories to produce *her* designs. They began to sell. And so Mei opened a factory, back in China – putting her sister in charge of production.

***

Like many of the businesses we met before, Mei's – Pacific Trade International – serves American consumers. Mei filled a gap in the homeware market which no local had managed to spot, because she came at things with an outsider's perspective.

Her company also employs Americans. Technicians in Rockville, manage the design process. And in 2010, Mei opened a factory in Maryville, to process urgent orders.

But her enterprise only got off the ground, because Mei was able to tap into the Chinese factory scene – using her knowledge of that nation, and the contacts she'd accrued in her youth. People who'd only ever lived in America, wouldn't have been able to do such a thing. (Guest, 2011).

***

Foreign entrepreneurs might also get ahead by serving *other immigrants*.

We touched on this whilst discussing the South Asian restaurants which are popular in the United Kingdom. They started off by serving curries to people who'd moved from the Indian subcontinent. Then they expanded their customer base – attracting a local clientele.

I've had personal experience of this myself: When we lived in Bulgaria, my wife missed the comfort foods she'd enjoyed in her youth. Each time I visited the capital, she insisted that I visit a Filipina immigrant, who'd opened an import business. I had to pay inflated prices for some very basic items – specific brands of noodles and soy sauce – to give my wife a little taste of home.

That trade kept an immigrant in business. But it must've also been a boon for the exporters she used in the Philippines, and for a handful of couriers.

It should be easy to see why it works: Filipinos know what other Filipinos will want. They know where they can source those items.

Can you imagine what would've happened, if a Bulgarian had tried to serve that same demographic? They might've succeeded in the end, but I expect they'd have made several costly errors along the way.

***

This "Nostalgia Trade" is big business...

The average Filipino, Honduran and Ethiopian – who resides in the USA – spends *$1,000* a year, importing things from the land of their birth. They create a massive market for immigrants to supply. (Newland, 2010).

***

But immigrants don't only import things *from* the lands of their birth. They also send items *back* the other way.

Mei Xu also fits into this category: After establishing herself in the USA, Mei opened a second business – "Blissliving" – which sells brightly-coloured furniture *in China*. (Guest, 2011).

This is circumstantial. But it's a part of a broader trend.

A study commissioned by the Canadian government, found that

immigrant-led businesses were more likely to export. They derived 14.3% of their earnings from exports, whereas Canadian-run businesses only generated 10.8% of their revenues from abroad. They also exported further afield: Canadian firms tended to rely on the USA for the vast majority of their export earnings. But immigrant-run enterprises sent their products around the world – receiving around three-tenths of their foreign income from Asia. (Blanchet, 2021).

Research which looked at Spanish exports, over a fifteen-year period, found that increases in immigration led to a significant increase in trade: Each time the number of immigrants from a specific country grew by one tenth, exports *into* that country increased by between 0.5% and 1%. (Peri & Requena-Silvente, 2010).

And a report published in the Journal of World Business, which analysed Chinese immigrants in over two-hundred nations, found that those people who were *less integrated* were *more likely* to be exporters. They retained their ties with China, and so found it easier to sell their merchandise back in that Asian nation. (Cai et al, 2021).

***

These immigrants use their intimate knowledge of other places, to find *customers* – opening up markets abroad. In the process, they attract foreign currency – helping to improve their nations' balance of trade.

But they don't only export goods. They also export *services*...

In Bulgaria, I was friends with an Englishman named Matt. His company, "Bansko Chalets", served British holidaymakers – collecting them from Sofia airport – providing them with accommodation, ski hire, breakfast, dinner and wine.

On the face of it, you might assume they were operating in a bubble – English people were providing a service to English consumers. But Matt's wife, who helped him to run the show, was Bulgarian. Matt sourced his food, linen and cleaning supplies from Bulgarian firms. His customers frequented Bulgarian-run bars, bought their lunches at Bulgarian restaurants, and visited the hot springs which were operated by local workers.

That business didn't just sell a service – a ski holiday – to a group of foreigners. They enticed consumers, who exchanged their pounds for leva, and spent that money *at Bulgarian businesses* – benefitting the local community.

Matt was able to do this because he was British. He knew what British holidaymakers desired: A package deal, with communal dining, and a cosy ambience. This type of "Chalet" holiday hadn't been available in the town before Matt arrived. But Matt knew what British customers wanted, and he knew how to market his business back in Britain.

That gave him a competitive advantage, which explains why he managed to succeed.

And it's hard to see a downside. Matt's company didn't compete with local businesses. It attracted *customers*, who spent their money in the local area.

***

Before we move on, it's also worth noting that foreign *employees* can also offer certain advantages: They supply local knowledge, which can be vital for firms which export.

Let's consider the case of the Ford Motor Company...

Ford was struggling to sell cars in India, but they couldn't understand why, until one of their Indian employees explained what they were doing wrong: People in India who can afford to buy new cars, tend to employ chauffeurs. Car owners sit on the *back seats*. But Ford had put the controls for the windows in the *front*. The solution was simple: They just had to move those switches around. But Ford's managers only worked this out, because they spoke to a foreign member of staff.

These days, Ford employs people from India to provide this kind of insight. These overseas workers help businesses like Ford to gain traction in foreign lands. (Guest, 2011).

DIASPORA NETWORKS!

Consider this statement from Mohan Trika, the chief executive of a Xerox venture named InXight:

"(I can approach) any company in the Bay Area, and find two or three contacts... Any software company must have at least two or three Indian or Chinese employees... And because they are there, it's very easy for me, or my technical officer, to create that bond, to pick up the phone and say: 'Swaminathan, can you help me, can you tell me what's going on?'... He'll say: 'Don't quote me, but the decision is because of this, this, and this'.

"Based on this, you can reformulate your strategy, your pricing, or your offer. *Such contacts are critical for start-ups.*"

***

Immigrants arrive in these distant lands – these places which have different laws, customs and cultures. They don't know how things are done, or what they should do themselves. But they're usually not alone. *Other people have already made similar journeys.* They'll empathise. They'll help. And this can create a virtuous cycle:

"(Diaspora networks) provide a safety net around you – the feeling that you can approach somebody to get some help... Your ability to manage risk is improved by these networks. If there are no role models, (and no) confidence builders to look at, then the chances of taking risk are not there. That's what we are saying: 'Come on with me, I'll help you.' This quickly becomes a self-reinforcing process: You create five or ten entrepreneurs, and those ten create *another* ten."

It feels like this is the case in general: When my great-grandmother first arrived in England, a fellow Eastern European took her in – providing her with accommodation (she slept on the floor), and with employment (she sewed buttonholes into clothing). When I moved to Bulgaria, it was a Brit who helped my wife to process her documents.

But immigrant entrepreneurs take things to another level, as Gerry Liu explains:

"When I was thinking of starting my own business, I went around to call on a few senior, established Chinese businessmen, to seek their advice. I called David Lee. I contacted David Lam and Winston Chen. I called up Ta-lin Hsu. They did not know me, but they took my calls. I went to their offices or their homes. They spent time with me telling me what I should or shouldn't be doing."

It doesn't stop here...

Fellow expats have also been known to provide *funding* for their compatriots' start-ups. They've taken *directorships*, offered *guidance*, made personal *introductions*, and helped them to secure *contracts*.

A MULTITUDE OF OTHER ADVANTAGES

We began this chapter by asking *why* immigrants achieve so much. We've gone on to give several reasons. And there are several more...

If you've turned your back on your homeland, sold everything you own, made an arduous journey, and resumed your life in a new location – then the chances are you're going to do everything you can to succeed. You're not going to surrender everything you had, only to settle for mediocrity. You're going to expend blood, sweat and tears – to ensure your circumstances are *better* than before. You're going to push on through, rise to any challenge, and refuse to take "No" for an answer.

You might be a *risk-taker*. You made a gamble when leaving home. Your journey may have been fraught with danger, but you endured it nonetheless. It's unlikely that you'll become risk-averse, once you've reached your destination. You'll take other risks – securing a job in a new industry, studying for a change of career, or opening a business – dedicating yourself to a fledgling industry, attempting to sell foods that no local has ever tried, or performing music that sounds strange the first time it's played.

You might also be driven by *curiosity*. You moved because you were interested to see what life was like in another country. The chances are you'll be curious enough to try new things even after you've arrived. Why not pour some tomato soup on top of a piece of tandoori chicken? Wouldn't you like to know how it tastes?

You might not have a choice.

Do you remember those pioneers of Hollywood? They were locked out of traditional professions, because they were Jewish. They *had* to establish a new industry, to create a niche for themselves.

But they were free to carve out that niche.

They'd freed themselves from the rules of their native land. They weren't fixed in place, within the fabric of their new society. They were marginal figures – outsiders in a peculiar place – *not bound by convention* – free to go wild and try new things. Nothing was holding them back. (Hirschman, 2013).

And they had access to more opportunities, *because* they'd just migrated.

They found themselves in a land which was home to a growing industry – with firms which were manufacturing cinematic equipment, and skilled workers who could use it – with access to talented writers, producers, directors, performers and designers. They were in a large consumer market, with millions of fans who were willing to buy tickets to see their films.

If the Warners had attempted to establish "Warner Brothers" while they were still living in Poland, the chances are they'd have failed, because they didn't have access to these suppliers, workers or consumers. That firm didn't become a household name because the Warners were such brilliant individuals. It succeeded *because the Warners had moved abroad.*

IN DEFENCE OF FREEDOM

"Fascism arrives as your friend. It will restore your honour, make you feel proud, protect your house, give you a job, clean up the neighbourhood, remind you of how great you once were, clear out the venal and the corrupt, remove anything you feel is unlike you... It doesn't walk in saying, 'Our programme means militias, mass imprisonments, transportations, war and persecution'."

Michael Rosen

It's easy to see the appeal...

It begins with a narrative of fear: An alien people are crossing the border. They're going to take your job, suppress your wages, and meddle with your way of life.

And then it offers a solution: A strong leader will prevent that from happening! They'll save you from those faceless hoards. They'll protect you, your family, your income, and your culture.

So what if you have to forgo a few of your liberties? So what if armed guards will be marching along the border, with virtual impunity under the law? So what if you'll have to pay a load of tax, to fund those militias?

You're going to be protected! That fear and unease, which was whipped up by a cabal of politicians, will be eased by those very same politicians!

***

The case for authoritarianism is simple: The powerful state will save you from the bogeymen, so long as you grant it control.

But this comes at a cost to one's freedom. It requires a Big Brother state...

The authorities will have to snoop on firms, to see if they're employing undocumented workers. They'll have to regulate landlords – forcing them to keep track of their tenants' visas. And they'll have to monitor universities – compelling them to comb through each of their students' papers.

States with hard borders don't only control immigrants, they control *their own citizens* – anyone who might help, house or employ a foreign national. (Kukathas, 2017).

**

What, then, about the alternative to authoritarianism? What about the *philosophical case* for open borders, free movement, and freedom in general?

Can't freedom be a good thing? An end in itself? Rather than delegate control over our lives to a government which claims a monopoly on violence – with its gun-wielding goons, detention centres, cages, deportations and lawfare – couldn't we, you know, just be free to live our lives, in whichever places we choose?

It's not such an outlandish idea.

Indeed, the philosophy of freedom has adherents across the political spectrum...

THE CAPITALIST CASE FOR FREE MOVEMENT

The "Second Treatise" – the book that inspired the American Revolution – was written by an English physician name John Locke...

Rebels quoted from Locke's writings while protesting against the Stamp Act. Thomas Jefferson wrote that Locke was a great inspiration for the USA's Declaration of Independence. And Locke's concept of "Inalienable rights" was borrowed by the authors of the American Constitution – a document which enshrined the right to *freedom* of speech, *freedom* of the press, and *freedom* of assembly.

At the time, Locke was considered a radical. He supported a revolution, after all. But Locke penned the ideas which shape today's political establishment.

According to Locke, we're all born into a state of freedom – we should be allowed to do whatever we want, however we want, *wherever* we want to do it – subject to the physical laws of nature.

These "Laws" do make a difference.

They mean that whilst you might be free to pillage a neighbouring village, *your actions will inspire a reaction*: Those villagers are likely to retaliate, and people will come to blows. They might even kill you. And you wouldn't want that!

These laws of nature, therefore, impose a limit upon one's freedom.

Locke argued that we can do whatever is physically possible, so long as it doesn't violate *anyone else's* "Inalienable" rights – their rights to "Life, liberty and property".

You don't have the right to attack me, because that would impinge on my right to life. Or, as Oliver Wendell Holmes once put it: "The right to swing my fist, ends where the other man's nose begins."

And you don't have the right to curtail my ability to move, because that'd impinge upon my right to "Liberty".

***

Locke's defence of property puts him on the more conservative end of the political spectrum. He aligned himself with the capital-owning classes. Thomas Jefferson even went as far as to amend Locke's list, when penning the Declaration of Independence – omitting this right to "Property", and replacing it with the right to "The pursuit of happiness".

Locke did believe in government, albeit one with a limited scope: To act as a guardian of our "Inalienable" rights.

But he also championed "Liberty" – "To be free from restraint and violence from others" – including, one would presume, the violence which is dished out at our borders. Locke even went as far as to defend our *right to revolt* against any government which attempted to suppress our freedoms.

In fact, Locke was even more explicit than this: He stated that if a person felt that a community's rules had become too onerous, then that person *had a right to leave*. He appears to have been demanding refugee rights, more than two-hundred years before they were enshrined by the United Nations. (Locke, 1689).

***

Locke's philosophy inspired the USA's founding fathers, including Thomas Paine, who wrote another famous treaty: The "Rights of Man".

In that book, Paine stated: "Independence is my happiness, and I view things as they are, without regard to place or person. *My country is the world*, and my religion is to do good." (Paine, 2010).

***

But Locke's writings didn't only hold sway over the American Revolution. His philosophy also inspired Adam Smith.

Smith argued for free movement from a purely economic standpoint – demanding that workers be allowed to go wherever there was demand for their labour:

"The *free circulation of labour* from one employment to another and from one country to another is *essential*." (Goldin, 2011).

"Anything that obstructs the free circulation of labour from one employment to another, similarly obstructs the movement of stock, because the quantity of stock that can be employed in any branch of business greatly depends on the quantity of labour."

Smith also called out the double standard which made it easy for entrepreneurs to do business in new locations, but much harder for workers to seek employment in those very same locales:

"It is always much easier for a wealthy merchant to obtain the privilege of trading in a town-corporate, than for a poor artificer to obtain the privilege of working in it." (Smith, 1776).

***

Smith's work returned into fashion with the rise of the "Neoliberals", in the late 1970s.

The neoliberals were led by Milton Friedman, who argued that companies had a single moral imperative: "The social responsibility of business is to increase its profits". Firms should seek to employ the most efficient workers – those people who can make them the most "Profit" – no matter where they happened to have been born. They shouldn't be bogged down in bureaucracy – dealing with a "Nanny State", with its bureaucracy and borders – artificial "Barriers to trade". They should be freed to fulfil their "Social responsibility": Recruiting the best staff, whatever their nationality – putting them to work in the most efficient manner – using them to maximise corporate profits. (Friedman, 1970).

***

After the neoliberal revolution, came the "Third Way" politics of Clinton and Blair, along with its *globalist* philosophy.

This is a quote from David Held, one of its leading proponents:

"Pollution, drugs, human rights and terrorism are amongst an increasing number of *transnational policy issues* which cut across territorial jurisdictions and existing political alignments, and which require *international cooperation.*"

Held was saying that some issues – such as the environment – affect us all, no matter where we live. We have "Overlapping communities of fate" – we all need to work together, no matter where we were born, to deal with these matters.

But national governments only exist to serve their own citizens. They're not tasked with the job of serving *everyone* on the planet.

Globalists argue that we need international organisations, which sit above national parliaments – to ensure that they act in the interests of the *global* population. (Held & McCrew, 1998).

***

Proponents of globalism tend not to focus on freedom of movement for *people*. But the organisations they celebrate haven't been so shy...

The World Economic Forum champions the rights of "Workers to migrate from countries where jobs are scarce, to others where jobs are many". They argue that free movement in Europe has reduced unemployment by up to 6%. (Hutt, 2016).

The International Monetary Fund has released a document on "Globalization" – for the "Free flow of ideas, *people*, goods, services and capital." It states: "The IMF believes that globalization has great potential to contribute to the growth that is essential to achieve a sustained reduction of global poverty." (IMF Staff, 2002).

And the World Bank echoes this philosophy, writing: "The rich have many assets, the poor have only one – their labour. Because good jobs are slow to come to the poor, the poor must move to find productive employment. Migration is, therefore, *the most effective way to reduce poverty and share prosperity* – the twin goals of the World Bank." (Georgieva, 2018).

THE ANTI-CAPITALIST CASE
FOR FREE MOVEMENT

Adam Smith was championing a sort of equality, in which labour and capital – people and firms – had an equal right to move. But he did so from the *perspective of capital* – arguing that businesses should have the right to attract workers from overseas, so that capitalists could exploit them in whatever location they choose.

At the other end of the political spectrum, Marxists also believe that labour should have as many freedoms as capital. But they argue from the *perspective of labour*.

When Karl Marx observed how British capitalists were pitting English workers against their Irish peers, he documented what he'd seen:

"In order to oppose their workers, the employers either bring in workers from abroad, or else transfers manufacture to countries where there is a cheap labour force."

This kind of thing might have been music to the ears of Adam Smith. But it appalled Karl Marx.

Still, Marx didn't wish to fight this capitalist internationalism with any kind of nationalism. He wished to challenge it with a new kind of *socialist internationalism*:

"Given this state of affairs, if the working class wishes to continue its struggle with some chance of success, the national organisations must become *international*." (Engels, 1867).

You've probably heard of Marx and Engel's famous demand – that "The workers of the world unite". They weren't pitting American workers against Mexican workers. They weren't calling for British workers to unite in isolation. They were calling upon people of *every nationality* to stand together as one.

They were calling upon workers to forget about notions of nationality:

"The working men have no country."

And they were saying that working-class people had common cause with other working-class people, in every other nation on Earth:

"National differences and antagonism between peoples are daily more and more vanishing, owing to the development of the bourgeoisie, to freedom of commerce, to the world market, to uniformity in the mode of production." (Marx & Engels, 1848).

This was key.

Marx and Engels differentiated between people on the basis of their *class*, rather than their *nationality*. Marxists believe that people of all nationalities are equal – we should treat each other as family, no matter where we were born.

If capitalists import foreign labour on lower wages, then domestic and foreign workers shouldn't turn on each other. They should unite, and challenge those capitalists – forcing them to pay the foreigners as much as the locals.

This battle – the *class war* – was the only war worth fighting.

***

But Marxism isn't the only anti-capitalist philosophy in town...

Anarchists want to create societies without nation-states – in which governance comes from the bottom-up, by the people – usually through some variant of direct democracy, or a chain of citizens' councils. Anarchists reject the violent apparatus of statehood – with its police, prisons, militarism and borders. They reject supranational organisations, like the IMF and the World Bank. They want people to be free to live their lives, unhindered by top-down control, *in whatever location they choose.*

The Anarchist Library has even produced a "No Borders Manifesto", which proclaims:

"Freedom of movement is not a right – it's a real living force. Despite all the obstacles that states put in people's way – all the barriers of barbed wire, money, laws, ID cards, surveillance and so on – millions cross borders every day. For every migrant stopped or deported, many more get through and stay, whether legally or clandestinely. Don't overestimate the strength of the state and its borders. Don't underestimate the strength of everyday resistance."

(TheAnarchistLibrary.Org).

***

Anarchists view things rather differently from statists...

Statists believe that nations have an innate right to exist – that their governments have a right to pass laws which restrict movement. If anyone dares to break those laws, *they* are doing something "Illegal". They're "Illegal immigrants", and they have to pay for their crime!

But anarchists believe that it's *people* who have that innate right to exist. *A person cannot be illegal.* If lawmakers decide to criminalise movement, then they're the ones in the wrong. Their *states* should be considered "Illegal".

***

This is particularly prescient in the New World, as Harsha Walia explains:

"In the context of settler-colonial states like Canada, a necessary corollary of *No One Is Illegal*, has been the assertion that *Canada Is Illegal*. Settler-colonial states are founded on the racist doctrine of discovery and terra nullius." (Dilts, 2015).

Walia is arguing that Canada is illegal, because it was established on stolen land. We shouldn't listen to what its government has to say because that government descends from a gang of thieves. Rather, we should show solidarity with the original peoples who'd lived on that land: Peoples who'd lived in stateless societies, without centralised governments or hard borders.

***

Like the Marxists, anarchists also take an anti-capitalist approach to migration. But David Graeber – the most prominent anarchist of recent times – shares something in common with Adam Smith. He also opposes the hypocrisy, which grants capital more freedom than labour:

"Activists have been trying to draw attention to the fact that the neoliberal vision of 'Globalisation' is pretty much limited to the movement of capital and commodities, and actually increases barriers against the free flow of people."

Capitalists are moving production to sweatshops in faraway lands, both because capital *is* free to move abroad, and also because labour *is not*:

"If it were not possible to effectively imprison the majority of people in the world in impoverished enclaves, there would be no incentive for Nike or The Gap to move production there to begin with. Given a free movement of people, the whole neoliberal project would collapse" – because sweatshop workers would relocate to places where they could receive a higher wage.

Graeber goes on to reaffirm anarchists' commitment to a borderless world:

"The main achievement of the nation-state in the last century has been the establishment of a uniform grid of heavily policed barriers across the world. It is precisely this international system of control that we are fighting." (Graeber, 2002).

***

Most things in life *aren't* policed. We don't need permission to go to the theatre or a gallery. So long as we remain *within* a nation's borders, we can travel almost anywhere we like, with whomever we choose, using whichever mode of transport we can afford – during the morning, afternoon or night.

Indeed, many of us do relocate *within* our nation's borders: Around forty-million Americans move home *every single year*. A large chunk are youngsters, moving from one rental property to another, often within the same city. But this number also includes those individuals who move between American states – to study, work or retire – to find new opportunities, a better climate, or cheaper housing. (Sauter, 2018).

Just because there aren't laws to regulate this kind of movement, it doesn't mean that society falls apart. People get on with their lives, without harming anyone else. Because, in general, we're not a bunch of wallies!

In the same way, anarchists would argue that we don't need restrictions on *international* travel. The vast majority of people would still move about in peace, without causing any harm. Because most of us are good eggs. And because we can police the bad eggs, within our communities, without needing to be subjugated by a state. (Kukathas,

2017).

GOD LOVES MIGRATION

So much for the political philosophies. What do the scriptures say?

You've probably heard of Eve – the mother of all humanity. It was Eve who ate from the Tree of Knowledge – an act which enraged God so much, that he expelled her and her husband from the Garden of Eden.

What did God command they do next?

This is what it says in Genesis chapter one:

"God blessed them and said to them, 'Be fruitful and increase in number; *fill the Earth* and subdue it'."

God gave humankind *a divine mandate to migrate* – to spread out and "Fill" the Earth.

And when he saw the tower of Babel, he took matters into his own hands: He "Scattered" humanity "Over the face of all the Earth".

***

A little further down the line, but still in the book of Genesis, we're introduced to the story of Lot...

When Lot spots a couple of wayfaring strangers, he invites them into his home – providing them with a bed for the night and a meal. Later that evening, a gang of unruly men knock on Lot's door and demand to rape his visitors. But Lot is defiant! He offers up *his own virgin daughters* in place of his guests.

It all sounds rather vulgar. But there's a moral to the story: In the end, we discover that those strangers were angels of God. They take vengeance on the sinners – turning them blind – thereby protecting Lot and his daughters.

The next day, God destroys the city of Sodom – punishing the ne'er-do-wells who lived in that town. But the angels lead Lot and his daughters to safety – rewarding them for the welcome they'd extended to their foreign guests.

***

The Torah also talks of Jews' obligation not to discriminate against foreigners...

Exodus chapter twenty-three commands: "You shall not oppress a stranger, since you yourselves know the feelings of a stranger, for you also were strangers in the land of Egypt". And this demand is repeated in Leviticus chapter nineteen, which says: "The foreigner residing among you must be treated as your native-born. Love them as yourself, for you were foreigners in Egypt".

The order to love foreigners comes up again in Deuteronomy chapter ten, which says: "You are to love those who are foreigners".

Deuteronomy chapters sixteen and twenty-six, both command the Israelites to include foreigners in their *festivals*.

In Numbers chapter thirty-five, the Lord orders Moses to create six towns which will be a "Refuge for Israelites and for foreigners".

And the Torah also demands that *charity* be extended to outsiders: Deuteronomy chapter fourteen asks farmers to store their crops, so that "The foreigners... who live in your towns may come and eat". Likewise, Leviticus chapter twenty-three asks: "Do not reap to the very edges of your field or gather the gleanings of your harvest. Leave them for the poor and for the foreigner residing among you".

The Torah doesn't judge non-nationals on the basis of their skills, savings and qualifications. There's no points-based system – just a divine command to love, protect, include and feed other people – no matter where they were born.

***

This sentiment is repeated in the New Testament...

Christ also asked his followers to "Love thy neighbour" – to welcome them with open arms. And Hebrews chapter thirteen begins by repeating this message: "Keep on loving one another as brothers and sisters. Do not forget to show hospitality to strangers".

Romans chapter twelve speaks of our duty to refugees: "Share with the Lord's people who are in need. Practice hospitality."

And Galatians chapter three speaks of a world without

nationalities, in which we all belong to the kingdom of Christ: "There is no longer Jew or Greek, there is no longer slave or free, there is no longer male and female; for all of you are one in Christ Jesus."

***

Inspired by these teachings, the Catechism of the Catholic Church calls for nations to open their doors to refugees who are fleeing from danger or poverty: To "Welcome the foreigner in search of the security and the means of livelihood which he cannot find in his country of origin."

But this is hardly surprising, when you consider the story of Jesus's life.

Christ was born unto parents who originally came from Bethlehem, but who'd moved to another place – making a home for themselves in Nazareth. The family became refugees in the Egyptian desert – fleeing from Herod, when that client king ordered the slaughter of all the male infants. And Jesus went on to become a wandering preacher himself: When he crossed into Samaria, he shocked his entourage by treating the Samaritans as though they were his kith and kin.

***

The early Christians were inspired by this lifestyle choice, as we can see in this excerpt from the "Letter to Diognetus", which was written in the second or third century:

"Christians are indistinguishable from other men either by nationality, language or customs. They do not inhabit separate cities of their own, or speak a strange dialect, or follow some outlandish way of life... They follow the customs of whatever city they happen to be living in, whether it's Greek or foreign.

"And yet there is something extraordinary about their lives. They live in their own countries as though they were only passing through. They play their full role as citizens, but labour under all the disabilities of aliens. *Any country can be their homeland.*"

This is significant: If those early Christians hadn't moved about, "Passing through", Christianity wouldn't be the religion it is today. The Christian Bible spread across the world, because these *nomadic* preachers took it from one place to the next – promoting their doctrine wherever they wandered.

***

Islam also champions freedom...

The "Universal Islamic Declaration of Human Rights", provides a framework for rights which are granted by God, and which therefore override national laws, because "God alone is the law giver and the source of all human rights".

This declaration reads as though it's been copied from John Locke.

It proclaims that "Man is born free", and "Has the inalienable right to freedom in all its forms – physical, cultural, economic and political... Every oppressed individual or people has a legitimate claim to the support of other individuals."

This includes the freedom to move, at least within Islamic states:

"Every Muslim shall have the right to freely move in and out of any Muslim country. No one shall be forced to leave the country of his residence, or be arbitrarily deported therefrom without recourse to due process of law."

***

What about Hinduism?

There are five freedoms in Hinduism. Whilst these don't include an explicit freedom to move, they do include a "Freedom from violence". Given that you cannot have borders without violence – borders are maintained by armed guards – this might be seen as a call to abolish borders, albeit in a roundabout way.

When UNESCO was formulating its Charter of Human Rights, it surveyed leading philosophers from around the world. Shrikrishna Puntambekar was asked to speak on behalf of Hindus. He obliged, penning an essay entitled "The Hindu Concept of Human Rights", in which he challenged the Western framework, which he found too materialistic – arguing that human rights should "Introduce higher spiritual aims".

Puntambekar was explicit, when stating Hinduism's support for free movement:

"We also want freedom from an all-absorbing conception of the state – the community and the church coercing individuals to particular and ordered ways of life. Along with this, we desire freedom of thought and expression, of *movement* and association." (Puntambekar, 2019).

***

And finally, what about Buddhism?

Buddhists believe that everything is interconnected – that we're all a part of a singular unity, which a religious person might call "God", and which a non-religious person might call the "Universe".

It therefore doesn't make any sense to draw lines on the planet, and say "You're Australian, so you belong within this set of borders", and "You're Botswanan, so you belong over there". The Australian and the Botswanan are both parts of the same overriding whole. They both belong everywhere, all the time.

***

These religions all have one thing in common: A version of the "Golden Rule"...

The Mahābhārata – a Sanskrit epic, revered by Hindus – states that: "One should never do something to others that one would regard as an injury to one's own self". The Talmud says, "What is hateful to you, do not do to your fellow". The Gospel of Matthew repeats this message: "Do to others what you want them to do to you". The Hadith repeats it again: "As you would have people do to you, do to them". And the Udānavarga states: "Hurt not others in ways that you yourself would find hurtful".

Let's apply this rule to those people who wish to migrate.

Put yourself in *their* position.

How would you feel, if someone said that *you* couldn't live in the land of your choice – that you had to remain in a warzone, somewhere afflicted by perpetual floods, or a place where you were only paid a dollar a day? Would you be fine with that? Would you be happy to suffer, simply because you'd been born in that particular location? Of course, you wouldn't! You'd want to move.

Well, if we're treating others as we'd wish to be treated – then we should grant others the same right to move, that we'd wish to have ourselves.

We wouldn't want other people to force *us* to remain in a dangerous place, an impoverished enclave, or a society where we were unfulfilled. And so we shouldn't force *others* to remain in those locations.

We should open our borders and allow those people to relocate, because we'd wish to move ourselves, if we ever found ourselves in their position.

IN THE NAME OF EQUAL OPPORTUNITIES

John Rawls, the American moral philosopher, is famous for his "Veil of Ignorance" – a thought experiment, which requires people to imagine they don't know anything about themselves – as though they were about to be reborn, into a random family, anywhere on the planet. You wouldn't know if you were going to be tall or short, disabled or able-bodied. You might be born into a rich home or a poor one. You could be any race, gender or sexual persuasion. You might have some natural talent. Then again, you might not.

Given these conditions, you must ask yourself a question: How would you design society?

Rawls argues that people would choose two things: They'd allow a degree of inequality – so long as *everybody* benefitted. And they'd want a certain amount of liberty – fair conditions, with *equal opportunities for all* – enabling everyone to fulfil their potential. (Rawls, 2001).

***

Equality of opportunity hasn't always been in vogue...

Under feudalism, if you were born into the nobility, you became a noble. If your parents were peasant farmers, you'd probably become a peasant yourself. Serfs were tied to the land. They were forbidden from seeking opportunities in other locations. That'd have caused the system to collapse!

These days, equality of opportunity is seen as a cornerstone of a just and fair society. A Gallup poll from 2011, found that 88% of Americans believed that their government should enact policies to "Increase the equality of opportunity for people to get ahead". If a person wishes to chase their dream, nothing should stand in their way! (Newport, 2011).

Yet such opportunities do not exist on an *international* level. People who are born in some countries, have fewer opportunities than people who are born in others.

This fails the "Veil of ignorance" test: If you didn't know your nationality – if there was a chance you might be born in an impoverished land – you'd probably want open borders. You'd want the right to move to a country where you'd be paid twenty times as much for the very same kind of work.

These are the words of contemporary philosopher, Joseph Carens:

"Citizenship in Western democracies is the modern equivalent of feudal class privilege – an inherited status that greatly enhances one's life chances. To be born a citizen of a rich state in Europe or North America is like being born into the nobility (even though many of us belong to the lesser nobility). To be born a citizen of a poor country in Asia or Africa, is like being born into the peasantry... Like feudal birthright privileges, contemporary social arrangements not only grant great advantages on the basis of birth, but also entrench these advantages by legally restricting mobility, making it extremely difficult for those born into a socially disadvantaged position to overcome that disadvantage, no matter how talented they are, or how hard they work."

In the late Middle Ages, reformers campaigned for freedom of movement *within* nations – arguing that people should be allowed to move around, in search of a better life. Carens believes we should launch a similar campaign today – demanding that people be granted the right to move *between* nations:

"Modern practices of state control over borders tie people to the land of their birth almost as effectively (as under feudalism). Limiting entry to rich democratic states is a crucial mechanism for protecting a birthright privilege. If the feudal practices protecting birthright privileges were wrong (in the Middle Ages), what justifies the modern ones?" (Carens, 1987).

Carens argues that if there are no natural hierarchies of birth, if we all have equal moral worth, then we should be freed to achieve whatever we can. But for this to happen, we have to be able to move:

"Freedom of movement is an essential prerequisite for equality of opportunity."

If someone wishes to practice a particular religion, they should be allowed to move to a land which tolerates that religion. If a person wishes to live under a particular political system, they should be allowed to travel to a country where that system already exists. If an individual wishes to marry a person of the same gender, they must be allowed to move to a nation which welcomes homosexuals. If they wish to become a rocket scientist, they should be permitted to go to a place which has a space program. If their dream is to become a professional cricketer, they should be allowed to migrate to a country where cricket is played. And if they wish to flee from war, poverty or natural disasters – then they should be permitted to move to places which aren't blighted by these afflictions.

Sometimes, these places exist within the same nation. Countries like the USA are so vast, you can find different opportunities by moving from one region to another. But what if you were born into a microstate such as Tuvalu? Should you allow yourself to be imprisoned within Tuvalu's twenty-six square-kilometres? Should you be forced to work in one of only a few industries? (Pretty much everyone on the Pacific Island either works in the public sector, coconut farming, fishing or tourism). Shouldn't you be free to seek out opportunities in other places?

Individuals who were born in poor nations, don't have the same opportunities as people who were born in wealthy nations. Individuals who were born in microstates, have far fewer opportunities than those people who were born in larger, more diverse lands.

And that's inherently unjust:

"Freedom of movement would contribute to a reduction of existing political, social, and economic inequalities. There are millions of people in poor states today who long for the freedom and economic opportunity they could find in Europe or North America. Many of them take great risks to come. If the borders were open, millions more would move. The exclusion of so many poor and desperate people seems hard to justify from a perspective that takes seriously the claims of all individuals as free and equal moral persons." (Carens, 2013).

IN THE NAME OF PEACE AND JUSTICE

Most of our legal structures stick to the principle of "Innocent until proven guilty" – that we should treat people as though they're innocent, unless it's been *proven* that they've done something wrong. This principle can be found in the statutes of several nations, the Talmud, the Roman records, and the Universal Declaration of Human Rights.

Yet it doesn't seem to apply to travellers.

Borders operate under the assumption that non-nationals are guilty.

When a foreigner arrives at a border, the onus is on *them* to prove their innocence. They have to demonstrate that they're worthy of admittance, that they'll contribute to society, and that they won't do anything naughty. They have to show that they have a place in a university, a contract of employment, a pension or savings.

This turns the entire principle of justice on its head.

It also creates a double standard, whereby not everyone is considered equal under the law: A person who's born in a country, is usually granted citizenship – no questions asked. They're considered innocent and worthy. But someone who moves to that place, must endure a barrage of questions, forms and procedures – just to claim that very *same* kind of citizenship. They're treated as though they're guilty of a crime.

There's one rule for one set of people, but another rule for everyone else. And that's a travesty of justice.

***

There does seem to be an exception – another double standard, this time based on *wealth*...

Whilst everyday folk have to beg for admittance, the super-rich are met with a red carpet whenever they land their private jets.

At least twenty-four countries have "Citizenship Investment Programs", which grant long-term residency and citizenship to anyone who invests a certain sum – usually around $200,000. If it wasn't formulated in law, you might say they were "Bribing" their way through the borders.

You're also more likely to be granted a *business visa* – such as the USA's "B Visa" – if you happen to be wealthy.

Even if you overstay your welcome, the chances are that the officials will turn a blind eye, so long as you're pocketing a hefty salary: In 2008, it was revealed that twenty-thousand people were receiving more than $100,000 a year, while employed in the States – even though they didn't have the legal right to work there. The authorities didn't seem particularly bothered about *those* undocumented workers. (Ossola, 2021).

And wealth can also be used to discriminate between *tourists*.

In Bhutan, holidaymakers must pay $200 for every night they stay. That's pocket change for the world's billionaires, but a major deterrent for the rest of us.

Open borders would eliminate these double standards. They'd grant *everyone* the equal right to move – no matter if they're rich or poor.

***

Borders are inherently unjust...

Consider the Iron Curtain: A government with a nuclear arsenal had erected a seven-thousand kilometre barrier – a melee of fences, walls, watchtowers and minefields. It was stopping its *own citizens* from moving away!

We see something similar in North Korea.

This goes against everything we're told to expect: A government is supposed to *nurture* its people. It isn't supposed to trap them.

Yet borders which stop people from *entering*, are just as coercive as borders which prevent people from *leaving*. And the right to leave means nothing, if we're unable to enter another land.

This is why the Geneva Convention talks about the obligations of states to *welcome* refugees. They must issue them with a set of identity papers, offer them "Administrative assistance", and "The possibility of assimilation and naturalisation".

But wouldn't it be great, if they granted the same rights to humans who *weren't* refugees?

Imagine this: A person is suffering from cancer, but they cannot afford the treatment they need to survive. As things stand, they're going to suffer a painful, premature death. And so they'd like to find a job in a richer country. They'd be paid more in that place. They'd be able to save some of that extra money, and use it to pay for the healthcare which would save their life.

In this scenario, the person is left with two options: Stay put and die, or move and remain alive. For them, migration is a matter of life and death.

This sort of thing happens here, in the Philippines, albeit in a roundabout way: People go abroad to work, they send remittances home, and those remittances are used to pay for someone else's healthcare. One person emigrates, and it saves another person's life.

But these people aren't classed as refugees, under the Geneva Convention – which only protects people who have a "Well-founded fear of being persecuted for reasons of race, religion, nationality, membership of a particular social group or political opinion." These people aren't being "Persecuted" by their diseases. They'd be classed as "Economic migrants", because they're moving to earn more money, to pay for healthcare. And "Economic migrants" aren't granted the same rights as refugees, *even when their poverty is going to kill them*.

How on Earth can that be right?

STOICISM, DUTIES AND OUTCOMES

It'd be wrong to talk of the philosophy of freedom, without mentioning that rebel thinker of the ancient world: Diogenes.

Diogenes was a bit of a rascal. When Alexander the Great offered to help the fellow, Diogenes responded by asking Alexander to move out of the sun! And when Alexander asked Diogenes why he was inspecting a pile of human bones, the philosopher replied: "I am searching for the bones of your father, but cannot distinguish them from those of a slave".

More to the point, Diogenes was also recorded as saying, "I am not an Athenian or a Greek, but a citizen of the world".

It might sound a little corny today, but it was a revolutionary statement at the time. And it was inspirational too. People began to call themselves "Cosmopolitans" – a portmanteau which combined the word "Cosmos", meaning the entire world, and "Polites", meaning citizen – a "Citizen of the world".

Diogenes was championing a new political philosophy – challenging the system of city-states, who waged war on each other – demanding that people unite with their fellow human beings, no matter where they were born.

And his ideas were inspirational: They gave rise to *Stoicism*.

Stoics believe that humans belong to two communities – our *local* communities, and the entire *human* community. Indeed, they sometimes use a metaphor – referring to humanity as a body. In the same way that we wouldn't only care about one of our limbs, or a few of our organs – Stoics argue that we shouldn't only care about ourselves, or our own society. We should care about *every* human, wherever they are, because we're all a part of the same body – the natural world – the global community.

For Stoics, it makes little sense to chop that world up, and say "Keep the Nigerians here, and put the Bolivians over there". That'd be like chopping up our body, putting our toes in one place, and putting our fingers in another. It'd cause needless suffering and pain.

We must take care of our entire body. And we must take care of all humanity – acting in a virtuous manner, to achieve the "Common good". (Langness, 2014).

***

Let's finish this chapter by considering two more schools of thought: Deontology and Consequentialism...

"Deontology", the philosophy of *rights* and *duties*, traces its roots back to the German philosopher, Immanuel Kant – who was also inspired by Diogenes.

It argues that some things are morally right. We have a *duty* to perform these actions, regardless of the consequences.

A deontologist might argue, therefore, that we have a duty to welcome other people, even if it results in some adverse effects. We can never be entirely sure of the consequences of our actions. But we can be sure of our intentions. We should *intend* to be kind, by welcoming anyone who appears at our borders.

***

Kant goes further – arguing a person has "A duty to maintain one's life". If someone feels threatened in one region, they have a *duty* to move to a safer place – to do whatever they can to stay alive. Kant also argues that this is natural – that we have a "Direct inclination" to preserve our lives.

And he goes further still, adding that "To secure one's own *happiness* is a duty" – because people who are forlorn, are likely to neglect their other duties, and descend into immorality. And so Kant isn't only making the case for refugees, who move to secure their safety, but for *anyone* who is unfulfilled, and who might find happiness in another location. (Kant, 1785).

***

Kant demands that we acknowledge the "Natural law of equality" – arguing that every person has an equal right to dignity and respect, no matter where they were born.

And Jacques Derrida takes this to the extreme, when he talks of "Unconditional hospitality":

"Let us say 'Yes' to who or what turns up, before any

determination... before any identification... (whether it is) a foreigner, an immigrant, uninvited guest, or unexpected visitor... the citizen of another country, a human, animal, or divine creature, a living or dead thing, male or female... Give the new arrival all of one's home, all of oneself... without asking (their) name, or compensation, or fulfilment, or even the smallest condition."

Derrida accepts that this is a risky business. Those guests might harm their hosts. But he argues that we must be willing to take this risk.

For Derrida, hospitality is a good thing *in itself*. We must welcome outsiders, because it's the moral thing to do – no matter what happens next. As Søren Kierkegaard once put it, we must love our neighbours with "Closed eyes" – without judging them for who they are, or what they're about to do. (Derrida et al, 2000).

***

More moderate deontologists might argue that nations have a *conditional* duty to help those people they've harmed.

Nations that wage war, have a duty to their innocent victims. If the United States wishes to bomb Libya, then it has a duty to house the Libyan refugees who flee from their bombs.

Nations that pollute, have a duty to the victims of that pollution. If the global north wants to burn fossil fuels, then it should open its doors to everyone who is affected by the floods, cyclones, and crop failures which are sure to ensue.

***

At the very least, you might argue that we have a duty not to harm other people.

This is what Kant called, the principle of "Universal Hospitality":

"'Hospitality' signifies the claim of a stranger entering foreign territory, to be treated by its owner *without hostility*. The latter may send him away again, if this can be done without causing his death. But, so long as he conducts himself peaceably, (the stranger) must not be treated as an enemy... He has *a right of visitation*." (Kant, 1795).

This principle – not to do harm – is nicely demonstrated by the "Starving Marvin" dilemma, which was posed by Michael Huemer:

"Suppose that, through no fault of mine, Marvin is in danger of starvation. He asks me for food. If I refuse to give him food, I thereby fail to confer a benefit on Marvin and, at the same time, allow Marvin to go hungry. If Marvin then starves to death... (you could say that I've) merely allowed him to die. And some believe that this is much less wrong than killing, possibly not even wrong at all.

"But now consider a different case. Suppose that Marvin, again in danger of starvation, plans to walk to the local market to buy some food. In the absence of any outside interference, this plan would succeed. The market is open, and there are people willing to trade food for something that Marvin has.

"Now suppose that, knowing all this, I actively and forcibly restrain Marvin from reaching the market. As a result, he starves to death. In this situation, I would surely be said to have killed Marvin, or at least done something morally comparable to killing him."

This argument can be extended to non-nationals: Even if you don't believe we have a duty to help new arrivals, you might still believe we have a duty *not to harm them*. Stopping people at the border might indeed cause them harm – it's the equivalent of stopping a starving person from going to the market.

We should steer clear of such behaviour:

"My charge is not that the US government fails to give Third World inhabitants what they need. It is that the government actively and coercively prevents many Third World inhabitants from taking a course of action that they otherwise would undertake, and that would in fact succeed in enabling them to meet their needs. This is much closer to *inflicting* a harm than it's to merely *allowing* a harm to occur." (Huemer, 2010).

***

Such an argument might convince a deontologist. But not everyone is motivated by a sense of duty.

Consequentialists argue that our intentions don't matter. You can have the best will in the world, but if you end up hurting a bunch of people, they're not going to give two hoots about that. For consequentialists, it's the *consequences* of your actions which count.

John Stuart Mill was one of the foremost consequentialists.

Mill would have taken issue with Huemer's first point, since the English philosopher believed that, "A person may cause evil to others not only by his actions, but by his *inaction*". We shouldn't stand by as others suffer. We should give food to a starving person, if that action would have a positive *consequence* – helping to reduce their pain.

Likewise, we shouldn't stand by and do nothing as people struggle to leave or enter our nations. If it'd have a positive consequence – if it'd make the world a better place – then we should get off our arses and help those people to move. (Mill,1859).

***

"Utilitarianism" is the most famous form of consequentialism.

This philosophy argues that we should maximise the total amount of "Utility" or "Value" in the world – performing a kind of "Cost-benefit analysis", and choosing whichever action "Produces the greatest good, for the greatest number":

"The general object that all laws have or ought to have in common, is to increase the total *happiness* of the community... (And) exclude, as far as possible, everything that tends to reduce that happiness." (Bentham, 1789).

Governments would have the right to place controls on movement, if those controls increased global happiness. But do they?

Based on the evidence of this book, it seems they do not. *Open borders would make the world a happier place.* They'd help to boost global GDP, and increase people's wages – eliminating poverty for good. They'd allow people to flee from climate change, war and persecution – reducing bloodshed, suffering and pain. They'd allow people to find satisfaction, in whichever societies work for them.

Borders stop this from happening. They're one of those things "That tends to reduce happiness" – one of those things that utilitarians would argue ought to be "Excluded".

***

These two schools of thought – deontology and consequentialism – often come into conflict. People who care more for intentions, and people who care more for consequences, can reach dramatically different conclusions.

But that's not the case in this situation: Both deontologists *and* consequentialists have argued in favour of open borders, because they both favour *liberty*.

"Freedom is necessary to morality", as Nikolai Berdyaev once proclaimed. Morality only makes sense if you're free to choose how to act – to choose between good and evil. And borders impinge upon that freedom: Borders limit people's ability to go to those places where they'll be best placed to fulfil their duties, *and* where they'll be able to do the greatest amount of good. They're *anti-moral*.

A ROADMAP FOR CHANGE

"The difficulty lies, not in the new ideas, but in escaping from the old ones."

John Maynard Keynes

When India was partitioned, in 1947, around fifteen-million people found themselves adrift. Muslims in India hurried towards East or West Pakistan. Hindus passed them by, whilst heading in the opposite direction.

A plague of sectarian violence ensued...

There were massacres, forced conversions and abductions. Villages were set on fire. 75,000 women were raped. Pregnant women were attacked – their breasts were carved off, their midriffs were slashed open, and their unborn babies were removed. Young children were roasted on spits. Up to two-million people lost their lives.

The imposition of a border, inspired a genocide. It also led to Bangladesh's war of independence, which resulted in more bloodshed – and to the troubles in Kashmir, which continue to this day.

Had that border not been imposed, millions of lives would've been saved. (Hajari, 2016).

***

This is an extreme example. But it's not unique.

Borders kill. And the death toll grows larger by the day...

The "Missing Migrants" project keeps track of all those "People who die in the process of (international) migration." Since 2014, they've recorded the deaths of 56,912 people. By the time you read this, that number will be even higher.

Of these, the most common cause of death was drowning: 34,382 people died at sea – 21,977 of them in the central Mediterranean. Over 40% of their bodies were never recovered. (MissingMigrants.Iom.Int).

But this phenomenon didn't originate when that website began its tally. Between 1997 and 2017, over 33,000 people lost their lives whilst moving to Europe. (Cowell, 2017).

Nor is this a uniquely European issue. Missing Migrants also documents 7,866 traveller deaths in the Americas, including 1,432 in

2022 alone. And these are just the official numbers. The actual toll is likely to be much higher.

As one American border guard put it: "I would say for every (corpse) we find, we're probably missing five." (Fernandez, 2017).

PROHIBITION DOESN'T WORK

Borders create divisions, these divisions inspire hatred, and this hatred can lead to violence. Sometimes, it leads to murder – as was the case in India and Pakistan. Sometimes, it leads to a kind of "Social murder" – as we see in the Mediterranean, and on the Mexican border.

If you remove those borders, and allow people to move, then fewer people would die.

***

It's not as though these borders prevent migration.

Prohibition almost never works.

Take a look at the USA, back when alcohol was illegal. The law didn't eliminate consumption – there was a *demand* for whisky and beer, and entrepreneurs were willing to *supply* those drinks. That legislation only pushed the industry underground. Safety standards went out the window. Some dubious characters lined their pockets. And still, the liquor flowed.

We see something similar today: People still wish to migrate. There's a *demand*. And there's a group of entrepreneurs – "Smugglers" – who are willing to satisfy that demand.

It's basic economics – a case of demand and supply.

And it's big business: A 2016 report by Interpol and Europol, estimated that nine out of every ten undocumented people who entered the European Union, were assisted by the members of a "Criminal network". They calculated that the industry was worth somewhere between $5b and $6b every single year. (Wainwright, 2016).

But that's a conservative estimate.

According to the United Nations, at least 2.5 million people were helped across borders in 2016 alone. Between them, they paid an estimated *$7b* to shady gangs.

Those smugglers also facilitated other crimes – arranging fake marriages, supplying phoney contracts, forging travel documents, and bribing officials. (Kangaspunta & Me, 2018).

And even *these* figures have been disputed. The International Organization for Migration estimates that the people smuggling industry may be worth as much as *$35b* a year! (Bugge, 2017).

***

People who are determined to migrate, usually end up in their desired location...

When researchers interviewed the families of over a thousand Mexican immigrants, they found that the wave of authoritarian policies, unleashed by Bill Clinton, had "Not stopped nor even discouraged unauthorized migrants". More people were being apprehended. But this didn't dampen their enthusiasm. Up to 97% of the people who were returned to Mexico, simply dusted themselves down and made their journeys again. Almost all of them reached their destination at the second or third attempt.

It's easy enough to understand, when you consider the benefits.

Migration offers a life-changing payoff, even if it comes at a price. If you tell someone that their income will increase ten-fold, that they'll escape from their poverty and help their families, but there's a one-in-three-hundred chance that they'll die along the way – then there's a good chance that they'll be willing to take that risk. Death is a heavy price to pay – but the chances of dying are minimal. There's a much greater chance that they'll survive, and the rewards will be immense.

It's an investment. And a part of that investment, involves paying those "Coyotes" who help humans to cross the border.

When lawmakers in Washington DC enact policies which make it harder to migrate, it doesn't stop people from coming. But it does give those traffickers an excuse to up their rates. Those criminals *make more money*.

The politicians who'd intended to make migration more *difficult,* only make it more *lucrative.* They're a boon for the criminal classes. (Cornelius & Lewis, 2006).

***

We see a similar tale across the world...

It's in people's rational self-interest to take the safest and most direct routes, each time they embark upon a journey. When officials close these channels, they're forced to take more circuitous and dangerous routes. They'll spend more time in the desert, sail atop rougher seas, and push through even denser forests. It becomes increasingly likely that they'll employ the services of an unlawful group. And it becomes increasingly likely that they'll die. (Jones, 2016).

When European border agents attempted to clamp down on those people who were crossing the Mediterranean, between 2015 and 2018, those travellers continued to come. But they *changed course* – sailing out into the choppiest waters. The results were tragic: Before the clampdown, one person died at sea for every 269 who made it across. Afterwards, one-in-fifty lost their lives. (UNHCR, 2018).

We see a similar tale on land.

In 2016, a campaign targeted those pilgrims who were crossing from Niger into Libya, whilst on their way to Europe. It was a heavy-handed operation. Smugglers were thrown into jail, vehicles were impounded, and over two-thousand people were deported. The mission seemed to have achieved its goal: Migrants stopped crossing into Libya. But they kept on coming: Taking a different, more precarious route – crossing into Chad, and traversing some of the remotest parts of the Sahara. Several thousands died. The smugglers *abandoned* them – leaving them to perish. But the majority still made it into Europe. (Penney, 2017).

***

These policies can even be counterproductive: Since Britain left the European Economic Area, it's become harder for Europeans to enter the country. But net migration has actually *increased*: Back in 2015, it stood at 329,000 people per year, according to figures from the Office for National Statistics. By 2022, that figure had jumped up to 606,000 – *an all-time high*! (Ravikumar & M, 2023).

And these policies can have another unintended consequence: They might encourage people *to stay in the country for good*...

Back in the 1960s, seventy-million Mexicans crossed into the USA. They did their work, earned their money, and then the vast majority – seventeen out of every twenty – turned back and headed home.

Now that the border has become a military zone, just 7% of undocumented people return to Mexico.

It's understandable: If you've paid traffickers a load of money, and if you've risked your life whilst crossing the desert, you're not going to pop home to visit your family for Christmas! You're not going to put yourself through that ordeal *a second time* the next time you want to work. You're going to stay where you are forever.

It's lose-lose-lose...

Hard borders don't deter people from moving. *And they do encourage people to stay!* Controls on movement force people to employ people smugglers – thereby enriching a criminal underclass. Some of those criminals commit acts of rape, theft and extortion. Some of their charges are exploited for sex or sold into slavery. Tens-of-thousands die along the way.

It's like when alcohol was outlawed in the States. People still drank. Prohibition only benefitted the criminal classes.

And just look at that industry now: Jack Daniels isn't a criminal gang. Moet doesn't have a bad reputation. Revenues from the sale of Guinness aren't used to fund other illegal activities.

These are regular businesses. They provide a product which some people enjoy, and they employ staff in a legitimate fashion. The state doesn't spend a fortune to police those brewers and distillers. It *receives* taxation from those organisations.

The people-smuggling industry could undergo a similar transition: If we opened our borders, legitimate firms would emerge to help people move around. These companies would also employ people. They'd also pay tax.

But how would we make this transition?

First, we'd need to win the public's support...

CHANGING THE NARRATIVE

When the Migration Observatory combed through the pages of every mainstream British newspaper, for the ten years leading up to 2016, they found that 69% of the articles about European migration were wholly negative. Three-quarters of the columns about so-called "Illegal" immigration didn't mention a single benefit. Those columns documented the *problems* associated with human movement – emphasising the number of people who travelled, the rules they flouted, the crimes which related to migration, and the suffering that travellers endured. But they didn't mention any of the amazing things that happen as a result of immigration. (Allen, 2016).

Another study, which analysed over 43 million words in the British press, concluded that, "Most common portrayals cast immigrants and asylum seekers in a very negative light". The papers were awash with emotive words, such as "Flood", "Wave", "Flock" and "Influx". And they focused on asylum seekers and "Illegals" – rather than students, workers and their relations – even though those other groups were far larger. (Blinder & Allen, 2016).

And a report from the London School of Economics, which analysed coverage of the so-called "Migrant Crisis", in the European press, found that most reports dehumanised people on the move: Their *nationalities* were mentioned in three-fifths of newspaper articles. But fewer than one-in-six mentioned their *names*, and just one-in-fourteen included their *professions*. Refugees were rarely allowed to speak. Women, in particular, were silenced. And the tone was shorn of emotion. Those humans were "Othered" – presented as a nameless, faceless, homogenous blob. (Georgiou & Zaborowski, 2017).

***

This bias has skewed our perceptions...

An IPSOS Mori survey, revealed that the average Brit thought that almost a quarter of British residents had arrived in the UK from abroad. The true figure was just 13% – barely half the perceived amount.

When the researchers conducted the same survey in thirty-seven other nations, the average respondent thought that 28% of their neighbours were non-nationals. The actual figure was just 12%. (Skinner, 2018).

And in Bulgaria, Romania and Poland – the average person overestimated the true proportion by a *factor of eight*. (European Commission, 2018).

***

We have other misconceptions...

When researchers surveyed over twenty-thousand people, across six wealthy nations, they found that people also overestimated the *unemployment rate* among international residents, and the rate at which foreigners claimed *welfare*. The general population believed that people born overseas were less *integrated*, in terms of religion and culture, than was really the case. And they underestimated the amount of *education* which the average globetrotter had received. (Alesina et al, 2022).

***

It's a slippery slope...

First, the press begins to *scaremonger*. They run a slew of front-page headlines, such as these: "Asylum seekers ferried around in stretch limos". "40% surge in ethnic numbers". "Migrant chaos all summer". "Migrants rob young Britons of jobs". "500,000 migrants get social housing". "Workers are fired for being British".

These stories result in the sorts of *misconceptions* we just introduced.

These misconceptions whip up *hatred* against foreign nationals.

And this hatred is used as a reason to introduce the sorts of anti-freedom *policies* which have been proliferating in recent years.

***

But what if we turned things on their head?

What if the papers were to lead with a slew of *pro-migration* headlines – bombarding us with information about all the great things that immigrants do for us? Wouldn't that whip up a new wave of love for our foreign guests? And wouldn't that encourage our governments to take more of a *pro*-freedom position?

In the introduction, we presented a hypothetical speech by Hillary Clinton, in which she celebrated the fact that foreign nationals had established a ton of businesses, which had created millions of jobs for American workers. That speech wasn't meant to be satirical. It was based on fact.

We should be shouting these facts from the rooftops.

It's not enough to go on the defensive. When the anti-freedom mob says, "Immigrants take our jobs" – we shouldn't debate them *on their terms* – focusing on the lie. We must go on the offensive. We must speak with confidence and pride, saying: "They *create* our jobs".

We must say that immigrants do the work we're not willing or able to do, that they staff our public services, that they build the homes we so desperately need, that they pick the fruit we eat, and that they staff our hospitals – saving our lives.

When people say, "Immigration reduces wages", it's not enough to argue the toss. We must say that immigration leads to *higher* wages. Immigrants bring skills which complement the skills we already have. They innovate, fuel economic growth, pay a load of tax, reduce the government's deficit, reduce the national debt, open up export markets, rebalance our demographics, and yes – they help to increase our wages.

And when people say, "They're affecting our way of life", we must remind them that our way of life has *always* been changing – it'll continue to change, whether they like it or not. New ideas present themselves, technology evolves, and people respond – behaving in different ways. But immigrants can complement that change – helping to make things *better*. They bring a taste of the exotic and an outsider's perspective. Immigrants introduced fish and chips to England. They took football to Brazil. They built Hollywood. How amazing is that?

Finally, we must personalise the narratives we use in our articles – to remind people that our foreign-born brethren aren't statistics.

They aren't "Hoards", a "Flood" or an "Invasion – "Asylum Seekers", "Refugees" or "Economic Migrants". They're living, thinking, feeling human beings – with their own personalities and stories – and with DNA which is almost identical to our own. They're Marie from Tijuana, with a slight lisp, a passion for embroidery, two pet hamsters, and a dream of working in pharmaceutical research. They're Pavel from Poland, who plays football seven nights a week, and who cooks the spiciest pierogi you've ever tasted. And they're little Daisy, with those dimpled cheeks, that coquettish giggle, and that walk which morphs into a skip.

And if you really must bunch them all together, when making a general point, at least use positive words: Call them "Expats" rather than "Migrants". Call them "Globetrotters", "Jet-setters", "Explorers" or "Citizens of the World".

***

Things can change.

There was a time when the power of kings seemed insurmountable. To a Roman, living in the height of Caesar's reign, it must've seemed like Rome would never fall. Generations of serfs lived their lives, without ever expecting to hike beyond the boundaries of their master's land.

Kings were overthrown. Rome fell. Serfs were freed.

Other worlds were possible back then, and they remain possible today. We *can* liberate ourselves from the borders which divide us. And we *can* win the public's support, *if we speak the truth*.

Ingar Haaland and Christopher Roth proved this, in a study from 2020...

Those two academics recruited over three-thousand Americans – taking extra care to ensure that their sample was representative. Then they told those participants about the "Mariel Boatlift": In 1980, Fidel Castro reduced restrictions on emigration. Within a few months, 55,000 workers had left Cuba and arrived in Miami. The low-skilled workforce in that city had risen by around a fifth.

The participants in Haaland and Roth's study were then asked what effect they thought this might have had on wages and unemployment.

The vast majority believed it would've led to a decrease in wages and an increase in unemployment, for *low-skilled* Miamians. They didn't think it would've affected the high earners.

At this point, participants were also asked if they thought the government should allow more or fewer immigrants to enter the country.

In the second stage of the study, Haaland and Roth provided some new information: They quoted from a study, which concluded that the Mariel Boatlift had pretty much *no effect* on wages *or* unemployment – in the short-term or the long-run – for either low-skilled or high-skilled Miamians.

The researchers posed their questions again.

In light of the new information, people *did* change their views. They were less likely to believe that immigration led to lower wages and higher unemployment. They also showed more support for low-skilled immigration: Participants who'd been shown the additional information, were 69.2% more likely to sign a live government petition, asking the authorities to increase "The annual cap on low-skilled guest workers" – when compared to those participants who hadn't been informed of the facts.

And this wasn't a flash-in-the-pan affair.

When the researchers conducted a follow-up study, a week later, they achieved identical results. The new information had led to a *permanent* shift in opinions. (Haaland & Roth, 2020).

***

Another project reached a similar conclusion...

The researchers recruited nineteen-thousand respondents from across Europe and North America. Those participants were split into two groups: Half were told the actual number of immigrants in their nation. The other half was not. Then everyone was asked if they thought there were *too many* immigrants in their land.

The results were unsurprising: Those people who'd been presented with the facts, were far less likely to believe that there were too many foreigners, when compared to those people who hadn't been supplied with the relevant information. (Grigorieff et al, 2016).

***

Opinions do evolve...

Back in 2009, 65% of Brits said that locals should be given jobs before immigrants. Fast forward to 2022, and that number had dropped to just 29%. The UK's population had gone from being one of the least tolerant in Europe, to one of the most welcoming – all in the space of thirteen years. (Booth, 2023).

When asked *why* they'd changed their views, 52% of people said it was because, "I have become more aware about the role of migrants in key services such as health and social care". 42% said it was because, "The discussions since the vote to leave the EU have highlighted how much immigrants contribute to the UK". (Skinner et al, 2022).

The shift in opinion wasn't only caused by a change of narrative. Back in 2009, the country was suffering in the aftermath of the Global Economic Crash. People wanted "British jobs for British workers", because it felt like there weren't enough jobs to go around. In 2022, however, there were over a million vacancies. The country *needed* more foreign workers.

Still, it does show that people can be open-minded. We *do* change our views – both when our circumstances change, *and* when we're presented with new information.

***

This provides cause for optimism. But we should offer a word of caution: Yes, opinions can change. And yes, we can help to shift the narrative – when we post on social media, and when we converse with our peers. We can boycott newspapers which spread misinformation. But we're not the billionaire moguls who control the media. It'll be difficult to get *them* to change their ways.

Furthermore, just because facts can change minds, doesn't mean that they do so *all the time*. We humans can be stubborn buggers. As Mark Twain once remarked: "It's easier to fool a person, than it is to convince them that they've been fooled."

Other studies have reached different conclusions: In one long-running project, people were informed about the number of non-nationals who were living in their country. This did affect their perceptions. They stopped exaggerating the figures. But they still supported the same policies as before. (Hopkins et al, 2019).

It's seldom enough to *tell* – to lecture people about the benefits of free movement. People don't like being told what to think. We must also *show*. We must bring our peers into contact with their foreign-born peers...

COMING INTO CONTACT

I can't help but feel that my love of free movement has a lot to do with the positive experiences I've enjoyed, whilst interacting with members of different nations.

My greatest achievement on a football field came when I won the championship with the London School of Economics' seventh team. Okay, we were only playing in Division Four of a university league. It's not like we won the World Cup! (And no-one needs to know that second-placed SOAS didn't play all their fixtures. Shush!) But for me, it was a major landmark, after decades of sporting failure.

What stood out, however, was the cosmopolitan nature of that team.

Our goalkeeper was a Canadian whose only previous shot-stopping experience had come on an ice rink. You couldn't pass to him, because he refused to kick the ball, but his reflexes were the stuff of legend. Our left back and central midfielder both came from Hong Kong. Our playmakers were both Norwegian. We attracted players from the USA, France, Germany and Scotland.

I associate that achievement, and the happiness it brought, with my foreign teammates – the people who made it happen. And that makes me feel good about foreigners in general.

But my views haven't only been shaped in such a passive fashion – whilst waiting for people to move closer to me. I've also had positive experiences while I was abroad.

In Yoff, in Northern Senegal, I was invited to join a game of beach football. When we finished, I was taken to one of the player's homes, where I was introduced to every member of their family, and bombarded with sugary tea. When my wallet disappeared, in Guinea Bissau, a Ghanaian man tracked me down – just so he could introduce me to the people who'd found it. When I got lost, while trekking in the Nepalese mountains, a poor villager allowed me to stay in her wooden hut. I stayed with a Palestinian family in a historic building, in the centre of Hebron. And I stayed with some Zionist settlers in a makeshift cabin nearby. Both families were kind, welcoming and sincere. They had more in common than I doubt either of them would ever care to admit.

***

I think I've always been a freedom-lover. I've been rebelling against authority for as long as I can remember – I even got expelled from primary school! But these experiences – meeting foreigners at home and abroad – certainly helped to fix my ideas in place.

The reverse can also be true: If you *don't* come into contact with people from other nations, you're *not* going to have these positive experiences, and so you'll be *less* likely to support free movement.

It's interesting to note that Donald Trump's anti-freedom rhetoric garnered the best response in those places which were *less* cosmopolitan.

The states which Donald Trump won in 2016, had a *lower-than-average* score on the "Diversity Index". Most of them ranked in the bottom twenty states.

This means that people in those states which had *fewer* immigrants, were *more* likely to fear immigration, and to be enticed by a candidate who was standing on an anti-immigration ticket. (Edsall, 2017).

We see something similar in Britain.

Eric Kauffman and Gareth Harris studied the data from British "Wards" – areas with a population of around seven or eight thousand people. In those wards where the populace was almost entirely Caucasian, around nine-in-ten white Brits wanted to reduce immigration. But in those wards where minorities made up over half the population, only seven-in-ten white Brits wanted immigration to fall.

Many factors were at play. But contact must've made a difference: People who met non-nationals on a daily basis – who formed relationships with their foreign neighbours – became more tolerant over time. (Kauffman & Harris, 2015).

***

This relationship is seen whenever two groups are brought into contact. Indeed, this is why it's called the "Contact Hypothesis".

It was demonstrated in the film, "Remember the Titans".

Starring Denzel Washington as Coach Herman Boone, that movie was based on a true story: In 1971, a black school and a white school were merged. A black coach – Boone – was tasked with the job of integrating the American football team.

He got down to work.

When two buses arrived, to transport the youngsters to a training camp, the black players climbed onto one, and the white players stepped on board the other. But Boone intervened – forcing the youngsters to mix.

That camp helped the squad to bond.

Boone built a team that was stronger than before, because it featured all the best black players *and* all the best white ones – the cream of both crops. Together, they won the state championship.

Those kids arrived at their new school with a number of prejudices. But when they came into *contact*, they realised that they weren't so different: Some had been labelled "Black", and others had been labelled "White". But they were a similar age. They were studying similar courses at the very same school. They loved the same sport. And they all wanted to win. This goal brought those youths together.

What's more, it also brought the *town* together: As the team improved, it garnered support from the wider community. The antipathy towards the merger faded away.

***

A more formal study of this relationship was conducted by Muzafer and Carolyn Sherif, back in the 1950s.

Those psychologists invited two groups of eleven and twelve-year-old boys to a summer camp, in the Robber's Cave State Park. The lads bonded, within their separate groups, while participating in activities such as swimming and hiking. They named themselves the "Eagles" and the "Rattlers", established their own social norms, and created their own logos, shirts and flags.

At this point, the two groups were introduced, and invited to compete in a series of sporting contests. The winners were rewarded with prizes. But the losers went home with nothing.

The hostilities were almost instantaneous: The boys made threatening remarks. When one group turned up late to a picnic, the other group ate their food. The Eagles burned the Rattlers' flag. The Rattlers responded by ransacking the Eagles' cabin.

In the final stage of the experiment, the two groups were encouraged to come together. But the lads had little interest in playing games with their sworn enemies!

That was when the Sherifs upped the ante: They stopped the water supply, blamed it on "Vandals", and encouraged the two groups to collaborate to identify the issue. This time, they *did* respond – working together to find a sack, which had been forced inside the water pipe. The two gangs collaborated a second time, to remove that obstruction.

When they completed the task, the two groups celebrated *together*. And they cooperated once more, a little later on – pooling their money, so they could afford to screen a film. (Sherif, 1956).

***

If black and white athletes can put their differences aside, to excel at sport – and if enemy gangs can work together, to secure the supply of a vital resource – then, so the theory goes, *anyone* from *any* *background* should also be able to unite. Together, they'll achieve more.

We might see this in the workplace: A foreign doctor and a local nurse might form an efficient team, because they share a common goal – helping to cure their patients.

We might see this in the community: Two people from different nations might form a bond whilst helping to run a youth group, because they're driven by the same passion – helping youngsters to learn a musical instrument, play a sport, or go on expeditions.

And we might see this as consumers: A local might get to know an immigrant, by consuming their food, music or dance. They'll derive a great deal of pleasure from these things, and learn to respect foreigners in general.

***

The Contact Hypothesis was first posited by Gordon Allport, who studied American army units during the Second World War: In those rare instances where black and white soldiers fought together, Allport discovered that prejudice towards black soldiers was nine times *lower* than in segregated units. Those militiamen became comrades. They formed genuine bonds, and they began to see past the colour of each other's skin.

Allport believed there needed to be four conditions for *contact* to result in this kind of *acceptance*: People had to have equal status – with similar incomes, roles and characteristics. They had to abide by the same set of customs. They needed to cooperate, rather than compete. And they had to share a common objective. (Allport, 1954).

The Robber's Cave experiment fulfilled these criteria: The two gangs were all children – they all had "Equal status" and similar "Customs". And those youngsters came together, when they were forced to "Cooperate" to achieve a "Common objective" – securing the water they needed to drink. That "Superordinate" goal superseded their own "Individual" goals – compelling them to overcome their prejudices. (Sherif, 1956).

We see something similar in army units, where fellow soldiers perform the same life-or-death missions. We see this in universities, where academics must collaborate to make scientific breakthroughs. And we see this in hospitals, where surgeons must work together to save lives.

***

It all sounds rather lovely, doesn't it? We just have to encourage everyone to mix. They'll form relationships, and their prejudices will fade away.

But things are rarely so simple.

We began by mentioning a study which showed how attitudes towards migration were more positive in diverse British wards. But even there, 70% of white Brits still wanted to *reduce* immigration.

Furthermore, this relationship went into reverse, when the researchers turned their attention to "Regions" – areas with around a hundred-thousand people. When these larger zones were more diverse, people were *less* likely to support free movement.

The most diverse wards were still more welcoming, but the more homogenous wards – which tended to surround them – were *far less* tolerant than the norm. The people in those places were close enough to perceive a kind of "Threat" – the foreigners who were only a short distance away. But they weren't close enough to form genuine relationships with those people.

For contact to have an effect, it's not enough to be relatively near to a group of foreign nationals. You have to be *incredibly near*. (Kauffman & Harris, 2015).

It's not enough to form superficial relationships with international residents – seeing them in passing – in the workplace, in public or at school. In isolation, this can lead to hostility. Attitudes only improve when locals establish *genuine friendships* with foreign individuals. (Magnus & Bentsen, 2021).

Time is also a crucial factor: When outsiders first arrive in a relatively homogenous community, negative sentiment tends to follow. The states which voted for Trump may not have been home to that many foreigners. But their number was on the *rise*. Things were changing. And for the locals, that was a little scary. They needed time to adapt.

But people *do* adapt. What once felt novel, will begin to feel normal. What once seemed alien, will become a part of the local culture. The anxiety and fear that individuals can experience when they first encounter foreign people, will disappear when they bond, and realise that they have a lot in common.

ACT! (WITHIN THE LAW)

You can tell your compatriots about the benefits of freedom, and you can bring them into contact with people from different lands. These things *have* won hearts and minds...

According to a report from the Cato Institute, just over half of Americans consider migration to be a "Basic human right". Over two-thirds acknowledge that inward migration has helped to boost economic growth. And over six-in-ten agree that "Immigration enriches American culture".

42% of Americans say that immigration has been "Mostly good", whilst only 16% say that it's been "Mostly bad". (Ekins & Kemp, 2021).

The number of Americans who wish to see *less* immigration, is lower today than at any time since Gallup began to ask the question, back in 1965. Brits have become steadily more open to immigration, throughout the early years of this millennium. More than nine-in-ten Germans are happy to have neighbours with different backgrounds. And racial tolerance is at an all-time high in France. (Kuper, 2023).

There *is* already a groundswell of support for immigration. But this hasn't influenced our out-of-touch politicians, who continue to wage their war on free movement.

The lesson should be obvious: It's not enough to win the public's backing, sit back, and expect things to change. We have to *push* for that change ourselves.

Fortunately, some organisations are already leading the way...

***

No More Deaths was established by a coalition of community and faith groups. Operating in the deserts around Tucson, Arizona – a sweltering wilderness, characterised by rocky gullies, listless mountains, cacti and scrub – the group is on a mission to "End death and suffering in the US Borderlands".

They do all the things you might expect: Their volunteers *record* the suffering which travellers endure, they *publicise* these atrocities, and they *lobby* for humane policy. But they also make a difference in the here and now – trekking around the desert, depositing humanitarian aid – things such as food, socks, blankets, and jugs of water. They mark these items with supportive words, such as "Solidarity and love".

The organisation distributed more than thirty-thousand gallons of water, during a three-year period. They found that 86% of it was used, which highlights the genuine need for refreshments: We know that at least 270 people died near the Mexican border, in 2020 alone. A little water might've saved them.

But our politicians don't want to save lives: Lawmakers in Washington have adopted a policy dubbed "Prevention through deterrence" – closing the safest routes into the country, on the basis that: "Illegal traffic will be deterred, or forced over more hostile terrain".

It's that "Hostile terrain" which is killing our fellow civilians.

For the bloodthirsty ghouls in government, this is an achievement. A document produced by the Government Accountability Office, suggested that the "Deaths of aliens attempting entry" could be used to measure "The effectiveness of the strategy". A higher death toll was, in their view, a proof of success.

It's a philosophy that No More Deaths have witnessed firsthand: Four-hundred of their water bottles were vandalised within the space of three years. The organisation suspects that state officials were to blame. Those thugs continue to harass their volunteers – they "Surveil, detain, interrogate, threaten arrest, and (threaten) physical violence."

No-one said that making a stand for freedom would be easy. It's a fight against our governments – massive organisations, that claim a monopoly on violence, and who have far more resources than our people-powered organisations.

But the likes of No More Deaths persevere, compelled by the righteousness of their task: They provide resources to pilgrims, *before* they leave Mexico. They send search parties to rescue people who are lost in the desert. And they provide emergency treatment – both in the desert and back at their base.

Whenever travellers are seized by the state, No More Deaths arrange legal aid. They also ensure that those people are reunited with their possessions, once they've been released. (NoMoreDeaths.org). (Crawford, 2023).

***

Care for Calais plays a similar role in the UK, France and Belgium...

The charity champions an "Inclusive attitude towards refugees and asylum seekers", and tries to influence "The public's perception". But, first and foremost, they exist to *help* migratory people, as they battle the UK's army of border guards and petite bureaucrats: "Our focus is to provide warm clothing, bedding, food and medical assistance to people in desperate need. We also provide social support and interaction, including language lessons, and sports and music workshops."

As the name suggests, their work is centred around Calais, on the French side of the English Channel – where they operate a day centre and volunteer with children. They also visit refugee camps up the coast in Dunkirk – delivering firewood, tea and food. Once a week, they take supplies to a camp in Brussels. And once refugees have made it to the UK, they provide them with "The basics" – things like shoes, winter coats, legal assistance and medical aid.

They don't just challenge the narrative and campaign for reform – they help people to survive their arduous journeys, and thrive once they've reached their destination. (Care4Calais.org).

***

Other groups have been fighting for our rights elsewhere...

The *Sans Papiers Movement* was born in Paris's Saint Bernard Church, when the parish priest provided refuge for around three-hundred human beings. Things were going swimmingly, until a thousand axe-wielding police smashed down the doors, and manhandled the people inside – dragging them away, and locking them up behind bars.

Yet, if the authorities thought that would be the end of the story, they were in for a rude awakening!

This violence inspired a backlash. Several *other* sanctuary movements popped up across France. Activists began to protect different groups of migratory people. They staged sit-ins, and demanded political change.

***

The Sans Papiers had been inspired by the *Sanctuary Movement* in the States – in which five-hundred religious communities had provided safe spaces for non-nationals.

Abolish ICE remains active in the States today – campaigning to close the USA's Immigration and Customs Enforcement agency. (Nail, 2018).

Ya Basta, in Italy, is a protest movement with three demands: A guaranteed basic income for everyone on Earth, free access to new technology, and "Global Citizenship" – allowing people to live wherever they choose. It's been campaigning since 1994. (Graeber, 2002).

The *No Border Network* is an alliance of independent groups, who've staged protests across Europe – establishing campsites in Sicily, Strasbourg, Sweden and Spain – Gatwick, Germany and Greece. Their members have dressed as border guards. They've made bridges from boats. When Lufthansa tried to deport people, they blockaded Frankfurt's airport with the help of a classical orchestra! They've also blockaded the UK's Border Agency, and created a squat in the Netherlands. (Graeber, 2002).

At the time of writing, *Cornwall Resists* was staging protests against the Bibby Stockholm – a "Prison ship", used to detain refugees – stating: "People who have fled their homes in search of safety deserve our compassion, dignity and respect. They do not deserve to be scapegoated, detained by the state, and treated as less than human."

The likes of *No-One Is Illegal* (Canada) and *We Are Here* (the Netherlands), have held protests and sit-ins. They also provide legal assistance to the foreign victims of authoritarian laws. (King, 2016).

ACT! (IN DEFIANCE OF BAD LAWS)

Shortly before my gran passed away, I asked her to speak about her life. I wanted to document our family's past – to save her memories from oblivion. I wanted to preserve her voice.

Unfortunately, my laptop broke. Those recordings disappeared. But one of my gran's anecdotes stuck in my mind: She spoke of a relative who'd saved hundreds of children from the Holocaust. He'd even appeared on a television show – "That's Life".

While writing this book, I tried to identify that gallant individual. The closest I came was when I discovered a chap named Nicholas Winton.

Winton was certainly a hero. He rescued 669 children. And he did appear on "That's Life".

An emotional clip from the episode can still be seen on YouTube. In it, the presenter retells Winton's story, before introducing one of the people he'd saved – Vera Gissing. The cameras pan to Vera, whilst the host continues to speak: "Hello Vera. And I should tell you that you are actually sitting next to Nicholas Winton."

Smiling, Vera turns to Winton, and embraces the man who'd saved her. It's emotional stuff. But the show moves to another level, a few moments later, when the presenter asks: "Is there anyone else in our audience tonight, who owes their life to Nicholas Winton? If so, could you please stand?" Several rows of the audience get to their feet. You'd have to have a heart made of stone, not to feel an emotional response.

I haven't been able to unearth any evidence which suggests my gran was related to Winton. Perhaps he was a family friend, or perhaps my grandma was speaking about someone else. Still, his tale deserves to be told...

It was late 1938, and Europe was on the brink of war. The German army had just marched on the Sudetenland, and Prague was awash with people who'd fled from that region. They were safe, for the meantime, but the Nazis were on their way. Those refugees needed to continue their journeys. And they needed help.

That help arrived in the form of a twenty-nine-year-old, sports-loving stockbroker: Nicholas Winton. Upon hearing about the persecution of Jews and other dissidents, the Londoner had used his two-week vacation to travel to Prague, to see what he could do:

"I went out into the camps, where the people who had been displaced had been put. And it was winter. And it was cold."

It seemed there was no way out: The world had closed its doors on these people. Conditions were brutal, especially for the children. And no-one had come to their aid.

Winton set up shop in a hotel – giving himself a simple mission: To get as many youngsters out of the country, as quickly as he could.

His services were in demand: People kept on arriving, saying: "Take my child! Take my child!" There weren't enough hours in a day. Winton worked until two in the morning, barely slept, and then began again at dawn.

He returned to London with a list of children's names. But he had to convince the authorities to grant them entry. So he took some headed paper from a charity – The British Committee for Refugees from Czechoslovakia. And that was when he committed his first crime: *Fraud*. Winton added the words "Children Section", a bogus department, and gave himself a false title – the "Chairman" of this non-existent bureau.

The American authorities rejected Winton's appeals – a decision that might've cost thousands of lives. But the British acquiesced on one condition: Winton had to find families who were willing to house the children, before they were allowed to travel.

Winton was up to the task. But the government dragged its feet – taking forever to issue the all-important documents. And so Winton committed a second crime: *Forgery*. He faked the necessary papers.

At around the same time, he performed a third and a fourth crime: Winton *blackmailed* and *bribed* officials, to get the authorization he needed to proceed.

"It worked," he explained. "That was the main thing!"

The first twenty children left Prague during the Spring of 1939.

The Czech capital was occupied by German soldiers the very next day, and the persecution of Jews was quick to follow: They were attacked, their property was confiscated, and they were bundled into camps.

But Winton continued on.

During that spring and summer, seven trains left Prague – taking children through Germany and onto the Netherlands, where they embarked upon ferries and set sail for Britain.

An eighth train was due to shuttle another 250 children to safety. But war was declared on the day it was scheduled to leave. It never pulled out of the station.

Most of those children would've been taken to the Theresienstadt concentration camp, before being moved to Auschwitz, where they would've been murdered.

***

Winton was a modest guy. He didn't publicise his deeds:

"I didn't really keep it a secret. I just didn't talk about it!"

For fifty years, he focused on other projects – helping people with disabilities, and building homes for the elderly. The children he'd saved had no idea who he was, before he appeared on "That's Life":

"It was the most emotional moment of my life, suddenly being confronted with all those children, who weren't children anymore."

***

Winton is considered a hero in the Czech Republic. He was knighted in 2003. But there can be no escaping the facts: The man was a criminal. He broke the law on *three* separate occasions – committing acts of fraud, forgery, blackmail and bribery.

This isn't meant as a slur, although it'd be easy to misinterpret it as such.

If you're anything like me, you'd have undergone a kind of indoctrination while you were a child – in which you were made to think that those people who respected the law were good, and that those people who broke the law were bad. The police might've visited your school – making speeches during your assemblies. They might've held stalls at local fairs – handing out stickers, allowing you to wear their uniforms, and taking your fingerprints. Politicians like to speak of "Good, law-abiding citizens" and the police who "Protect" us. The media portrays these sentiments as though they're undisputed facts. You rarely hear people speak of "Good criminals" or "Bad laws".

But this is ideological – a kind of pro-law extremism. This belief that criminals are *always* the bad guys, and that law enforcers are *always* good, lacks any sort of nuance.

I certainly wouldn't wish to come at things from the opposite extreme – suggesting that criminals are always good. I only wish to promote a more *moderate* approach – arguing that the so-called "Criminals" might be righteous, *in certain situations*. Law enforcers might be the real threat. We need to judge these things on a case-by-case basis.

In this case, Winton – the criminal – was a good guy because he saved hundreds of lives. The policemen and soldiers who were responsible for the Holocaust, were in the wrong, even though they were upholding their government's laws.

***

Winton wasn't alone...

You may have heard of the Dutch family who hid Anne Frank in their attic. You may have seen the film about Irene Sendler, who smuggled Jewish children out of the Warsaw Ghetto.

These people follow in a long line of "Good criminals" – including those individuals who helped to liberate slaves, who ignored segregation laws, or who attacked the institutions of apartheid.

I've chosen to recount Winton's story, because it's relevant to this book: Winton broke the law, to *help people to move across international borders*.

***

We can apply the same logic to the modern world...

Borders are murderous constructs. They force people to endure the sorts of poverty which might kill them. They force people to remain in war zones, in places which are being decimated by environmental disasters, and in nations which are ruled by oppressive regimes.

Under a system based on freedom, people who were born in

such locations, through no fault of their own, would be able to move elsewhere. But borders deny them that right – condemning them to premature deaths.

These borders may be "Legal", but the guards who police them are the bad guys. We need more Nicholas Wintons – more rebels, who are prepared to bend the law, to help others to escape.

The smugglers we mentioned at the beginning of this chapter are deemed "Bad", because they're profiteers – they operate for personal gain. Some of them abandon or abuse the very people they're supposed to be helping. But if they were to behave more benevolently – like Winton – then *they'd* become the good guys. They might forge papers, and give them away for *free*. They might smuggle people across borders in a *humane* fashion – not to make money, but because it's the right thing to do.

We should encourage this sort of behaviour. We should support it wherever we can.

***

These aren't the only ways we can break the law, to help our foreign-born kith and kin...

When they arrive in our neighbourhoods, we can *hide* them from the authorities. That's what Miep Gies did, in Amsterdam, when he hid the Franks in his attic. It's what a parish priest did in Paris, when he provided sanctuary for hundreds of people.

We might also *vandalise* the walls which divide us – resigning them to the same fate that befell the Berlin Wall. Those walls are evil. They deserve to be destroyed.

The laws which underpinned the slave trade, segregation, apartheid, the Holocaust and colonialism – were murderous monstrosities, which ruined lives and condemned people to a premature death. The laws which maintain hard borders, fall into the same category as those spiteful laws. They're genocidal. And they deserve to be broken. The so-called "Criminals" who disobey them, will be remembered as heroes in the decades to come.

Accuse them of "Arson", "Vandalism", "Smuggling", "Trafficking" or "Forgery". It doesn't matter. Lives are at stake.

We need these rebels – these vigilantes who break bad laws.

THE CARROT NOT THE STICK

Even if after reading all this, you'd still like to see a little less immigration, it doesn't mean we should maintain the policies which exist today. We could take a softer approach, and achieve similar or better results.

We touched on this in the "Necessity" chapter: If you don't want people who are fleeing from war to end up in your country, then don't start wars in *their* countries! If you don't want people to flee from the bombs which were manufactured by your compatriots, then abolish the arms industry. If you don't want people to flee from their poverty, then help to enrich their nations. And if it annoys you when people escape from the effects of climate change, then stop polluting yourself!

Until this happens, people are going to move. You might *try* to stop them, but they'll still find a way to come. And in the meantime, you'll cause a load more hatred, violence and death.

So, here's a radical idea: Rather than go with the stick – saying, "If you come here, we'll capture, detain and deport you" – why not try the carrot? Why not say, "You could have an even better life *over there*"?

We saw how some nations are encouraging certain types of migration, in the "Nurture" chapter: Canada and Japan are enticing migrants, to rebalance their ageing demographics. China is wooing its diaspora – encouraging emigrants to return, open businesses, and create new jobs.

But we can go even further than that.

Whilst climate change is making some places uninhabitable, other areas are beginning to benefit: By 2080, over half the permafrost in Siberia will have melted. There'll be longer growing seasons, and the land will be able to sustain a much larger population. Antarctica is set to gain seventeen-thousand square-kilometres of new land. Alaska looks like it'll be the safest place to live, within the borders of the United States. And Canada is going to gain over four-million *square-kilometres* of arable farmland. It could end up with one-fifth of the world's freshwater. (Vince, 2022).

As things stand, only 20% of the Earth's land is taken up by urban expanse and cropland. Around half the planet's terrain is "Relatively untouched". We do have the space. We *can* house our peers in safe and suitable locations. (Riggio et al, 2020).

We're going to end up with some very hospitable terrain, in regions which remain sparsely populated today. These places could be the perfect destination for the next tranche of nomadic individuals. We just need to build the infrastructure, and encourage people to go to *those* particular locations.

We need to use the *carrot*, not the stick.

***

There is a historical precedent for this type of policy...

Roman residents were offered full citizenship, if they moved to the Empire's borderlands. And the American government passed the Homestead Act, in 1862 – gifting up to 160 acres of public land, to anyone who was willing to head west. That policy persuaded *1.6 million* "Pioneers" to relocate. And it was a win-win affair: Those families received hundreds-of-millions of acres of land, and the nation secured its frontiers. (Potter & Wynell, 1997).

This should provide an inspiration for policymakers *today*.

Indeed, the Russians are already in on the act...

The "Law on the Far Eastern Hectare" was passed by Vladimir Putin's government in 2016. That country is now gifting a hectare of land to any individual who chooses to move to its eastern region – an area which has very little infrastructure, but a lot of potential – with a population of just 7.4 million people, and more than ten-million square-kilometres of land.

This program means that a family of five could claim twelve acres! And even foreigners can claim their lot. In fact, immigrants are being *wooed* – granted five years of tax exemption, should they choose to relocate. Russia feels it needs those people – it wants a larger population in the region, to discourage Chinese expansion. And so those families are being welcomed in a way which must seem unimaginable on the Mexican border, or the fringes of the Mediterranean Sea. (Palmer, 2016).

Of course, we wouldn't want to develop *every* square metre of land. We need to preserve our wildlands – to protect the ecosystem. (Riggio et al, 2020).

But we can encourage certain migrations into underpopulated areas, whilst caring for our surroundings...

The Canadians are creating "Flash Forests" – using drones to plant a hundred-thousand trees a month, atop of their newly thawed terrain. They could build communities within those forests – providing spaces for both people *and* nature.

As things stand, Greenland has a relatively small population – with just under sixty-thousand residents. But it has a landmass which is considerably larger than Germany's. And its habitable land is growing as its ice sheets melt – meaning that Greenland could provide homes for tens or even hundreds of millions of people. What's more, it could do so in an environmentally friendly way: Greenland has the potential to produce massive amounts of hydro, geothermal, and wind power. Its ice melt provides more water than its residents will ever be able to drink. (Khanna, 2021).

BUILD THE INFRASTRUCTURE FOR FREEDOM

In the Netherlands, animals such as deer and badgers can traverse six-hundred custom-made corridors – enabling them to pass over train tracks, business parks and sports facilities. More than forty structures loop above a highway in Montana – allowing black bears, mountain lions and bobcats to avoid the speeding traffic. Conservationists have dug tunnels for toads, built bridges for squirrels, and erected ladders for fish. Architects have designed green roofs, covered in plants and flowers, which provide respite for butterflies and birds. (Shah, 2020).

If we can go to such lengths to create channels for migratory animals, don't you think we could build a similar infrastructure to help members of *our own species*?

We don't have to cover our borders in razor wire and watchtowers. We don't have to employ guards to harass people who don't conform to our government's definition of a "Legal" human being.

Indeed, open borders *do* already exist today: A person can cross from Texas into Louisiana, without showing any papers. The border between England and Scotland is little more than a "Welcome" sign on the side of a road. People from the thirty countries inside the European Economic Area, can cross into any other EEA nation, without so much as a pit-stop.

The idea of open borders isn't all that extreme. It just takes these existing arrangements, and seeks to expand them. But there is a challenge: Even with open borders, states will still want to govern the people who reside within their jurisdictions. Migratory people might wish to access public services, find gainful employment, or establish a business. So we'd still require an *administrative infrastructure*, which would enable our brethren to do these kinds of things. And right now, that infrastructure is a bit of a mess.

***

I'm speaking from personal experience...

When I moved to India, to start my career as an author, I was granted a six-month visa. When that visa expired, the law compelled me to leave the country. I had to travel for the best part of two days, to reach Nepal. It didn't help that the Maoists had called a national strike, enforced roadblocks, and left us with little choice but to spend a night on the side of the road! But that was just the start. After I'd waited for two weeks, I discovered that the Indian Embassy had issued the wrong visa. I had to kick my heels for another two weeks, before receiving the correct accreditation.

This sort of ball-ache is par for the course. I expect you'll find that things are far worse if you're a refugee, or if you don't have a passport from a wealthy nation.

As a Brit, it was pretty easy for me to claim Bulgarian residency. But it was much harder for my (now) wife, simply because she'd been born somewhere else.

She had to fly to Vietnam – because there's no Bulgarian Embassy in the Philippines – apply for a tourist visa, and stick around for three weeks while her application was being processed. That gave her the right to enter Bulgaria.

We could only apply for her residency *after* we'd entered the country. But it turned out that the only way to do this, was to either register as a business or get married. So we were forced into wedlock, to satisfy the criteria on a bureaucrat's list.

Even this was a palaver. We had to pass *four* medical examinations, and get documents sent over from abroad. And after all that, my wife was only granted *temporary* residency.

None of this would've been necessary, had there been a better *infrastructure* in place. All that should've been required, was a website – allowing us to declare our existence, and register our address. It shouldn't have taken more than five minutes. It shouldn't have cost a dime. The criteria should have been the same for everyone, no matter where they were born.

***

Anyone who's ever moved from country to country, will be familiar with the bureaucratic nightmares which pop up, even *after* you've submitted your papers, traipsed between offices, taken photos, passed your police checks, and endured your medical examinations.

Voting can be an issue...

Consider the case of James Preston, a realtor who worked for a British firm in Madrid. In 2011, Preston discovered that anyone who'd lived outside the UK for more than fifteen years, lost their right to vote (unless they'd worked for the British government). Preston was unable to elect a representative – either in the UK *or* in Spain. (Campbell, 2011).

Preston was taken by surprise, because he hadn't attempted to vote before. And that's not so unusual. In the US presidential election of 2012, 72% of eligible voters who'd been born in the USA, went out to cast a ballot. But only 48% of eligible immigrants did the same. It appears that foreign nationals are less likely to vote, even when they can. And that's hardly surprising: If you're new to a country, and unfamiliar with its politics, it can be difficult to know which candidate to choose. (Caplan, 2019).

But we should still have the *right* to vote, whether we use it or not. And in some countries, we already do...

The swanky name for this is "Non-citizen suffrage", but it tends to be conditional. In Chile and Columbia, for example, non-nationals can only vote after they've stuck around for a full five years. Hong Kong enfranchises all its "Permanent residents", but only after they've resided there for *seven* years. EU citizens have the right to vote in local and European elections, while living in other EU nations. In Greece, these rights have been extended to residents who come from outside the EU. But you'll struggle to find a nation where you can simply turn up, register, and vote in *every* election from day one.

And things get even trickier when we consider *standing* for election.

In theory, I could run for office here in the Philippines. But I'd have to secure citizenship, which is something very few foreigners manage to achieve. I'd also have to rescind my British citizenship, which might cost me my state pension.

At the same time, I could still stand for office in Britain. But that seems fairly implausible. How would I campaign, while living so far away? Who would vote for a candidate who'd gone to live abroad?

In reality, it seems unlikely that I'll ever hold political office.

The whole system needs to be overhauled. We need a new infrastructure – one that allows people to vote and stand for election wherever they choose.

***

Foreigners are the victims of several other forms of discrimination...

Purchasing land can be an issue: We had to buy our plot in my wife's name, even though I supplied the money. She's from the

Philippines, so she has the right to buy Philippine land. Some "Hacienderos" have taken this right to extremes – hoarding thousands of hectares. But I cannot own a regular parcel of land, because I was born in a different place.

Prices are another issue: You may have heard of the "Skin tax" – this idea that a seller might quote a higher price to a person who looks foreign – assuming they're wealthy and can afford to pay more. Here in the Philippines, one healthcare provider charges foreigners double the price for a vasectomy. And some governments use this scam: To visit the Taj Mahal, foreigners have to pay ten-times as much as an Indian national.

Healthcare can be a major concern: Twelve EU nations refuse primary and secondary care to undocumented people. Another six only grant them emergency healthcare.

This can have devastating consequences: International people tend to be healthier than their hosts, when they first arrive in a new land. But their health deteriorates soon after. In the Netherlands, for example, Iraqi refugees suffer from more psychiatric disorders and chronic physical ailments, the longer they're made to wait for their papers. (Spencer & Hughes, 2015). (Laban et al, 2008).

Then there's the sticky issue of the *driving licence*: If you visit a country for a short while, you're usually allowed to drive with a foreign licence. Stay a while longer, and you'll lose that right. You'll have to exchange your licence for a local one – paying some fees, completing some paperwork, waiting around, and maybe losing some of the categories. Move on again, and you'll have to exchange your licence a second time. And a third. And a fourth.

It's all so utterly pointless.

Couldn't we just create a system, that allows people to vote in whichever country they choose, stand as a candidate in any election, buy a certain amount of land in any location, pay the same prices no matter where they were born, and be granted equal access to healthcare? Couldn't we have an international driving licence, which allows people to drive on any road, anywhere on the planet?

We need a new *infrastructure for freedom* – one that would allow people to live, work and travel – wherever they darned well like!

***

Such an infrastructure has already been mooted by the French philosopher, Etienne Balibar. He's called for "New representative institutions", which serve *everyone*, wherever they happen to be. (Balibar, 2003).

Balibar was writing before the United Nations negotiated their "Global Compact for Safe, Orderly and Regular Migration", in December 2018. This is a "Non-legally binding, cooperative framework... (designed to foster) international cooperation among all relevant actors on migration, acknowledging that no state can address migration alone, and upholds the sovereignty of states and their obligations under international law."

Okay, it's a bit of a word salad! The "Non-legally binding" part means it's a bit of a damp squib. And it's certainly not a manifesto for open borders. It calls for nations to "Manage borders in an integrated, secure and coordinated manner."

But it is well-intentioned.

The thirty-four page document goes on to state: "We commit to facilitate and ensure safe, orderly and regular migration for the benefit of all."

It provides a kind of *Migrants' Bill of Rights*, with twenty-three "Objectives". These call for states to share data about their international inhabitants, and provide them with "Proof of legal identity and adequate documentation". It calls for governments to give foreign residents access to "Consular protection", "Basic services" and "Safer and cheaper transfer of remittances". And it demands that host nations allow migratory peoples the right to retain whatever social security they'd earned while living overseas. (United Nations, 2018).

When the compact was put to the vote, at the UN's General Assembly, hundreds of countries voted in favour. Only five were opposed.

Since then, plenty of other nations have decided *not* to ratify the treaty. But it still provides a starting point – something we can build upon in the years to come. (Shah, 2020).

THE RIGHT TO INTERNATIONAL CITIZENSHIP

The United Nation's "Compact" encourages nations to regularise people's *immigration status*. And that'd be a start. But those of us who support open borders, are calling for something way more profound. We believe that there shouldn't be such a thing as "Immigration status". It shouldn't matter where you were born. You should be treated as an equal – a fellow human being – no matter where you're standing.

My idea is pretty simple: Adults should be given a free choice – to be "Nationals" or "Internationals".

If you want to be nationalistic, then that's fine. You can have your cake, you can put a cherry on top, and you can eat it whenever you like. Use your national passport, wave your nation's flag, and sing your national anthem. You need never leave the land of your birth.

But if you're not that way inclined, if you'd rather be *a citizen of the world*, then you should have the right to register for *international citizenship*, and claim a passport that would allow you to live, travel, work, study, retire, consume, drive, vote, stand for election, claim welfare and access healthcare in any place – without having to complete any forms, pay any fees, wait in any lines, get married, exchange your driving licence, or jump through any other bureaucratic hoops.

***

International passports do already exist...

Diplomatic passports allow embassy staff to hop across borders, with "Immunity" from prosecution. Monarchs, presidents and prime ministers have special passports, which grant them entry into whichever countries they visit. Queen Elizabeth didn't even have a passport! But that never stopped her from travelling wherever took her fancy. Interpol's employees have ID cards, which grant them entry into almost any nation on the planet. And members of some associations, such as the World Health Organisation, can get their hands on the United Nations' *Laissez-Passer*, which affords them certain privileges, and visa-free access to a raft of different nations. (Noble, 2022).

So we're not talking about creating something new. We're talking about democratising something that *already exists* – taking the kinds of passports which are used by the rich and powerful, and offering them to regular folk.

***

As things stand, people can create *their own passports*...

When the Australian government refused to provide legal status for four-hundred asylum seekers, imprisoned in a detention centre near Papua New Guinea, Aborigine elders created a new document – the "Aboriginal passport" – and issued it to those marginalised people. (Faa, 2019).

And the "World Citizen Government" issues a "World Passport", which looks like a regular passport – with a black cover, laminated information page, and thirty sides which can be used for stamps and visas. The document doesn't indicate a person's nationality. "It is therefore a neutral, apolitical document of identity and (a) potential travel document."

The key word is "Potential". The World Passport looks and feels like a regular passport. It's been used to gain entry into 185 nations, over the course of sixty years. But passport holders still have to apply for visas. The World Passport doesn't grant the right to travel, work or live in any particular nation. It's more "Nation-neutral" than "International". Only six nations respect the booklet without asking any questions. And it'll set you back a cool $125. (WorldService.org).

***

We need something more – an "International citizenship", which would grant us the right to go wherever we choose, *without* visas, authorization, violence or bureaucracy.

Indeed, we can already enter one particular territory, without securing any of these things: In *Svalbard*, an Arctic archipelago to the north of Norway, anyone can show up without prior notice, and stay for as long as they like – no questions asked. New arrivals are automatically granted the right to work. They just have to register, by showing an identity card. And that's the end of that.

If it's possible in Svalbard, it can be possible anywhere. We just need the political will.

***

These things should be easier than ever before, because we live in a digital age...

New technology allows us to do most of our administrative tasks in the cloud. Several jobs can already be performed online, from any location – as we saw when we met the digital nomads. We can store our money in e-wallets, which aren't registered at a physical address. Nomads in Estonia are given a USB key, which grants them access to *all* the country's services. There's no reason why everybody couldn't be given that same sort of key – and granted access to every service, in every nation on Earth.

Perhaps we'd all get an international ID, which we'd scan whenever we arrived at a new destination. Or perhaps we'd register online. A simple calculation would work out what taxes we owed to what governments. We'd make a single payment, which would be sent on to the relevant exchequers. In return, we'd be granted access to healthcare and welfare, in any location on Earth. Our pensions would be protected, no matter where we lived.

The system could work out the place where we'd lived for the longest, and grant us the right to vote and stand in its elections.

We could issue driving licences which are valid on every road, anywhere on the planet.

***

Right now, *everything* is set up to serve those individuals who have a nationalistic mindset. And they can keep their systems. They can have their national citizenships, their national passports, their visas and their borders.

But the nationalists shouldn't be allowed to impose their systems onto everyone else. Internationalists should be allowed to live their lives in a way that suits them – so long as they don't harm anyone else. We should have the option to claim *international citizenship* – securing ourselves the right to reside wherever we like, for however long we choose. Because some of us long to be free. And because nobody else should be allowed to stand between us and our freedom.

REFERENCES

Abdalla, Safa; Cronin, Fran; Daly, Leslie et al. (September 2010). "All Ireland Traveller Health Study". University College Dublin.

Alesina, Alberto; Miano, Armando; Stantcheva, Stefanie. (January 2023). "Immigration and Redistribution". The Review of Economic Studies, Volume 90, Issue 1, Pages 1-39.

Allen, William. (7th November 2016). "A Decade of Immigration in the British Press." Migration Observatory.

Allport, Gordon. (1954). "The Nature of Prejudice". Perseus Books.

Alonso, Paola. (7th November 2020). "My Grandfather, The Bracero". Texas Woman's University.

Al-Saeed, Ashraf; El Khalil, Zeina. (1st June 2021). "Lebanon Sinking into One of the Most Severe Global Crises Episodes, amidst Deliberate Inaction". The World Bank.

Anderson, Nicholas (18th January 2023). "Basketball Gone Global: The Rapid Expansion of the Classic American Sport". The Science Survey.

Anderson, Stuart. (27th July 2020). "Immigrant Players Steal Bases And Basketballs, Not Jobs" Forbes.

Anderson, Stuart. (March 2016). "Immigrants and Billion Dollar Start-ups". The National Foundation for American Policy.

Anser, MK; Yousaf, Z; Nassani, AA et al. (5th June 2020). "Dynamic linkages between poverty, inequality, crime, and social expenditures in a panel of 16 countries". Economic Structures, Volume 9, Article Number 43.

Auer, Daniel; Tetlow, Daniel. (July 2020). "Brexit, Collective Uncertainty and Migration Decisions". WZB Berlin Social Science Center , Discussion Paper SP VI 2020–102.

Auton, A.; Brooks, L. D.; Durbin, R. M. et al. (1st October 2015). "A global reference for human genetic variation". Nature Journal, Volume 526, Issue 7571, Pages 68-74.

Balibar, Etienne. (14th December 2003). "We, the People of Europe? Reflections on Transnational Citizenship". Princeton University Press.

Ballard, Roger. (2011). "Indian, Pakistani, and Bangladeshi Migrants in Great Britain since 1947" in "The Encyclopaedia of Migration and Minorities in Europe". Cambridge University Press.

Bankston, Carl; Zhou, Min. (Summer 2002). "Being Well vs. Doing Well: Self Esteem and School Performance Among Immigrant and Non-immigrant Race and Ethnic Groups". International Migration Review, Volume 36, Number 2, Pages 389-415.

Barbujani, G; Magagni, A; Minch, E; Cavalli-Sforza, LL. (1997). "An apportionment of human DNA diversity". Proceedings of the National Academy of Sciences, Volume 94, Issue 9, Pages 4516-4519.

Barfield, Thomas. (January 1991). "Tribe and state relations: The Inner Asian perspective" in "Tribes and State Formation in the Middle East". University of California Press, Berkley.

Basta, Hannah. (Spring 2017). "Slaves, Coloni, and Status Confusion in the Late Roman Empire". Journal of the National Collegiate Honors Council.

Bastani, Aaron. (11th June 2019). "Fully Automated Luxury Communism". Verso Books.

Batalova, Jeanne. (14th May 2020). "Immigrant Health-Care Workers in the United States". Migration Policy Institute.

Batalova, Jeanne. (21st July 2022). "Top Statistics on Global Migration and Migrants". Migration Policy Institute.

Beard, Mary. (27th April 2016). "Ultimate Rome: Empire Without Limit". Timeline, Episode 1.

Beard, Mary. (11th May 2016a). "Ultimate Rome: Empire Without Limit". Timeline, Episode 3.

Beine, Michel; Docquier, Fréderic; Rapoport, Hillel. (April 2008). "Brain drain and human capital formation in developing countries: winners and losers". The Economic Journal, Volume 118, Number 528 pages 631-652.

Bennet, James. (3rd June 2010). "The open society and its discontents". The Economist.

Bentham, Jeremy. (1789). "An Introduction to the Principles of Morals and Legislation" Early Modern Texts.

Beyer, John. (2021). "Immigrants Are Vital to the U.S. Economy". Joint Economic Committee, US Senate.

Bianconi, Eva; Piovesan, Allison; Facchin, Federica et al. (2013). "An estimation of the number of cells in the human body". Annals of Human Biology, Volume 40, Issue 6, Pages 463-471.

Bier, David. (21st February 2023). "Immigrating to the US Is The Main Way To Escape Poverty in Dozens of Countries". Cato Institute.

Bier, David. (26th July 2016). "Why Unemployment Is Lower When Immigration Is Higher". Cato Institute.

Bivens, Josh. (23rd January 2019). "Updated employment multipliers for the US economy". Economic Policy Institute.

Black, Julia. Golindo, Jorge; Damasco, Diego; Gallo, Jorge. (12th September 2023). "US-Mexico Border World's Deadliest Migration Land Route". Missing Migrants Project, International Organization for Migration.

Blanchet, Nancy. (18th July 2021). "Immigrant-led SME Exporters in Canada". Economist, Trade and Economic Analysis Division, Government of Canada.

Blinder, Scott; Allen, William. (2016). "Constructing Immigrants: Portrayals of Migrant Groups in British National Newspapers, 2010-2012". International Migration Review, Volume 50, Issue 1, Pages 3-40.

Bloom, Laura. (31st January 2022). "Work From Home or Anywhere: Top 30 Companies For Remote Jobs In 2022". Forbes.

Bloomberg, Michael. (June 2012). "Patent Pending: How Immigrants are Reinventing the American Economy". A report from the Partnership For a New American Economy.

Boin, Douglas. (9th June 2020). "Alaric the Goth: An Outsider's History of the Fall of Rome". W. W. Norton & Company.

Booth, Robert. (23rd February 2023). "UK now among most accepting countries for foreign workers, survey finds". The Guardian.

Borjas, George. (2003) "The Labor Demand Curve Is Downward Sloping: Re-examining the Impact of Immigration on the Labour Market." Quarterly Journal of Economics,

Volume 118, Number 4, Pages 1335-74.

Boskamp, Elsie. (15th February 2023). "40+ Vital Outsourcing Statistics [2023]: How Many Jobs Lost To Outsourcing?" Zippia.

Bregman, Rutger. (14th March 2017). "Utopia for Realists: How We Can Build the Ideal World". Little, Brown and Company.

Bremmer, Jan. (1st August 2021). "Becoming a man in Ancient Greece and Rome". Mohr Siebeck Tübingen.

Bridle, James. (1st April 2022). "The speed of a tree: how plants migrate to outpace climate change". The Financial Times.

Bundy, Colin. (26th April 2018). "South Africa's African National Congress in Exile". Oxford Research Encyclopaedias.

Bryc, Katarzyna; Durand, Eric; Macpherson, J. Michael; Reich, David; Mountain, Joanna. (8th January 2015). "The Genetic Ancestry of African Americans, Latinos, and European Americans across the United States". American Society of Human Genetics Journal, Volume 96, Issue 1, Pages 37-53.

Bugge, Axel. (31st May 2017). "People smugglers make $35bn a year on migrant crisis". Reuters.

Burley, Leo. (13th July 2022). "The Real Mo Farah". Atomized Studios, British Broadcasting Corporation, Red Bull Studios.

Cai, Hongbo; Meng, Yinghua; Chakraborty, Suparna. (February 2021). "Migrants and exports: Decomposing the link". Journal of World Business, Volume 56, Issue 2.

Calnitsky, David; Gonalons-Pons, Pilar. (18th March 2020). "The Impact of an Experimental Guaranteed Income on Crime and Violence". Social Problems, Volume 68, Issue 3, Pages 778-798.

Campbell, Duncan. (29th March 2011). "Most Brits in Spain say no gracias to integration". The Guardian.

Campbell-Whittle, Iain. (2023). "Donohoe and Bangu, Proctor and Stark". Scots Football Worldwide.

Caplan, Bryan. (29th October 2019). "Open Borders: The Science and Ethics of Immigration". First Second.

Card, David; and Peri, Giovanni. (December 2016) "Immigration Economics by George J. Borjas: A Review Essay." Journal of Economic Literature, Volume 54, Number 4, Pages 1333-49.

Carens, Joseph. (2013). "The Ethics of Immigration". Oxford University Press.

Carens, Joseph. (Spring 1987). "Aliens and Citizens: The Case for Open Borders". Review of Politics, Volume 49, Number 2, Pages 251-273.

Carotenuto, Francesco; Tsikaridze, Nikoloz; Rook, Lorenzo et al. (June 2016). "Venturing out safely: The biogeography of Homo erectus dispersal out of Africa". Journal of Human Evolution, Volume 95, Pages 1-12.

Carrier, David. (March 2007). "The Short Legs of Great Apes: Evidence for aggressive behaviour in australopiths". International Journal of Organic Evolution, Volume 61, Issue 3, Pages 596-605.

Chen, I-Ching; Hill, Jane; Ohlemüller, Ralf et al. (19th August 2011). "Rapid Range Shifts of Species Associated with High Levels of Climate Warming". Science, Volume 333, Issue 6045, Number 1024-1026.

Chen, Shuai. (24th November 2008). "What percent of DNA is different between a European and an Asian?". The Tech Interactive.

Chote, Robert; Parker, Graham; Bean, Charles. (July 2018). "Fiscal sustainability report". Office for Budget Responsibility.

Claudian. (1922). "The Gothic War". The Loeb Classical Library.

Clemens, Michael. (Summer 2011). "Economics and Emigration: Trillion-Dollar Bills on the Sidewalk?" The Journal of Economic Perspectives, Volume 25, Number 3, Pages 83-106.

Clemens, Michael; Hunt, Jennifer. (30th January 2019). "The Labor Market Effects of Refugee Waves: Reconciling Conflicting Results". ILR Review, Volume 72, Issue 4, Pages 818-857.

Clemens, Michael; Lewis, Ethan; Postel, Hannah. (June 2018). "Immigration Restrictions as Active Labor Market Policy: Evidence from the Mexican Bracero Exclusion". American Economic Review, Volume 108, Number 6, pages 1468-87.

Clemens, Michael; Pritchett, Lant. (September 2008). "Income per Natural: Measuring Development for People Rather than Places". Population and Development Review, Volume 34, Number 3, Pages 395-434.

Commission For Racial Equality. (May 2006). "Common Ground: Equality, good race relations and sites for Gypsies and Irish Travellers".

Connor, Philip. (29th June 2021). "How are immigration and GDP growth connected?" FWD.

Cooper, Mary-Beth. (2022). "Where Basketball was Invented: The History of Basketball". Springfield College.

Cornelius, Wayne; Lewis, Jessa. (2006). "Impacts of Border Enforcement on Mexican Migration: The View from Sending Communities". Lynne Rienner Publishers.

Cornelius, Wayne; Salehyan, Idean. (June 2007). "Does border enforcement deter unauthorized immigration? The case of Mexican migration to the United States of America". Regulation & Governance Journal, Volume 1, Issue 2, Pages 139-153.

Cowell, Alan. (13th November 2017). "German Newspaper Catalogs 33,293 Who Died Trying to Enter Europe". New York Times.

Crawford, James. (10th January 2023). "The Edge of the Plain: How Borders Make and Break Our World". W. W. Norton & Company.

Crawford, Nicholas; Kelly, Derek; Hansen, Matthew et al. (12th October 2017). "Loci associated with skin pigmentation identified in African populations". Science, Volume 358, Number 6365.

Crow, James Franklin. (Winter 2002). "Unequal by nature: A geneticist's perspective on human differences". Dædalus.

Crown, Daniel; Faggian, Alessandra; Corcoran, Jonathan. (2020). "High skilled immigration and the occupational choices of native workers: the case of Australia". Oxford Economic Papers, Volume 72, Issue 3, Pages 585-605.

Cruz, Melissa. (January 2021). "The Cost of Immigration Enforcement and Border

Security". American Immigration Council.

Davis, Mark; Chew, Matthew; Hobbs, Richard et al. (8th June 2011). "Don't judge species on their origins". Nature, Volume 474, Pages 153-154.

Davis, Mark; Thompson, Ken; Grime, J. Philip. (January 2001). "Charles S. Elton and the dissociation of invasion ecology from the rest of ecology". Diversity and Distributions Journal, Volume 7, Issue 1-2, Pages 97-102.

Davies, Robert. (16th September 2003). "Christian Slaves, Muslim Masters: White Slavery in the Mediterranean, the Barbary Coast and Italy, 1500–1800" London 2004. Palgrave Macmillan.

Dawson, Fabian. (6th March 2023). "New immigration operation centre in Philippines part of Canada's bid to attract more skilled workers". New Canadian Media.

De Cocker, Julie. (2023). "Kazakh Nomads of Mongolia: Eagle Hunters". Gorgeous Unknown.

De Meyer, Tim. (2017). "Attracting skilled international migrants to China: A review and comparison of policies and practices". Centre for China and Globalization (CCG).

De Queiroz, Alan. (7th January 2014). "The Monkey's Voyage: How Improbable Journeys Shaped the History of Life". Basic Books.

Derrida, Jacques; Dufourmantelle, Anne; Bowlby, Rachel. (1st September 2000). "Of Hospitality (Cultural Memory in the Present)". Stanford University Press.

Dillehay, TD, Ocampo C, Saavedra J, Sawakuchi AO, Vega RM, Pino M, et al. (18th November 2015). "New Archaeological Evidence for an Early Human Presence at Monte Verde, Chile". PLoS ONE Journal. 10(11): e0141923.

Dilts, Andrew. (5th January 2015). "Dismantle & Transform: On Abolition, Decolonization, & Insurgent Politics". Abolition Journal.

Dingle, Hugh. (10th September 2014). "Migration: The Biology of Life on the Move". Oxford University Press.

Dobbs, David. (January 2013). "Restless Genes". National Geographic Magazine.

Docquier, Frédéric; Ozden, Caglar; Peri, Giovanni. (February 2011). "The Wage Effects of Immigration and Emigration". Policy Research Working Paper 5556, The World Bank Development Research Group.

Domnich, Alexander; Panatto, Donatella; Gasparini, Roberto; Amicizia, Daniela. (September 2012). "The "healthy immigrant" effect: Does it exist in Europe today?". Italian Journal of Public Health, Volume 9, Number 3, eLocator e7532.

Donaldson, Erin; Devlin, Rachel; Stites, Chip et al. (2013). "Global Retirement Index". International Living.

Dowd, Lisa. (24th January 2022). "'Death threats are a way of life': Gypsies and Irish Travellers and Muslims 'least-liked' in UK, survey finds". Sky News Website.

Dowty, Alan. (1987). "Closed Borders: The Contemporary Assault on the Freedom of Movement". Yale University Press.

Duffy, Bobby; Frere-Smith, Tom. (January 2014). "Perceptions and Reality: Public Attitudes to Immigration". IPSOS Mori.

Dumitriu, Sam; Stewart, Amelia. (10th July 2019). "Job Creators: The Immigrant Founders of Britain's Fastest Growing Businesses". The Entrepreneurs Network.

Duncker, Karl. Translated by Lynne Lees. (1945). "On problem solving". Psychological Monographs, Volume 58, Number 5, Pages 1-113.

Dustmann, Christian; Frattini, Tommaso. (November 2013). "The Fiscal Effects of Immigration to the UK". Centre for Research and Analysis of Migration, Discussion Paper Series, CDP No 22/13.

Dustmann, Christian; Frattini, Tommaso; Preston, Ian. (2013) "The Effect of Immigration along the Distribution of Wages". Review of Economic Studies, Volume 80, Pages 145-173.

Dyson, Stephen L. (1985). "Roman border control rare The Creation of the Roman Frontier". Princeton Legacy Library.

Edsall, Thomas. (5th October 2017). "How Immigration Foiled Hillary". New York Times.

Eisenberg, Dan TA; Campbell, Benjamin; Gray, Peter B; Sorenson, Michael D. (10th June 2008). "Dopamine receptor genetic polymorphisms and body composition in undernourished pastoralists". BMC Evolutionary Biology, Volume 8, Article 173.

Ekins, Emily; Kemp, David. (27th April 2021). "E Pluribus Unum: Findings from the Cato Institute 2021 Immigration and Identity National Survey". Cato Institute.

Emmer, Pieter C. (2011). "West Indians in Great Britain, France, and the Netherlands since the End of World War II" in "The Encyclopedia of Migration and Minorities in Europe". Cambridge University Press.

Emmer, Pieter C.; Lucassen, Leo. (13th November 2012). "Migration from the Colonies to Western Europe since 1800". EGO-Redaktion.

Engel, Jeffrey. (1st June 2021). "American Immigration: Fear, Myth, and Reality". Dreamscape Media.

Engels, Friedrich. (July 1867). "On The Lausanne Congress". Marx Engels Collected Works, Volume 20, page 421.

Esipova, Nail; Pugliese, Julie; Ray, Anota. (2012). "Gallup World Poll: The Many Faces of Global Migration". Gallup.

European Commission. (April 2018). "Integration of Immigrants in the European Union." Directorate General for Communication, Special Barometer 469.

Everson, Miles; King, Steve; Ockels, Carolyn. (September 2022). "Working From The Road: The Aspirations and Reality for Digital Nomads". MBO Partners & Emergent Research.

Faa, Marian. (17th July 2019). "Refugees on Manus to receive Australian First Nations 'passports' from activists aboard sail boat". ABC News.

Feinblatt, John. (12th March 2019). "New Data Shows Immigrant-Owned Businesses Employed eight-million Americans". New American Economy.

Felbab-Brown, Vanda. (Aug 2017). "The Wall: The Real Costs of a Barrier between the United States and Mexico". Brookings Institution Press.

Fernandez, Manny. (4th May 2017). "A Path to America, Marked by More and More Bodies". New York Times.

Fernández-Reino, Mariña; Rienzo, Cinzia. (6th January 2022). "Migrants in the UK Labour Market: An Overview". The Migration Observatory, The University of Oxford.

Field, Martin, Bel, Sarah. (8th May 2015). "Global Burden of Armed Violence 2015: Every

Body Counts". Geneva Declaration on Armed Violence and Development (Report).

Finch, Jenn. (14th June 2020). "The Cultural Impact of Migration: The Impact of Sound System Culture on Britain". Halcyon Wax.

Finney, Ben. (June 1991). "Myth, Experiment, and the Reinvention of Polynesian Voyaging". American Anthropologist, Volume 93, Number 2, Pages 383-404.

Firestone, Ross. (17th January 1994). "Swing, Swing, Swing: The Life and Times of Benny Goodman". W.W. Norton & Company Press.

Fleagle, J.; Shea, J; Grine, F et al. (2010). "Out of Africa I: The First Hominin Colonization of Eurasia". Springer.

Fleming, Luke. (2011). "The Relationship Between Poverty and Crime: A Cross Section Analysis Luke Fleming". Bryant University.

Foster, Frederick; Collard, Mark. (28th August 2013). "A Reassessment of Bergmann's Rule in Modern Humans," PLOS One, Volume 8, Number 8, eLocator e72269.

Fouarge, Didier; Özer, Merve; Seegers, Philipp. (December 2019). "Personality traits, migration intentions, and cultural distance". Regional Science, Volume 98, Issue 6, Pages 2425-2454.

Fox, Alex. (13th April 2020). "Hares and Chickens Were Revered as Gods - Not Food - in Ancient Britain". Smithsonian.

Fraknoi, Andrew. (Spring 2007). "How Fast Are You Moving When You Are Sitting Still?". The Universe in the Classroom, Number 71.

Frausto, Maria. (11th April 2016). "National Volunteer Week: How Much Do Immigrants Volunteer?" New American Economy.

Fredrick, James. (4th August 2023). "Like traps meant for animals". The Guardian.

Freidman, Milton. (13th September 1970). "A Friedman doctrine: The Social Responsibility of Business Is to Increase Its Profits". The New York Ties, Section SM, Page 17.

Frydman, Alma Andino. (October 2022). "Work and Pleasure; Investigating the Rise of Digital Nomads in Mexico". Stanford Institute for Economic Policy Research, Stanford University.

Funk, Cary; Lopez, Mark. (14th June 2022). "Hispanic Americans' Trust in and Engagement With Science". Pew Research Center.

Gabler, Neal. (8th September 1989). "An Empire of Their Own: How the Jews Invented Hollywood". Anchor Books.

Galloway, Hamilton; Gambarin, Alice. (16th May 2023). "The State of the Creator Economy: Assessing the Economic, Cultural, and Educational Impact of YouTube in the US in 2022". Economic Consulting Team, Oxford Economics.

Gelin, Martin. (23rd June 2020). "Japan Radically Increased Immigration and No One Protested". Foreign Policy.

Georgieva, Kristalina. (2018). "Moving For Prosperity: Global Migration and Labor Markets". Policy Research Report, World Bank Group.

Georgiou, Myria; Zaborowski, Rafal. (March 2017). "Media coverage of the 'Refugee Crisis': A cross-European perspective". Council of Europe, Report DG1(2017)03.

Gerstle, Gary. (5th April 2022). "The Rise And Fall Of The Neoliberal Order: America and the World in the Free Market Era". Oxford University Press.

Gibson, Campbell. (June 1992). "The Contribution of Immigration to the Growth and Ethnic Diversity of the American Population". Proceedings of the American Philosophical Society, Volume 136, Number 2, Pages 157-175.

Gioia, Ted. (17th December 1998). "The History Of Jazz". Oxford University Press.

Gita-Carlos, Ruth. (29th November 2019). "Duterte promises 'sustainable' work, livelihood for OFWs in PH". Philippine News Agency.

Goldin, Ian. (11th October 2011). "Exceptional People: how migration shaped our world and will define our future". Lecture at the London School of Economics.

Goldin, Ian; Cameron, Geoffrey; Balarajan, Meera. (16th September 2012). "Exceptional People: How Migration Shaped Our World and Will Define Our Future". Princeton University Press.

Goodwin, Andrew; Serra, Margarida. (18th October 2022). "The impact of YouTube in the UK". Economic Consulting Team, Oxford Economics.

Gouveia, Alexandria. (13th April 2020). "Famous Immigrant Designers Who Pursued The American Dream". Vogue.

Graeber, David. (January/February 2002). "The New Anarchists". New Left Review, Volume 13.

Graeber, David; Wengrow, David. (19th October 2021). "The Dawn of Everything: A New History of Humanity". Allen Lane.

Grigorieff, Alexi; Roth, Christopher; Ubfal, Diego. (December 2016). "Does information change attitudes towards immigrants? Representative Evidence from Survey Experiments". IZA Institute of Labor Economics, Discussion Paper Series, Number 10419.

Grindon, AJ; Davison, A. (19th June 2013) Irish Cepaea nemoralis Land Snails Have a Cryptic Franco-Iberian Origin That Is Most Easily Explained by the Movements of Mesolithic Humans. Plos One Journal, Volume 8, Number 6.

Grishkevich, Vladislav; Yanai, Itai. (24th September 2024). "Gene length and expression level shape genomic novelties". Genome Research, Volume 24, Issue 9, Pages 1497-1503.

Griswold, Daniel. (18th February 2002). "Immigrants Have Enriched American Culture and Enhanced Our Influence in the World". Cato Institute.

Grøn, Ole. (2015). "Territorial Infrastructure, Markers and Tension in Late Mesolithic Hunter-gatherer Societies: An Ethnoarchaeological Approach". The 150th Aniversary of the Discovery of Mesolithic Shellmiddens, Volume 2, Chapter 16.

Guest, Robert. (8th November 2011). "Borderless Economics: Chinese Sea Turtles, Indian Fridges and the New Fruits of Global Capitalism". St. Martin's Press.

Gugliotta, Guy. (July 2008). "The Great Human Migration". Smithsonian Magazine.

Guimarães Lima, Margareth et al. (3rd December 2019). "Leisure-time physical activity and sports in the Brazilian population: A social disparity analysis". PloS One Journal, Volume 14, Number 12.

Haaland, Ingaar; Roth, Christopher. (November 2020). "Labor market concerns and support for immigration". Journal of Public Economics, Volume 191.

Hajari, Nisid. (21st June 2016). "Midnight's Furies: The Deadly Legacy of India's Partition". Mariner Books.

Hanson, Gordon; McIntosh, Craig. (Fall 2016). "Is the Mediterranean the New Rio Grande? US and EU Immigration Pressures in the Long Run". The Journal of Economic Perspectives, Volume 30, Number 4, Pages 57-81.

Hao, Lingxin; Bonstead-Bruns, Melissa. (July 1998). "Parent-Child Differences in Educational Expectations and the Academic Achievement of Immigrant and Native Students," Sociology of Education, Volume 71, Number 3, Pages 175-198.

Harmon, Amy. (17th October 2018). "Why White Supremacists Are Chugging Milk (and Why Geneticists Are Alarmed)". The New York Times.

Harris, Angel; Jamison, Kenneth; Trujillo. (November 2008). "Disparities in the Educational Success of Immigrants: An Assessment of the Immigrant Effect for Asians and Latinos". The ANNALS of the American Academy of Political and Social Science, Volume 620, Issue 1, Pages 90-114.

Harris, Jason; LaRocque, Regina; Chowdhury, Fahima et al. (9th Aril 2009). "Susceptibility to Vibrio cholerae infection in a cohort of household contacts of patients with cholera in Bangladesh". PLOS Neglected Tropical Diseases, Volume 2, Number 4, eLocator e221.

Hayden, Laura. (17th May 2018). "Max Levchin: The Making of a Tech Mogul". The Grainger College of Engineering.

Heather, Peter. (1st March 2012). "Empires and Barbarians: The Fall of Rome and the Birth of Europe". Oxford University Press.

Hebdige, Dick. (16th July 1987). "Cut `n' Mix: Culture, Identity and Caribbean Music". Routledge, London.

Held, David; McGrew, Anthony. (1998). "The End of the Old Order? Globalization and the Prospects for World Order". Review of International Studies, Pages 219-243.

Henriques, Julian. (8th September 2011). "Sonic Bodies: Reggae Sound Systems, Performance Techniques, and Ways of Knowing". Continuum.

Herodian. (1961). "History of the Roman Empire: From the Death of Marcus Aurelius to the Accession of Gordian III". University of California Press.

Hillman, Nick; Stern, Vivienne. (September 2021). "The costs and benefits of international higher education students to the UK economy". Higher Education Policy Institute, Universities UK International, London Economics.

Hirschman, Charles. (1st November 2005). "Immigration and the American Century". Demography, Volume 42, Issue 4, Pages 595-620.

Hirschman, Charles. (Summer 2013). "The Contributions of Immigrants to American Culture". Daedalus, Volume 142, Number 3, Pages 26-47.

Hodge, Channon. (27th November 2020). "A short history of American food (whatever that is)". CNN.

Holmes, John. (December 2009). "Losing 25,000 to hunger every day". United Nations Chronicle, Volume 45, Issue 3, pages 14-20.

Hong Gihoon; McLaren, John. (April 2015). "Are Immigrants a Shot in the Arm for the Local Economy?". National Bureau of Economic Research, Working Paper Number

21123.

Hopkins, Daniel; Sides, John; Citrin, Jack. (January 2019). "The Muted Consequences of Correct Information About Immigration". Journal of Politics, Volume 81, Number 1, Pages 315-20.

Horowitz, Joseph. (3rd March 2009). "Artists in Exile: How Refugees from Twentieth-Century War and Revolution Transformed the American Performing Arts". Harper Perennial.

Howington, Jessica. (2022). "25 Companies Embracing Permanent Remote Work-From-Home Jobs". Flex Jobs.

Hudjashov, Georgi; Kivisild, Toomas; Underhill, Peter et al. (2007). "Revealing the prehistoric settlement of Australia by Y chromosome and mtDNA analysis". Proceedings of the National Academy of Sciences of the United States of America, Volume 104, Pages 8726-30.

Huemer, Michael. "Is There a Right To Immigrate?" (July 2010). Social Theory and Practice, Volume 36, Number 3, pages 429-461.

Hunter, Philip. (12th September 2012). "The genetics of human migrations". EMBO Reports, Volume 15, Issue 10, Pages 1019-1022.

Hutt, Rosamond. (1st September 2016). "The free movement of people: what it is and why it matters". World Economic Forum.

Hysi, Pirro. Choquet, Hélène; Khawaja, Anthony. (April 2020). "Meta-analysis of 542,934 subjects of European ancestry identifies new genes and mechanisms predisposing to refractive error and myopia". Nature Genetics, Volume 52, Pages 401-407.

IMF Staff. (March 2002). "Globalization: A Framework for IMF Involvement". International Monetary Fund.

Jacobovici, Simcha; Samuels, Stuart. (22nd March 1998). "Hollywoodism - Jews, Movies and the American Dream". Associated Producers.

Jaumotte, Florence; Koloskova, Ksenia; Saxena, Sweta. (2016). "Impact of Migration on Income Levels in Advanced Economies". Spillover Task Force, International Monetary Fund.

Johnson, Luke; Kimmelman, Damian. (March 2014). "Migrant Entrepreneurs: Building Our Businesses. Creating Our Jobs". The Centre for Entrepreneurs & DueDil.

Johnson, Tracey. (28th March 2023). "54 Countries with Digital Nomad Visas – The Ultimate List". Nomad Girl.

Jokela, Markus. (February 2009). "Personality predicts migration within and between U.S. states". Journal of Research in Personality, Volume 43, Issue 1, Pages 79-83.

Jokela, Markus; Elovainio, Marko; Kivimäki, Mika; Keltikangas-Järvinen, Lüsa. (September 2008). "Temperament and Migration Patterns in Finland". Psychological Science, Volume 19, Issue 9, Pages 831-837.

Joly, K., Gurarie, E., Sorum, M.S. et al. (2019). "Longest terrestrial migrations and movements around the world". Scientific Reports Journal. Volume 9. Article 15333.

Jones, Reece. (11th October 2016). "Violent Borders: Refugees and the Right to Move". Verso.

Jordan, John-Erik. (11th August 2021). "English Words That Are Actually Spanish". Babel

Magazine.

Jorde, LB; Watkins, WS; Bamshad, M et al. (25th February 2000). "The distribution of human genetic diversity: A comparison of mitochondrial, autosomal, and Y-chromosome data". American Journal of Human Genetics, Volume 66, Number 3, Pages 979–988.

Kangaspunta, Kristiina; Me, Angela. (2018). "Global Study on Smuggling of Migrants". United Nations Office On Drugs And Crime.

Kant, Immanuel. (1785). "Grounding for the Metaphysics of Morals". Project Gutenberg.

Kant, Immanuel. (1795). "Perpetual Peace: A Philosophical Essay". Project Gutenberg.

Kao, Grace; Tienda, Marta. (March 1995). "Optimism and Achievement: The Educational Performance of Immigrant Youth". Social Science Quarterly, Volume 76, Number 1, Pages 1-19.

Kaufmann, Eric, Harris, Gareth. (October 2015). "'White Flight' or Positive Contact? Local Diversity and Attitudes to Immigration in Britain". Comparative Political Studies, Volume 48, Issue 12, Pages 1563-1590.

Keith, Felix. (15th April 2015). "The Unlikely Architects Of Brazilian Football". The Football Times.

Kennan, John. (August 2012). "Open Borders". National Bureau of Economic Research, Working Paper Series, Number 18307.

Kerr, William; Lincoln, William. (July 2010). "The Supply Side of Innovation: H-1B Visa Reforms and US Ethnic Invention". Journal of Labor Economics, Volume 28, Number 3, Pages 473-508.

Kerwin, Donald; Nicholson, Mike; Alulema, Daniela; Warren, Robert. (1st May 2020). "US Foreign-Born Essential Workers by Status and State, and the Global Pandemic". Center for Migration Studies.

Khan, Asma; Arokkiaraj, H. (3rd November 2021). "Challenges of reverse migration in India: a comparative study of internal and international migrant workers in the post-COVID economy". Comparative Migration Studies, Volume 9, Article Number 49.

Khanna, Parag. (12th October 2021). "Move: Where People Are Going for a Better Future". Scribner.

King, Natasha. (15th October 2016). "No Borders: The Politics of Immigration Control and Resistance". Zed Books.

Knaus, Verena; You, Danzhen. (2023). "Children displaced in a changing climate". United Nations Children's Fund (UNICEF).

Koch, Alexander; Brierley, Chris; Maslin, Mark M.; Lewis, Simon L. (2019). "Earth system impacts of the European arrival and Great Dying in the Americas after 1492" Quaternary Science Reviews, Volume 207, Pages 13-36.

Kosack, Edward. (March 2021). "Guest Worker Programs and Human Capital Investment: The Bracero Program in Mexico, 1942–1964. Journal of Human Resources, Volume 56, Issue 2, Pages 570-599.

Koulouris, Giorgos. (11th November 2019). "Poverty: The most pressing human rights issue". The London School of Economics.

Kowaleski-Wallace, Beth. (1994). "Tea, Gender, and Domesticity in Eighteenth-Century

England". Studies in Eighteenth-Century Culture, Volum 23, pages 131-145.

Ku, Leighton; Bruen, Brian. (19th February 2013). "The Use of Public Assistance Benefits by Citizens and Non-citizen Immigrants in the United States". Working Paper Number 13, Cato Institute.

Kukathas, Chandran. (2nd February 2017). "Anarchy, Open Borders and Utopia". The Institute of Art and Ideas News, Issue 53.

Kuper, Simon. (26th January 2023). "Why the world can benefit from contact theory". The Financial Times.

Kurdi, Tima. (17th April 2018). "The Boy on the Beach". Simon & Schuster.

Laban, Cornelis; Komproe, Ivan; Gernaat, Hajo et al. (July 2008). "The Impact of a Long Asylum Procedure on Quality of Life, Disability and Physical Health in Iraqi Asylum Seekers in the Netherlands". Social Psychiatry and Psychiatric Epidemiology, Volume 43, Number 7, Pages 507–15.

Langness, David. (22nd July 2014). "I Am a Citizen of the World". Bahai Teachings.

Le Roux, Johannes; Strasberg, Dominique; Rouget, Mathieu et al. (October 2014). "Relatedness defies biogeography: The tale of two island endemics (Acacia heterophylla and A. koa)". New Phytologist, Volume 204, Issue 1, Pages 230-242.

Leslie, Stephen; Winney, Bruce; Hellenthal, Garrett et al. (18th March 2015). "The fine-scale genetic structure of the British population". Nature Journal, Volume 519, Pages 309-314.

Leung, Angela; Maddux, William; Galinsky, Adam; Chiu, Chi-yue. (May 2008). "Multicultural experience enhances creativity: The when and how." American Psychologist, Volume 63, Number 3, Pages 169-181.

Lévi-Strauss, Claude. (1967). "The social and psychological aspects of chieftainship in a primitive tribe: The Nambikwara of northwestern Mato Grosso" in "Comparative Political Systems". Natural History Press, Pages 45-62.

Li, Jun; Absher, Devin; Tang, Hua; Southwick; Casto, Audrey; Ramachandran, Sohini; Cann, Howard; Barsh, Gregory; Feldman, Marcus; Cavalli-Sforza, Luigi; Myers, Richard. (22nd June 2008) "Worldwide human relationships inferred from genome-wide patterns of variation". Science, Volume 319, Issue 5866, Pages 1100-1104.

Li, Zheng-Xiang et al. (5th January 2008). "Assembly, configuration, and break-up history of Rodinia: A synthesis". Precambrian Research, Volume 160, Issues 1-2 , Pages 179-210.

Lindstrom, David; López-Ramírez, Adriana. (July 2010). "Pioneers and Followers: Migrant Selectivity and the Development of US Migration Streams in Latin America". Annals of the American Academy of Political and Social Science, Volume 630, Number 1, Pages 53-77.

Locke, John. (December 1689). "Second Treatise of Government". Awnsham Churchill.

López, Ana. (17th September 2021). "Brazil: Level of interest in football 2020". Statista.

Maciel, Cármen. (2011). "Angolan and Mozambican Labor Migrants in Portugal since the 1970s" in "The Encyclopedia of Migration and Minorities in Europe". Cambridge University Press.

Maddux, William; Galinsky, Adam. (2009). "Cultural Borders and Mental Barriers: The

Relationship Between Living Abroad and Creativity". Journal of Personality and Social Psychology, Volume 96, Number 5, Pages 1047-1061.

Magnus, Beint; Bentsen, Aamodt. (14th May 2021). "Intergroup Contact and Negative Attitudes Towards Immigrants Among Youth in Sweden". Journal of International Migration and Integration, Volume 23, Pages 243-266.

Maier, Elke. (February 2014). "A Four-Legged Early-Warning System". Max Planck Research, Pages 58-63.

Marcellinus, Ammianus. (1939 Edition). "The Roman History: Volume 3". Loeb Classical Library.

Mark, Veronika. (24th April 2020). "Common English Words with Foreign Origin". Saint-Petersburg School of Social Sciences and Area Studies.

Martisiute, Laura. (8th March 2018). "15 Gross Medieval Foods That People Actually Ate". All That's Interesting.

Marquardt, Felix. (8th July 2021). "The New Nomads: How the Migration Revolution is Making the World a Better Place". Simon & Schuster UK.

Marx, Karl; Engels, Friedrich – translated by Samuel Moore. (21st February 1848). "The Manifesto of the Communist Party" in "Selected Works". Progress Publishers, Moscow, 1969 edition.

Massey, Douglas S.; Arango, Joaquin; Hugo, Graeme; Kouaouci, Ali; Pellegrino, Adela; Taylor, J. Edward. (1998). "Worlds in Motion Understanding International Migration at the End of the Millennium". Oxford University Press.

Massey, Douglas. (September 2007). "Understanding America's Immigration "Crisis"". Proceedings of The American Philosophical Society, Volume 151, Number 3, Pages 309-327.

Mata, Fernando; Mata, Andreia. (19th July 2023). "Investigating the relationship between inbreeding and life expectancy in dogs: Mongrels live longer than pure breeds". PeerJ Journal, Volume 11, eLocator e15718.

Matthews, Luke; Butler, Paul. (2011). "Novelty-Seeking DRD4 Polymorphisms are Associated with Human Migration Distance Out-of-Africa After Controlling for Neutral Population Gene Structure". American Journal of Physical Anthropology, Volume 145, Pages 382–389.

McAllister, Sean. (13th January 2023). "There could be 1.2 billion climate refugees by 2050. Here's what you need to know". Zurich Insurance Group.

McAuliffe, M; Triandafyllidou, A. (2021). "World Migration Report 2022". International Organization for Migration (IOM).

McGranahan, Gordon; Balk, Deborah; Anderson, Bridget. (April 2007). "The rising tide: assessing the risks of climate change and human settlements in low elevation coastal zones". Environment and Urbanization, Volume 19, Issue 1, Pages 17-37.

McNeill, William H. (March 1984) "Human Migration in Historical Perspective". Population and Development Review, Volume 10, Number 1, Pages 1-18.

McWhorter, John. (14th December 2015). "How Immigration Changes Language". The Atlantic.

Mehlem, Ulrich. (2011). "Maghrebis in France after Decolonization in the 1950s and

1960s" in "The Encyclopedia of Migration and Minorities in Europe". Cambridge University Press.

Melnick, Ralph. (5th March 2007). "Senda Berenson: The Unlikely Founder of Women's Basketball". University of Massachusetts Press.

Mena, Rodrigo; Hilhorst, Dorothea; Peters, Katie. (2019). "Disaster risk reduction and protracted violent conflict: The case of Afghanistan". Overseas Development Institute (report).

Mill, John Stuart. (1859). "On Liberty". Project Gutenberg.

Miller, Todd; Buxton, Nick; Akkerman, Mark. (October 2021). "Global Climate Wall: How The World's Wealthiest Nations Prioritise Borders Over Climate Action". Transnational Institute, Amsterdam.

Mingroni, Michael. (January-February 2004). "The secular rise in IQ: Giving heterosis a closer look". Intelligence, Volume 32, Issue 1, Pages 65-83.

Mingroni, Michael. (2007). "Resolving the IQ Paradox: Heterosis as a Cause of the Flynn Effect and Other Trends". Psychological Review, Volume 114, Number 3, Pages 806-829.

Mishra, Prachi. (2014). "Emigration and wages in source countries: a survey of the empirical literature" in "International Handbook on Migration and Economic Development". Edward Elgar Publishing, Chapter 9, Pages 241-266.

Mitchell, Hillary. (10th February 2017). "14 Very British Things That Were Actually Created By Immigrants". BuzzFeed Staff.

Mize, Ronald; Swords, Alicia. (15th October 2010). "Consuming Mexican Labor: From the Bracero Program to NAFTA". University of Toronto Press.

Mlot Christine. (24th May 2013). "Are Isle Royale's wolves chasing extinction?" Science. Volume 340, Issue 6135, Pages 919-921.

Mooney, Harold; Cleland, Elsa. (June 2001). "Mooney H, Cleland E. The evolutionary impact of invasive species". Proceedings of the National Academy of Sciences, Volume 98, Issue 10, Pages 5446-51.

Mukherjee, Debabrata. (2nd November 2017). "The British Curry". History Magazine.

Muñoz-Rodríguez, Pablo et al. (23rd April 2018). "Reconciling Conflicting Phylogenies in the Origin of Sweet Potato and Dispersal to Polynesia". Current Biology, Volume 28, Issue 8, Pages 1246-1256.

Murphy, Cullen. (16th June 2007) "Roman Empire: Gold Standard Of Immigration". Los Angeles Times.

Myambo, Melissa. (1st May 2017). "Frontier Heritage Migration in the Global Ethnic Economy". Public Culture, Volume 29, Pages 261-285.

Nail, Thomas. (1st February 2019). "Sanctuary, Solidarity, Status!" in Reece Jones' "Open Borders: In Defense of Free Movement". University of Georgia Press.

Naudé, Wim; Siegel, Melissa; Marchand, Katrin. (9th March 2017). "Migration, entrepreneurship and development: critical questions". IZA Journal of Migration, Volume 6, Article Number 5.

Newland, Kathleen. (2010). "Diasporas: New Partners in Development Policy". Migration Policy Institute.

Newport, Frank. (16th December 2022). "Americans Prioritize Economy Over Reducing Wealth Gap". Gallup.

Nicholls, Robert; Marinova, Natasha; Lowe, Jason. (13th January 2011). "Sea-level rise and its possible impacts given a 'beyond 4°C world' in the twenty-first century". Philosophical Transactions of the Royal Society, Volume 369, Issue 1934, Pages 161–81.

Noble, Will. (12th January 2022). "The passports that open all doors". CNN.

Norris, Michele. (12th March 2008). "Bill Gates Targets Visa Rules for Tech Workers". NPR.

Nunn, Nathan; Qian, Nancy; Sequeira, Sandra. (10th March 2017). "Migrants and the Making of America: The Short and Long Run Effects of Immigration During the Age of Mass Migration". CEPR Discussion Paper Number 11899.

Obe, Mitsuru. (3rd February 2022). "Japan to require four times more foreign workers, study says". Nikkei Asia.

Oonk, Gijsbert. (17th November 2022). "Who Represents the Country? A Short History of Foreign-Born Athletes in the World Cup". Migration Policy.

Orrenius, Pia. (Spring 2016). "Benefits of Immigration Outweigh the Costs". The Catalyst Journal. Issue 02.

Ortiz, Gabe. (5th May 2016). "Donald Trump's Immigration Quotes Are Totally Unrecognizable From Past Republican Presidents". America's Voice.

Ossola, Alexandra. (3rd May 2021). "How the wealthy seem to immigrate as they please". Quartz.

Ottaviano, Gianmarco; Peri, Giovanni. (August 2006, revised May 2008). "Rethinking The Effects Of Immigration On Wages". Working Paper 12497, National Bureau of Economic Research.

Ottoni, C., Van Neer, W., De Cupere, B. et al. (19th June 2017). "The palaeogenetics of cat dispersal in the ancient world". Nature Ecology and Evolution Journal, Volume 1, Page 139.

Ovchinnikova, Anna; Krylova, Ekaterina; Gavrilenko, Tatjana et al. (February 2011). "Taxonomy of cultivated potatoes". Botanical Journal of the Linnean Society, Volume 165, Issue 2, Pages 107-155.

Pääbo, Svante. (11th February 2014). "Neanderthal Man: In Search of Lost Genomes". Basic Books.

Paine, Thomas. (13th February 2010). "The Writings of Thomas Paine, Complete". Project Gutenburg.

Palmer, Coburn. (7th May 2016). "Forget Canada, Russia Offers Political Asylum To Americans If Trump Wins Presidency". The Inquisitr.

Pan, Lynn. (15th June 1994). "Sons of the Yellow Emperor: A History of the Chinese Diaspora". Kodansha USA Publishing.

Parmesan, Camille. (17th March 2016). "Public Forum - Camille Parmesan, Plymouth University". Institute for Marine and Artic Studies.

Pearson, Raven. (8th Aril 2021). "The Kazakh nomads of Mongolia: Preserving a way of life three-thousand years old". The Lovepost.

Penney, Joe. (22md August 2017). "Why More Migrants Are Dying in the Sahara," New York Times.

Perez-Navarro, Grace. (30th November 2022). "Tax revenues rebounded as economies recovered from the COVID-19 pandemic, according to new OECD data". OECD.

Peri, Giovanni. (February 2012). "The Effect of Immigration on Productivity: Evidence from US States." The Review of Economics and Statistics, Volume 94, Number 1, Pages 348–58.

Peri, Giovanni; Requena-Silvente, Francisco. (November 2010). "The trade creation effect of immigrants: Evidence from the remarkable case of Spain". The Canadian Journal of Economics, Volume 43, Number 4, Pages 1433-1459.

Perreira, Krista; Mullan-Harris, Kathleen; Lee, Dohoon. (August 2006). "Making it in America: High School Completion by Immigrant and Native Youth". Demography, Volume 43, Number 3, Pages 511-536.

Phoonphongphiphat, Apornrath. (16th February 2023). "Thai rice exports to Philippines set to double as Vietnam cuts back". Nikkei.

Piazza, Roberto; Engler, Philipp; Honjo, Keiko et al. (April 2020). "The Macroeconomic Effects of Global Migration" in "The World Economic Outlook". International Monetary Fund.

Poloczanska, Elvira; Brown, Christopher Brown; Sydeman, William et al. (4th August 2013). "Global imprint of climate change on marine life". Nature Climate Change, Volume 3, Number 10, Pages 919-925.

Portnoy, Susan. (26th July 2017). "The last wanderers: Inside the lives of Mongolia's nomads". Adventure.

Potter, Lee; Wynell Schamel. (October 1997). "The Homestead Act of 1862". Social Education Volume 61, Number 6, Pages 359-364.

Priglinger, Elisa. (2019). "Different Aspects Of Mobility And Migration During The Middle Kingdom". Egypt and the Levant Journal, Volume 29, pages 331-354.

Pring, Cecilia; Roco, Irene. (January 2012). "The Volunteer Phenomenon of Nurses in the Philippines". Asian Journal of Health, Volume 2, Pages 95-110.

Pritchett, Lant. (15th September 2006). "Let Their People Come: Breaking the Gridlock on Global Labor Mobility". Center for Global Development.

Pritchett, Lant. (18th May 2010). "The Cliff at the Border" in "Equity and Growth in a Globalizing World". World Bank Publications.

Pugliese, Anita; Ray, Julie. (24th January 2023). "Nearly 900 Million Worldwide Wanted to Migrate in 2021". Gallup.

Puntambekar, Shrikrishna. (January 2019). "The Hindu Concept of Human Rights". The UNESCO Courier, Volume 2018, Issue 4, pages 27-29.

Quaker, Daisy. (31st March 2022). "Amazon Stats: Growth, sales, and more". Sell Amazon.

Ranker, Lynsie; Ubania, Ben; Woolhandler, Steffie; Himmelstein, David; Zallman, Leah. (April 2021). "Keeping Medicare Solvent How Immigrants Subsidize Medicare's Trust Fund for All US Seniors". New American Economy.

Ratha, Dilip. (6th January 2007). "Leveraging Remittances for Development".

Proceedings Journal, Pages 173-185.

Ratha, Dilip; Mohapatra, Sanket; Ozden, Caglar. (26th April 2011). "Leveraging Migration for Africa: Remittances, Skills, and Investments". World Bank Publications.

Ratha, Dilip. (November 2022). "Remittances Brave Global Headwinds: Special Focus: Climate Migration". Migration and Development Brief 37, The Global Knowledge Partnership on Migration and Development (KNOMAD).

Ravikumar, Sachin; M, Muvija. (25th May 2023). "Record net arrivals highlight UK's post-Brexit migration dilemma". Reuters.

Rawlins, Aimee. (11th March 2011). "Immigration Reform and US Economic Performance". Council on Foreign Relations.

Rawls, John (16th May 2001). "Justice as Fairness: A Restatement". Belknap Press.

Rayner, Jay. (19th January 2003). "Enduring love". The Guardian.

Read, Herbert Harold; Watson, Janet. (1975). "Introduction to Geology". Macmillan Publishers Limited.

Reich, David. (27th March 2018). "Who We Are and How We Got Here: Ancient DNA and the New Science of the Human Past". Pantheon.

Reid, Kathryn. (22nd July 2022). "Forced To Flee: Top countries refugees are coming from". World Vision.

Riggio, Jason; Baillie, Jonathan; Brumby, Steven et al. (August 2020). "Global human influence maps reveal clear opportunities in conserving Earth's remaining intact terrestrial ecosystems". Global Change Biology, Volume 26, Issue 8, Pages 4344-4356.

Rodriguez, Sabrina. (12th January 2021). " Trump's partially built 'big, beautiful wall'". Politico.

Rosas, Ana. (26th September 2014). "Abrazando el Espíritu: Bracero Families Confront the US-Mexico Border". University of California Press.

Rose, Steven. (8th September 2016). "How to Get Another Thorax". London Review of Books, Volume 38, Number 17.

Roy, Ananda; Conroy, Richard. "Toward mapping the human body at a cellular resolution". Molecular Biology of the Cell, Volume 29, Number 15, Pages 1779-1785.

Ruggles, Steven; Flood, Sarah; Sobek, Matthew et al (April 2020). "The Essential Role of Immigrants in the US Food Supply Chain (UPDATED)". Migration Policy Institute.

Rupp, Rebecca. (8th January 2015). "Are French Fries Truly French?" National Geographic.

Sattin, Anthony. (20th September 2022). "Nomads: The Wanderers Who Shaped Our World". W. W. Norton & Company.

Sauter, Michael. (5th July 2018). "Population migration: These are the cities Americans are abandoning the most". USA Today.

Savage, Michael. (20th April 2019). "Tony Blair: Migrants should be forced to integrate more to combat far right". The Guardian.

Saxenian, AnnaLee. (31st October 2007). "The New Argonauts: Regional Advantage in a Global Economy". Harvard University Press.

Scarpetta, Stefano. (2022). "International Migration Outlook". OECD Publishing, Paris.

Scott, James. (8th February 1999). "Seeing like a State: How Certain Schemes to

Improve the Human Condition Have Failed". Yale University Press.

Scott, James. (22nd August 2017). "Against the Grain: A Deep History of the Earliest States". Yale University Press.

Scott, Robert; Wilson, Valerie; Kandra, Jori; Perez, Daniel. (31st January 2022). "Botched policy responses to globalization have decimated manufacturing employment with often overlooked costs for Black, Brown, and other workers of color". Economic Policy Institute.

Shah, Sonia. (2nd June 2020). "The Next Great Migration: The Beauty and Terror of Life on the Move". Bloomsbury Publishing.

Shallby, Colleen. (15th September 2018). "The financial crisis hit 10 years ago. For some, it feels like yesterday". The Los Angeles Times.

Shaw, Artie. (1st January 1992). "The Trouble with Cinderella: An Outline of Identity". Fithian Press.

Shaw-Roberts, Maddy. (22nd June 2022). "How the Windrush generation changed British music and arts forever". Classic FM.

Sherif, Muzafer. (November 1956). "Experiments in Group Conflict". Scientific American, Volume 195, Number 5, Pages 54-59.

Shuttleworth, Ian; Stevenson, Clifford; Bjarnason, Þóroddur; Finell, Eerika. (April 2021). "Geography, psychology and the 'Big Five' personality traits: Who moves, and over what distances, in the United Kingdom?". Population Space and Place, Volume 27, Issue3, eLocator e2418.

Siculus, Diodorus. (1946 translation). "Library of History, Volume 4". Loeb Classical Library.

Simcoe, Mark; Valdes, Ana; Liu, Fan et al. (10th March 2021). "Genome-wide association study in almost 195,000 individuals identifies 50 previously unidentified genetic loci for eye color". Science Advances, Volume 7, Issue 11.

Singer, Colin. (1st November 2022). "Canada To Welcome Unprecedented 1.45 Million Immigrants In Next Three Years". Canadian Citizenship & Immigration Resource Center.

Skinner, Gideon. (6th December 2018). "The Perils of Perception 2018". IPSOS Mori.

Skinner, Gideon; Gottfried, Glenn; Day, Holly. (March 2022). "Attitudes towards immigration". IPSOS Mori and British Future.

Skorton, David J. (4th July 2018). "Immigrants helped build our nation. We need to embrace them, not exclude them." USA Today.

Smith, Adam. (1776). "An Inquiry into the Nature and Causes of the Wealth of Nations". Early Modern Texts.

Smith, James; Edmonston, Barry. (1997). "The New Americans: Economic, Demographic, and Fiscal Effects of Immigration". National Research Council, The National Academies Press.

Sohrabi, S. (14th January 2015). "The criminal gene: The link between MAOA and aggression". BMC Proceedings, Volume 9, Supplement 1.

Soni, Jimmy. (22nd February 2022). "The Founders: The Story of Paypal and the

Entrepreneurs Who Shaped Silicon Valley". Simon & Schuster.

Spencer, Sarah; Hughes, Vanessa. (July 2015). "Outside and In: Legal Entitlements to Health Care and Education for Migrants with Irregular Status in Europe". COMPAS, University of Oxford.

Springer, Kate. (7th August 2020). "Passports for Purchase: How the Elite Get Through a Pandemic," CNN.

Stantis, Chris; Kharobi, Arwa; Maaranen, Nina; Nowell, G.; Bietak, Manfred; Prell, Silvia; Schutkowski, Holger. (2020). "Who were the Hyksos? Challenging traditional narratives using strontium isotope (87Sr/86Sr) analysis of human remains from ancient Egypt". PLoS ONE Journal, Volume 15.

Stefanopoulos, George (13th May 2022). "Migration through History: Ancient Athens". So Close.

Stump, Scott. (22nd March 2016). "Donald Trump: Brussels is 'Catastrophic,' waterboarding Paris suspect 'Would be fine'". Today, NBC Universal.

Suchodolska, Liliana; Sargsyan, Gueram; Zinni, Belen; Parrot, Frederic. (28th September 2017). "Entrepreneurship at a Glance 2017". OECD Publishing, Paris.

Sumption, Madeleine; Forde, Chris; Alberti, Gabriella; Walsh, Peter. (15th October 2022). How is the End of Free Movement Affecting the Low-wage Labour Force in the UK?". The Migration Observatory.

T., L. (17th November 2016). "Why Africa's borders are a mess". The Economist.

Tarman, Dan, (4th June 2018). "A Look at the 'eBay Economy' in the US". eBay Impact.

Taylor, Paul; Cohn, D'Vera; Morin, Rich et al. (7th February 2013). "Second-Generation Americans: A Portrait of the Adult Children of Immigrants". Pew Research Centre.

Tilly, Chares. (January 1985). "War Making and State Making as Organized Crime". Cambridge University Press

Thompson, Ken. (20th March 2014). "Where Do Camels Belong?: The story and science of invasive species". Profile Books.

Ullman, Berthold. (November 1922). "Our Latin-English Language". The Classical Journal, Volume 18, Number 2, Pages 82-90.

UN Department of Economic and Social Affairs. (2019). "World Population Ageing 2019: Highlights". United Nations, New York.

UNHCR, The UN Refugee Agency. (2021). "Displaced on the Frontlines of the Climate Emergency". Story Maps.

UNHCR. (January-December 2018). "Desperate Journeys: Refugees and Migrants Arriving in Europe and at Europe's Borders". United Nations High Commissioner for Refugees.

United Nations. (13th July 2018). "Global Compact for Safe, Orderly and Regular Migration".

United Nations Development Programme. (16th May 2022). "Losing the ground beneath our feet". UNDP.

Vaidyanathan, Gayathri. (2nd September 2013). "Scientists trace origins of India's tigers, elephants and other large mammals". The Washington Post.

Van Campenhout, Gijs; Van Sterkenburg, Jacco; Oonk, Gijsbert. (2018) "Who Counts as a Migrant Footballer? A Critical Reflection and Alternative Approach to Migrant Football Players on National Teams at the World Cup, 1930–2018". The International Journal of the History of Sport, Volume 35, Number 11, Pages 1071-1090.

Vedder, Richard. (28th March 1994). "Immigration Doesn't Displace Natives". Wall Street Journal.

Vellend, Mark; Baeten, Landa; Myers-Smith, Isla. (28th October 2013). "Global meta-analysis reveals no net change in local-scale plant biodiversity over time". Proceedings of the National Academy of Sciences of the United States of America, Volume 110, Number 48, Pages 19456-9.

Vidal, Céline; Lane, Christine; Asrat, Asfawossen et al. (27th January 2022). "Age of the oldest known Homo sapiens from eastern Africa". Nature, Volume 601, Pages 579–583.

Viegas, Jennifer. (1st July 2006). "Pierre Omidyar: The Founder of Ebay (Internet Career Bios)". Rosen Young Adult.

Vigne, Jean-Denis; Zazzo, Antoine; Saliège, Jean-François et al (22nd September 2009). "Pre-Neolithic wild boar management and introduction to Cyprus more than 11,400 years ago". Proceedings of the National Academy of Sciences Journal, Volume 106, Number 38.

Vince, Gaia. (23rd August 2022). "Nomad Century: How Climate Migration Will Reshape Our World". Flatiron Books.

Volner, Ian. (11th June 2019). "The Great Great Wall: Along the Borders of History from China to Mexico". Abrams Press.

Wadhwa, Vivek; Rissing, Ben; Saxenian, AnnaLee; Gereffi, Gary. (11th June 2007). "Education, entrepreneurship and immigration: America's new immigrant entrepreneurs, Part II." Duke University, Berkley School of Information, Ewing Marion Kauffman Foundation.

Wadhwa, Vivek; Jain, Sonali; Saxenian, AnnaLee et al. (28th April 2011). "The Grass is Indeed Greener in India and China for Returnee Entrepreneurs: America's New Immigrant Entrepreneurs – Part VI". Social Science Research Network Electronic Journal.

Wainwright, Rob. (May 2016). "Migrant Smuggling Networks". Joint Europol-Interpol Report.

Walmsley, Terrie; Winters, Alan; Ahmed, Amer; Parsons, Christopher. (2005). "Measuring the Impact of the Movement of Labour Using a Model of Bilateral Migration Flows". Conference Paper 331440, Center for Global Trade Analysis, Purdue University.

Wang, Huiyao; Bao, Yue. (8th October 2015). "Reverse Migration In Contemporary China: Returnees, Entrepreneurship And The Chinese Economy". Palgrave Macmillan.

Wang, Nora. (2011). "Chinese Student Workers in France after World War I" in "The Encyclopedia of Migration and Minorities in Europe". Cambridge University Press.

Wang, Xiao. (2022). "Immigrant Income and Taxation Report". Boundless.

Ward, Paul. (June 2019). "Soundsystem Culture: Place, Space and Identity in the United Kingdom, 1960-1989". Historia Contemporánea Journal, Volume 2, Number 57, Pages 349-376.

Warren, Charles. (August 2007). "Perspectives on the 'Alien' versus 'Native' species debate: A critique of concepts, language and practice". Progress in Human Geography, Volume 31, Issue 4.

Warren, Robert; Kerwin, Donald. (2017). "Mass Deportations Would Impoverish US Families and Create Immense Social Costs". Center For Migration Studies.

Washington, John. (24th April 2019). "What Would an Open-Borders World Actually Look Like?". The Nation.

Waters, Mary; Gerstein-Pineau, Marisa. (November 2015). "The Integration of Immigrants into American Society". The National Academies Press, Washington DC.

Weil. Eric; Giulianotti, Richard. (2023). "Football around the world". Encyclopaedia Britannica.

Wenger, Stephanie. (12th May 2022). "Jeff Bezos Tears Up Recalling His Dad's Journey as a Cuban Immigrant Starting a Life in America". People Magazine.

Westermann, William Linn. (1945). "Between Slavery and Freedom." The American Historical Review, Volume 50, Number 2, Pages 213–27.

Wildavsky, Ben. (25th April 2010). "The Great Brain Race: How Global Universities Are Reshaping the World". Princeton University Press.

William, Wulf. (Winter-Spring, 2006). "Foreign-Born Researchers Are Key to US Prosperity and Security". The National Academies In Focus, Volume 6, Number 1.

Winchester, Simon. (19th January 2021). "Land". Harper Collins.

Winder, Robert. (4th November 2010). "Bloody Foreigners: The Story of Immigration to Britain". Abacus.

Wintour, Patrick. (22nd November 2018). "Clinton, Blair, Renzi: why we lost, and how to fight back". The Guardian.

Wolgin, Philip. (18th August 2015). "What Would It Cost to Deport 11.3 Million Unauthorized Immigrants?". The Center For American Progress.

Wood, Laura. (26th September, 2018). "Impact of punitive immigration policies, parent-child separation and child detention on the mental health and development of children". BMJ Paediatrics Open, Volume 2, Issue 1.

World Food Program. (March to July 2021). "Hunger Hotspots. FAO-WFP early warnings on acute food insecurity". Food and Agriculture Organization of the United Nations (Report), Rome.

Wu, Nan. (14th April 2022). "Immigrants Punch Above Their Weight as Taxpayers". Immigration Impact.

Wunsch, Nils-Gerrit. (14th December 2022). "Most popular British dishes in Great Britain Q3 2022". Statista.

Xenophon. (Translated August 27th 2008 by HG Dakyns). "On Revenues". Salzwasser-Verlag Gmbh.

Xu, Chi; Kohler, Timothy; Lenton, Timothy; Svenning, Jens-Christian; Scheffer, Marten. (26th May 2020). "Future Of The Human Climate Niche". Proceedings of the National Academy of Sciences of the United States. Volume 117, Number 21, Pages 11350-11355.

Xue, Cheng; Raveendran, Muthuswamy; Harris, Alan. (17th October 2016). "The population genomics of rhesus macaques (Macaca mulatta) based on whole-genome sequences". Genome Research Journal, Volume 26, Pages 1651-1662.

Yamano, Hiroya; Sugihara, Kaoru; Nomura; Keiichi. (17th February 2011). "Rapid poleward range expansion of tropical reef corals in response to rising sea surface temperatures". Geophysical Research Letters, Volume 38, Issue 4.

Yeung, Jessie; Bacani, Xyza Cruz. (November 2020). "When Love Is Not Enough". CNN.

Yglesias, Matthew. (12th August 2019). "Immigration makes America great". Vox.

Yuen, AWC; Jablonski, Nina. (1st January 2010). "Vitamin D: In the evolution of human skin colour". Medical Hypotheses, Volume 74, Issue 1, Pages 39-44.

Zeng, Lin; Ming, Chen; Li, Yan et al. (January 2018). "Out of Southern East Asia of the Brown Rat Revealed by Large-Scale Genome Sequencing". Molecular Biology and Evolution, Volume 35, Issue 1, Pages 149–158.

OTHER WORLDS WERE POSSIBLE

Sunny and his kinfolk were content with their way of life. During the dry season, their clan lived alone. They hunted whenever they chose, gathered an array of plants, told stories, and took part in debates. In the rainy season, they united with the rest of their tribe. They formed a temporary city, feasted, held dances and played games.

They could have lived like this forever. But a strange and foreign people had ideas of their own...

Appearing out of nowhere, these aliens looked completely different. They smelled different. They even dressed differently. And they had the most peculiar habits.

These people did not live with the earth. They exploited the earth, imposing monocultures and intensive farming. They were not content with their lot. They were possessed by an insatiable desire to consume. And they had no sense of freedom. They were beholden to a never-ending list of outlandish concepts; things such as "Hierarchy", "Patriarchy", "Monarchy", "Monogamy", "God", "Punishments", "Ownership", "Inequality", "Money", "Work" and "Tax".

Sunny and his kinfolk faced the toughest decision in their history...

They could wage war on these imposters. But their enemies were strong. They had killed hundreds-of-thousands of indigenous people.

They could flee. But these imperialists would surely follow. They would push them into the sea, the mountains or the desert.

Their clan needed another solution. But what could it be? Could they negotiate with this violent foe? Could they form a pact? Could they create a kind of alliance?

Sunny had no idea. But he was compelled by a duty to find out. This was his time. And he was willing to risk his life, to save the people he loved...

DEMOCRACY

A USER'S GUIDE

THEY SAY WE LIVE IN A DEMOCRACY. WE ARE FREE AND WE SHOULD BE GRATEFUL.

But just how "Free" are we? How democratic are our so-called "Democracies"?

Is it enough to simply elect our leaders and sit back, helpless, as they rule over us like dictators? What good is selecting our politicians, if we cannot control our media, police or soldiers? If we must blindly follow our teachers' and bosses' commands, whilst at school and in the workplace, is it not a little naïve to believe that we are the masters of our own destinies? And if our resources are controlled by a tiny cabal of plutocrats, bankers and corporations; can we honestly say that our economies are being run for us?

Could things not be a little bit more, well, democratic?

Indeed they can! "Democracy: A User's Guide" shows us how...

Within the pages of this story-filled book, we shall visit Summerhill, a democratic school in the east of England, before stopping off in Brazil to check out Semco, where workplace democracy is the name of the game. We will travel to Rojava, to explore life in a democratic army, and head to Spain, to see why Podemos is giving liquid democracy a go. We shall travel back in time, to see democracy at work in hunter-gatherer societies, tribal confederacies, the guilds and on the commons. We will consider the case for participatory budgeting, deliberative democracy, collaborative hiring, community currencies, peer-to-peer lending, and much much more.

The message is clear and concise: Democracy does not have to be a pipe dream. We have all the tools we need to rule ourselves.

INDIVIDUTOPIA

Beloved friend,

The year is 2084, and that famous Margaret Thatcher quote has become a reality: There really is no such thing as society. No one speaks to anyone else. No one looks at anyone else. People don't collaborate, they only compete.

I hate to admit it, but this has had tragic consequences. Unable to satisfy their social urges, the population has fallen into a pit of depression and anxiety. Suicide has become the norm.

It all sounds rather morbid, does it not? But please don't despair, there is hope, and it comes in the form of our hero: Renee Ann Blanca. Wishing to fill the society-shaped hole in her life, our Renee does the unthinkable: She goes in search of human company! It's a radical act and an enormous challenge. But that, I suppose, is why her tale's worth recounting. It's as gripping as it is touching, and I think you're going to love it...

Your trusty narrator,

PP

MONEY POWER LOVE
ALL WARS ARE BANKERS' WARS

"Breathtaking"
The Huffington Post
"Picaresque"
Scottish Left Review
"Unputdownable"
The Avenger
"Strangely kind"
The Tribune

Born on three adjacent beds, a mere three seconds apart, our three heroes are united by nature but divided by nurture. As a result of their different upbringings, they spend their lives chasing three very different things: Money, power and love.

This is a human story: A tale about people like ourselves, cajoled by the whimsy of circumstance, who find themselves performing the most beautiful acts as well as the most vulgar.

This is a historical story: A tale set in the early 1800s, which shines a light on how bankers, with the power to create money out of nothing, were able to shape the world we live in today.

And this is a love story: A tale about three men, who fall in love with the same woman, at the very same time...

THE LITTLE VOICE

Can you remember who you were before the world told you who you should be?

"The most thought-provoking novel of 2016"
The Huffington Post
"Radical... A masterclass... Top notch..."
The Canary
"A pretty remarkable feat"
BuzzFeed

Dear reader,

My character has been shaped by two opposing forces; the pressure to conform to social norms, and the pressure to be true to myself. To be honest with you, these forces have really torn me apart. They've pulled me one way and then the other. At times, they've left me questioning my whole entire existence.

But please don't think that I'm angry or morose. I'm not. Because through adversity comes knowledge. I've suffered, it's true. But I've learnt from my pain. I've become a better person.

Now, for the first time, I'm ready to tell my story. Perhaps it will inspire you. Perhaps it will encourage you to think in a whole new way. Perhaps it won't. There's only one way to find out...

Enjoy the book,

Yew Shodkin

INVOLUTION & EVOLUTION

This is the story of Alfred Freeman, a boy who does everything he can; to serve humankind. He feeds five-thousand youths, salves-saves-and-soothes; and champions the maligned. He helps paralytics to feel fine, turns water into wine; and gives sight to the blind.

When World War One draws near, his nation is plunged into fear; and so Alfred makes a stand. He opposes the war and calls for peace, disobeys the police; and speaks out across the land. He makes speeches, and he preaches; using statements which sound grand.

But the authorities hit back, and launch a potent-attack; which is full of disgust-derision-and-disdain. Alfred is threatened with execution, and suffers from persecution; which leaves him writhing in pain. He struggles to survive, remain alive; keep cool and stay sane.

'Involution & Evolution' is a masterpiece of rhyme, with a message which echoes through time; and will get inside your head. With colourful-characters and poetic-flair, it is a scathing critique of modern-warfare; and all its gory-bloodshed. It's a novel which breaks new ground, is sure to astound; and really must be read.